A GRAMMAR OF MAM, A MAYAN LANGUAGE

TEXAS LINGUISTICS SERIES

Editorial Board
Winfred P. Lehmann, Chair
Joel Sherzer
Carlota S. Smith

A Grammar of Mam, a Mayan Language

NORA C. ENGLAND

UNIVERSITY OF TEXAS PRESS, AUSTIN

Copyright © 1983 by the University of Texas Press
First paperback printing 2011

All rights reserved

For reasons of economy and speed this volume has been printed from camera-ready copy furnished by the author, who assumes full responsibility for its contents.

Requests for permission to reproduce material from this work should be sent to:
 Permissions
 University of Texas Press
 P.O. Box 7819
 Austin, TX 78713-7819
 https://utpress.utexas.edu/book-permissions/

Library of Congress Catalog Number 82-51115

ISBN 978-0-292-72927-8, paperback
ISBN 978-0-292-76246-6, library e-book
ISBN 978-0-292-76247-3, individual e-book

CONTENTS

Abbreviations Used in the Examples   ix

INTRODUCTION   3
The Language and People   4
Research   15
Personnel   16
Previous Studies   19
Overview of the Grammar   21

1. PHONOLOGY
Phonemic Inventory   24
Phonemic Description   25
Summary of Phonological Processes   36
Stress   37
The Syllable   38
Juncture   39
Notes   41

2. MORPHOPHONEMICS   43
Vowels   43
Glottals   51
Nasal Alternation   54

3. ROOTS AND WORDS   55
Verbs   55
Nouns   66
Non-Verbal Predicates   75
Summary of Inflection   78
Positionals   78
Adjectives   83
Affect Words   84
Measure Words   86
Particles   86
Canonical Shape of Roots   93
Notes   96

4. STEM FORMATION   98
Verb Stems   99
Noun Stems   117
The Infinitive Stem   123

Adjective Stems   124
Affect Stems   130
Measure Stems   131
Derived Adverbial Stems   131
Stem Formation Through Vowel Length and Glottal Stop Addition   132
Review of Derivation   133
Notes   138

5. THE NOUN PHRASE   139
The Structure of the Noun Phrase   141
Definiteness   151
Relational Noun Phrases   153
Pronominalization   155

6. THE VERB PHRASE   161
Aspect   161
Person   164
Directionals   167
Mode   172
Verb Stem   174
Structure of the Verb Phrase   174

7. SENTENCE FORMATION   177
Verbal Sentences   177
Non-Verbal Sentences   238
Negation   244
Question Formation   248
Coordination   254
Notes   256

8. COMPLEX SENTENCES   258
Dependent Person Marking   258
Dependent Aspect Marking   275
Relative Clauses   290
Complement Clauses   298
Syntactic Clitics   304
Notes   316

Appendix I. Vowel Disharmonic Suffixes   319
Appendix II. Exceptions to Morphophonemic Rules   324
Appendix III. Text   328
Bibliography   343
Index   349

FIGURES
1. The Mam Area in Guatemala 5
2. The Mayan Language Family 7
3. The Principal Divisions of the Mam Area 8
4. The Immediate Constituent Structure of the Noun Phrase 140

TABLES
1. Vowel Disharmonic Suffixes 48
2. Agent and Patient Incorporation 62
3. Passives 210
4. Antipassive Functions 221

ABBREVIATIONS USED IN THE EXAMPLES

Roots and stems are indicated by glosses in capitals; affixes and clitics are glossed in lower case. Single letter abbreviations for root, stem, or word classes are capitalized if they refer to a root class only.

a	adjective
abs n	abstract noun suffix
af	affect root, word
af vb	affect verb suffix
affirm	affirmative
agt	agent
agtv	agentive suffix
ap	antipassive suffix
atten	attenuator
ben	benefactive
caus	causative
cl	classifier
clt	clitic
com	comitative
cond	conditional
cont	contrary to fact
dat	dative
dep	dependent (aspects)
dir	directional
dist	distributive
ds	directional suffix
emph	emphatic
encl	enclitic
i	intransitive

ABBREVIATIONS USED IN THE EXAMPLES

imp	imperative
inf	infinitive
inj	interjection
inst	instrument
int	interrogative
intens	intensifier
LOC PRED	locative/existential predicate
n	noun
n→adj	noun to adjective derivational suffix
n→t	noun to transitive derivational suffix
neg	negative
ord num	ordinal number
p	positional
p→i	positional to intransitive derivational suffix
p→t	positional to transitive derivational suffix
part	participle
pas	passive
pas?	∅ passive or agentless transitive, depending on analysis
pat	patient
perf	perfective
pl	plural
pos	possessive
pos adj	positional adjective
pot	potential
proc	processive
proc imp	processive imperative
proc pas	processive passive
prog	progressive
rec	recent past
refl	reflexive
rel	relative marker

ABBREVIATIONS USED IN THE EXAMPLES

RN	relational noun
spec term	specific termination of action derivational suffix
t	transitive
1s	first person singular
2s	second person singular
3s	third person singular
1p	first person plural
1p ex	first person plural exclusive
1p in	first person plural inclusive
2p	second person plural
3p	third person plural
1sA, etc.	first person singular absolutive, etc.
1sE, etc.	first person singular ergative, etc.
1s emph, etc.	first person singular emphatic marker, etc.

Note: Person prefixes are marker 1, 2, 3 s/p although the interpretation depends on the enclitics. Enclitics are also marked 1, 2 s/p. Absolutive/ergative distinctions are marked on verbs. Nonverbal predicates are marked absolutive to distinguish the markers from the enclitics for person, which are contiguous. Noun possessive prefixes are not marked 'ergative' although the prefixes for possession are the same as the ergative markers.

Morphemes in the examples and glosses are separated by a -. A slash within a gloss is used to further qualify the gloss; e.g. RN/in means 'relational noun meaning _in_'.

A GRAMMAR OF MAM, A MAYAN LANGUAGE

INTRODUCTION

In response to an advertisement from the Proyecto Lingüístico Francisco Marroquín (PLFM) calling for linguists to work on Mayan languages, I arrived in Guatemala in August, 1971, with: a master's degree in anthropological linguistics and experience working on American languages, solid training in descriptive field linguistics, and a determination to successfully tackle my own first language in a "real" field situation. I also arrived without: being able to speak Spanish, knowing which Mayan language I was to work on, or having had any previous experience living outside the eastern United States. The PLFM taught me Spanish, Terrence Kaufman taught me about Mayan languages, and living in Guatemala for two and a half years taught me to love fieldwork, to love Mayan, and to respect and understand something about the people who speak Mayan languages.

During my stay in Guatemala I lived in the town of San Ildefonso Ixtahuacán, in the household of a Mayan family who speak Mam, for a total of several months, and visited friends in that and other villages on many occasions. People were very generous in permitting me to share in their daily and festival routines. These experiences, along with the teaching of Charles Wagley, Alexander Moore, and William Carter, and the field companionship and conversation with Anne Farber and Kay Warren, helped me to learn about the people. Linguistic training by Martha Hardman and Terrence Kaufman gave me the background for this study, which many other Mayan linguists, especially Will Norman, aided and abetted as our paths crossed and recrossed in the field and at meetings. The people of

San Ildefonso Ixtahuacan, especially Juan Maldonado Andrés, Juan Ordóñez Domingo, and Juan Ortiz Domingo (there are only 20 surnames and almost as few first names used in Ixtahuacán) enabled me to learn Mam. That I speak it indifferently is not their fault but mine; that I understand its structure is due to their patience and diligence in guiding me through its intricacies.

Intricate it certainly is. My purpose in writing a grammar of Mam has been to explain, as clearly as I can, how the language works. Mam has the (undeserved) reputation of being the most difficult of the Mayan languages. Once the sounds, which are indeed more troublesome than those of other Mayan languages, are learned it is no more nor less difficult than any other--which is to say that it is a complex language quite different from any European language and at times maddeningly opaque to the outsider, but learnable, speakable, and analyzable. This grammar is offered as a glimpse into a people's mind, as reflected in their language, and also as grist for the mill of linguistic theory.

Several colleagues were very kind and helpful in reading parts of the manuscript and sharing their comments with me. They are Judith Aissen, Colette Craig, Martha Hardman, Terrence Kaufman, William Ladusaw, and John Watanabe. Victoria R. Bricker encouraged me more than she perhaps knows to start, and finish, writing it. Laura Martin shared a great deal in the field. Susan Flinspach and Becky Miller compiled the index, and Cynthia Otis Charlton helped prepare the final copy.

1. THE LANGUAGE AND PEOPLE

Mam, spoken in the northwestern highlands of Guatemala (figure 1), is one of the twenty-four to thirty extant Mayan languages whose speakers live in Guatemala and Mexico (Kaufman 1974:

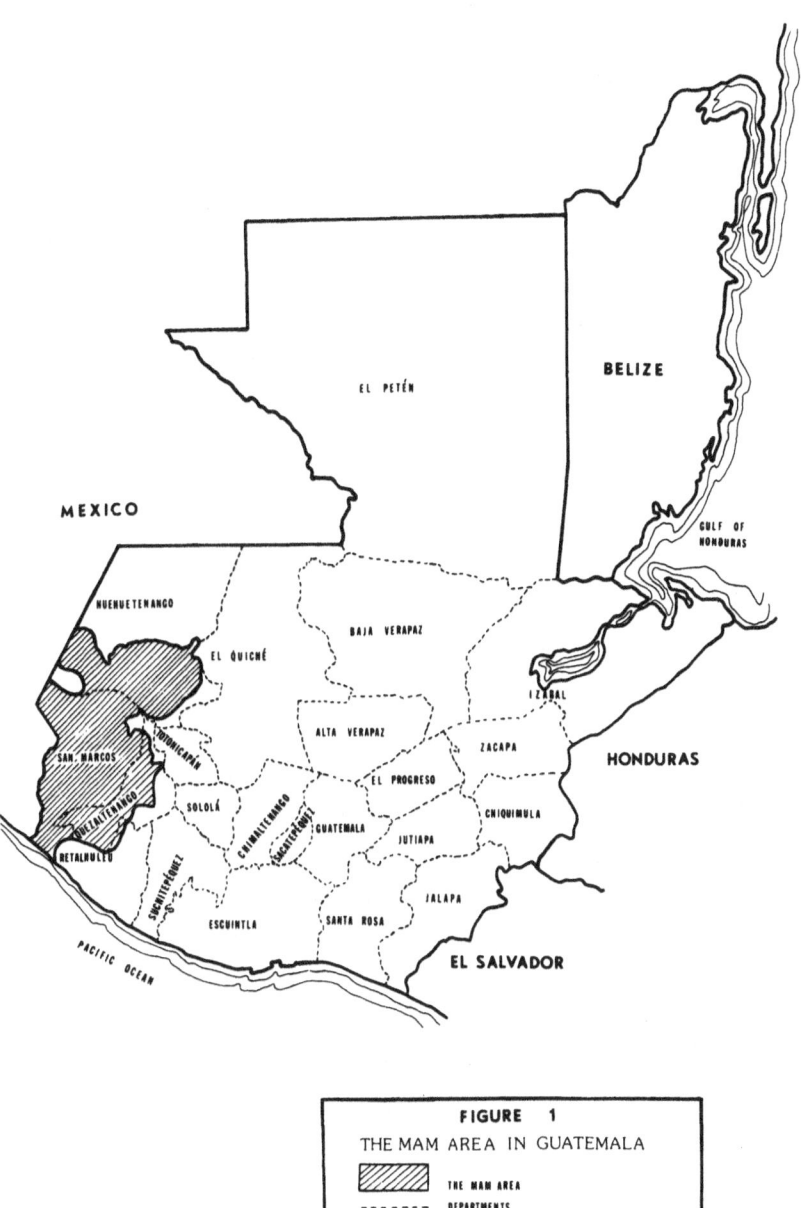

35). It belongs to the Mamean branch of the Eastern Mayan languages, along with its closest neighbors: Teco, Ixil, and Aguacatec (figure 2). Although an Eastern language, Mam is bordered on the north and west by Western Mayan languages and shares a number of characteristics with them which are not shared by the Quichean branch of the Eastern languages. It is the third largest of the Mayan languages, after Quiché and Cakchiquel, with more than 439,000 speakers living in 56 different towns and speaking at least 15 distinct dialects which can be divided into three major divisions (figure 3) (Kaufman 1976b and the 1973 Guatemalan census).

The dialect of Mam which this grammar describes is that spoken by 12,000 people in San Ildefonso Ixtahuacán, in the department of Huehuetenango, Guatemala. It belongs to the Northern group of Mam dialects. Languages in the Mamean group are few but quite distinct from each other. None are mutually intelligible with the possible exception of Teco and Western Mam. There is also considerable variation within Mam dialects. Intelligibility between the principal dialect divisions is reduced, although possible with practice. Of the three dialect divisions, Northern Mam is the least conservative (Kaufman, personal communication), and the Mamean branch is in general quite innovative. The data described in this grammar are representative of other dialects of Northern Mam, and share much with Southern and Western Mam, but specific details differ on all grammatical levels.

Why is there so much dialect diversification within a relatively small geographical area? The Mam people have occupied their territory continuously since long before the Spanish Conquest, perhaps from as early as 500 A.D. (Kaufman 1976a). Huehuetenango, partially occupied by Mam people today, may in fact have been the center of early Mayan dispersal,

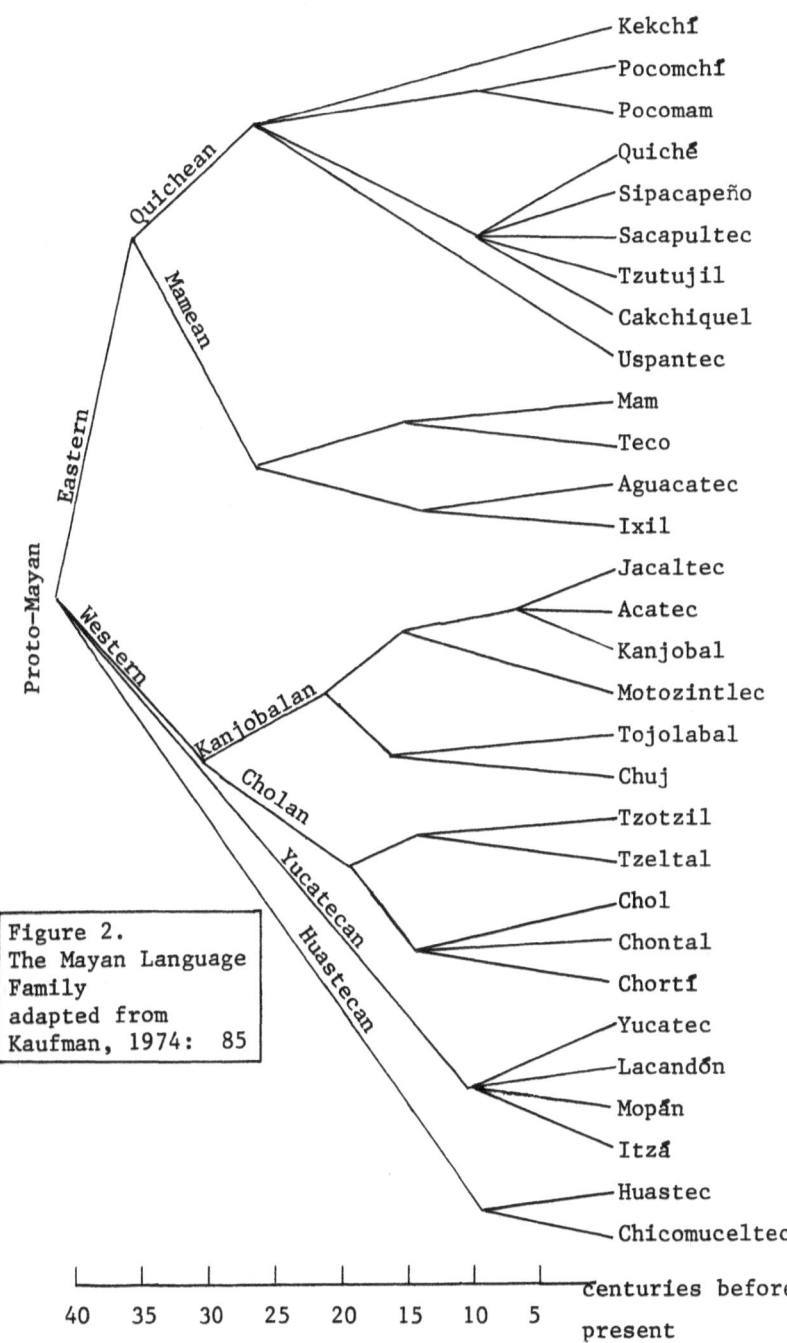

Figure 2.
The Mayan Language Family
adapted from
Kaufman, 1974: 85

8 INTRODUCTION

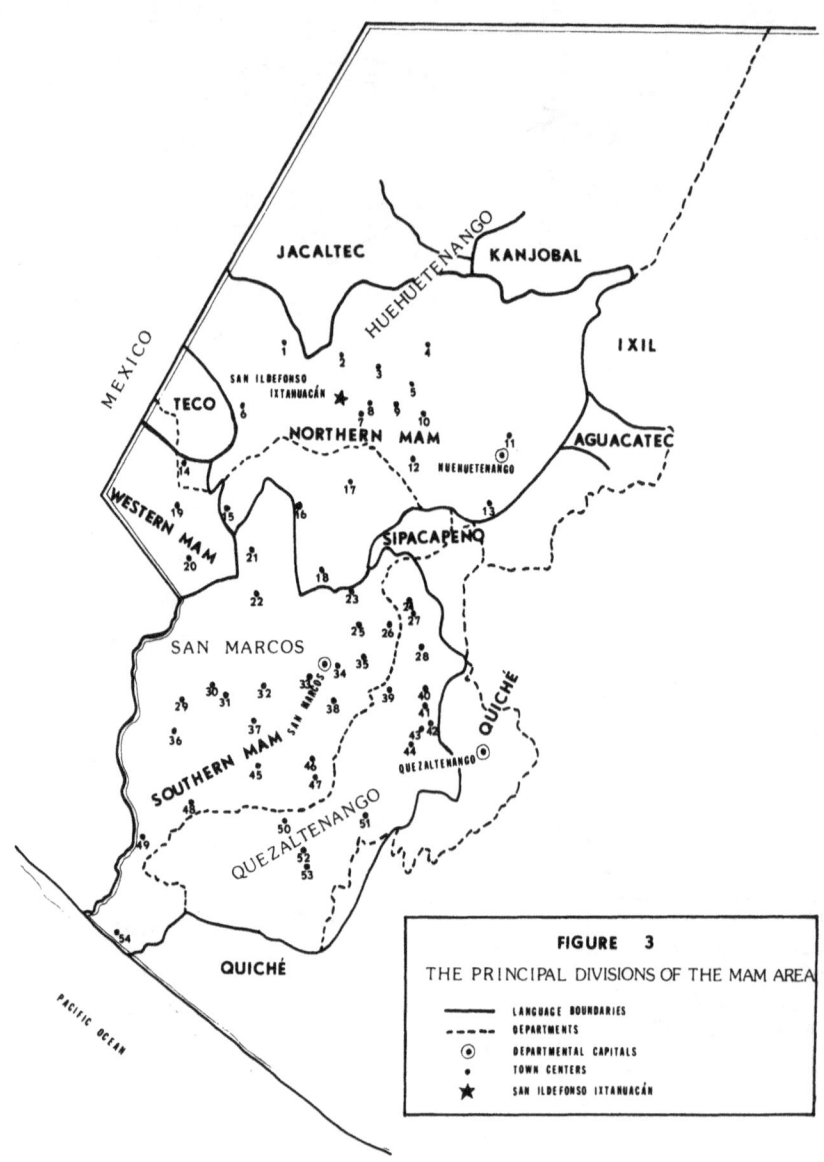

FIGURE 3
THE PRINCIPAL DIVISIONS OF THE MAM AREA

— LANGUAGE BOUNDARIES
--- DEPARTMENTS
⊙ DEPARTMENTAL CAPITALS
• TOWN CENTERS
★ SAN ILDEFONSO IXTAHUACÁN

Figure 3: Town Names

1. La Libertad
2. San Pedro Necta
3. Santiago Chimaltenango
4. Todos Santos Cuchumatán
5. San Juan Atitán
6. Cuilco
7. San Gaspar Ixchil
8. Colotenango
9. San Rafael Pétzal
10. San Sebastián Huehuetenango
11. Chiantla
12. Santa Barbara
13. Malacatancito
14. Tectitán
15. San José Ojetenam
16. Concepción Tutuapa
17. San Miguel Ixtahuacán
18. Tejutla
19. Tacaná
20. Sibinal
21. Ixchiguán
22. Tajumulco
23. Comitancillo
24. Cabricán
25. San Lorenzo
26. Rio Blanco
27. Huitán
28. Sibilia
29. Malacatán
30. San Pablo
31. El Rodeo
32. San Rafael Pie de la Cuesta
33. Esquipulas
34. San Pedro Sacatepéquez
35. San Antonio Sacatepéquez
36. Catarina
37. El Tumbador
38. San Cristóbal Cucho
39. Palestina de los Altos
40. Cajolá
41. San Miguel Sigüilá
42. San Juan Ostuncalco
43. Concepción Chiquirichapa
44. San Martín Sacatepéquez
45. Nuevo Progreso
46. La Reforma
47. El Quetzal
48. Pajapita
49. Ayutla
50. Coatepeque
51. Colomba
52. Flores Costa Cuca
53. Génova
54. Ocós

about 2600 B.C. (Vogt 1969b), so the Mam people and their forbears have a long history in one area where it would have been perfectly possible to have differentiated towns and groups very early. Many of the present day towns did in fact originate before the Conquest (Valladares 1957: 28) and each has a separate and distinct identity whereby people from one town regard people from other towns as strangers, even if they speak the same language (Wagley 1969: 55). Town endogamy, different styles of dress, and craft and agricultural specialization help establish and maintain the identity of each town. The rarity of intermarriage between towns, the isolation of one town from another, and the rugged mountainous terrain have been major contributing factors in language divergence and the establishment of dialect differences. Different dialects help to maintain separate town identity, so the process becomes circular. Mam speakers enjoy joking about the accents of people from neighboring towns and from the point of view of someone from Ixtahuacán there is nothing funnier than the way people from Colotenango talk (or what they do).

Because of traditional patterns of trade and commerce by which certain towns are linked to other towns, either as sources of certain specialized craft or agricultural items or as outlets for the goods produced locally, people have had limited contact with only a few other towns in the Mam area, and none at all with the more distant ones. People from Ixtahuacán seem to have had the greatest amount of contact with people from Colotenango, Concepción Tutuapa, San Juan Atitán, La Libertad, Cuilco, San Gaspar Ixchil, and San Miguel Ixtahuacán; less with other towns in the Northern Mam area, and practically none outside it.

There has been a distinct change in patterns of contact in the last ten years or so, as opportunities for travel have been increasingly used for various purposes. Many people from Ixtahuacán have recently become settlers in the frontier area of the Ixcán, an outlying <u>aldea</u> (hamlet) of the town of Barillas which is located in the far northwest corner of the department of El Quiché, in the lowlands. Here they have settled along with people from many other towns in Huehuetenango and El Quiché, and not only several dialects of Mam, but several other Mayan languages as well are spoken there. Settlers in the Ixcán return to their native town with frequency, but how much effect this contact will have on the old established towns is uncertain.

Another area of recently increasing contact is through education. Since most towns only have primary schools (although several do have an <u>instituto básico</u> or junior high) young people who wish to continue their education and have the economic resources to do so must travel to the departmental capital or some other large city to do it. There has been a recent surge in the number of people from Ixtahuacán, both men and women, who have been able to study in Huehuetenango. Again it is too early to know what effect the increase in travel and contact among young people will have on town customs or language. Certainly this group of people speaks Spanish much better than has been usual among Mam speakers. A superficial but noticeable innovation which is occurring among women students is that they are exchanging clothing. Mayans have, at least since the Conquest, worn clothing which is distinct for each town. This custom has died out among the men of many towns as they have changed to Western dress, but has been maintained by all Mayan women. Today, however, it is common to see young Mayan women in Huehuetenango wearing a blouse from one town, a skirt from another, and highheeled shoes. No matter how innovative in the area of dress, women still retain at least one piece of traditional clothing.

Recently expanded educational opportunities for Mayans also include the government program of <u>castellanización</u>, a preschool year designed to teach Spanish to Mayan children using the native language as the language of instruction, using speakers of the native language as teachers (<u>promotores bilingües</u>), and even teaching beginning reading and writing in the Mayan language. This program, which began in the late 1960's, has increased Mam contact with Spanish, and has also on occasion placed <u>promotores bilingües</u> in towns other than their own (at times to the dismay of the parents of school children, who may view the intrusion of another dialect as bastardization of their language). Further, Mayan school teachers are becoming qualified in greater numbers, and they also often receive posts in rural areas outside their native towns, according to supply, demand, and educational politics. The net result is that children who go to school have a greater opportunity than previously to have teachers who speak their language (instead of teachers who only speak Spanish) but who may well speak a different dialect of the language.

Finally, several development programs and political movements directed toward Mayans are involving an increasing number of people in jobs, meetings, or negotiations which take them outside their towns and put them in contact with people in other towns who have similar interests. These increased avenues of contact supplement the traditional activities involving contact within the Mayan highlands: trading and agricultural labor. Ixtahuacán has a weekly market which all townspeople attend on a fairly regular basis and which is the local center for economic, social, and certain ritual activities. Part-time vendors from other towns hawk their wares in the market. Men from Ixtahuacán also travel to nearby towns to sell their surplus agricultural or craft products,

and many people from Ixtahuacán attend the weekly market in
Colotenango to buy goods available there. Occasionally the
longer trip to Huehuetenango in undertaken in order to go to
the daily regional market, to shop in the stores, to attend
to legal matters, or to visit doctors.

Men, sometimes accompanied by their families or some members of their families, frequently travel to the coastal areas
of Guatemala and Mexico to work on the large plantations.
This is one of the few ways they are able to earn a cash income, which has traditionally been necessary to participate
in the ritual life of the town and is increasingly necessary
for such additional items as medical services, bus fares,
education for children, manufactured clothing, and a few
household goods. Seasonal agricultural labor is common but
is viewed as a last resort in times of need due to the poor
working conditions and dreaded lowland diseases (to which can
be added pesticide poisoning).

Whether increased contact between people from Ixtahuacán
and other Mayans and Ladinos (non-Mayans) will affect the
language in significant ways remains to be seen. Certainly
it is possible that it might result in the slow-down of dialect divergence, even in dialect convergence, or in an accelerated loss of Mam in favor of Spanish monolingualism. It
has been assumed by some anthropologists that cultural modernization among the Mayans inevitably leads to "Ladinoization,"
a view which is challenged by Brintnall (1979), who claims
that modernization can be carried on within an Indian framework. Similarly the assumption that modernization and increased bilingualism inevitably leads to language loss can be
questioned. If the Mam speakers, and other Mayans, are increasingly finding it advantageous and possible to learn
Spanish it does not necessarily imply loss of their own language.

First, steady bilingualism can be maintained where there is a differentiation of function for the two languages (e.g., Rubin 1968: 116). Second, Mayan languages, including Mam, have withstood over 450 years of pressure toward extinction from Spanish speakers, first as conquerers and representatives of Crown policy, then as settlers, and finally as the economically and politically dominant people in Guatemala. While a few of the Mayan languages in existence at the time of the Conquest have disappeared or have diminished, the majority have remained stable or have grown. With few exceptions, Mam speakers are numerically dominant in the towns where they live and are likely to remain so given the nature of the economic and land tenure structure of Guatemala. They are culturally conservative, although linguistically innovative, and have maintained much more than their language during the years of Spanish contact. Women are the mainstay of family life and tradition and are still, despite increasing educational opportunities, predominantly monolingual in Mam. Men, who have greater responsibilities in the public sphere of village life, speak Spanish more often and better than women, but the entire area has a very high level of monolingualism--perhaps as high as 85%. This of course is lower than the rate of monolingualism among native Spanish speakers in Guatemala, but higher than most other Mayan areas of the country except Alta Verapaz.

Factors which distinguish Mayans from Ladinos are strong in the Mam area. These include values about work. Mam speakers are primarily subsistence farmers who cultivate the familiar Mesoamerican crops of corn, beans, chiles, and squash. Such a high value is placed on agricultural work that men who do not farm are viewed askance. Ritual and religion, a complex synthesis of Catholic and traditional beliefs (Wagley

1949; Oakes 1951; Valladares 1957), functions to create and maintain a separate social identity for the Mam people. Endogamy, in addition to bolstering town identity, identifies members of the community on the basis of descent. Language and dress contribute to that identity, as does tension between Ladinos and Indians. Mam is a vigorous language spoken by a large and likewise vigorous group of people. It is unlikely that the language will die, or even diminish, in the foreseeable future.

2. RESEARCH

I undertook field research on Mam in August, 1971, and from then until December, 1973, continued that research as part of my job as a linguist with the PLFM, in a program supported by the U.S. Peace Corps. During that time I also taught linguistics to twelve students who were native speakers of Quiché, Cakchiquel, or Mam, and taught the Mam speakers at the PLFM how to read and write in Mam, make dictionaries, and collect texts. I began work in Mam with about a month of straight lexical elicitation to learn the phonology, vocabulary, and inflectional paradigms. As I took notes on the sessions, Juan Maldonado and Juan Ordóñez, seated across from me at our work table, copied, upside-down, what I wrote. So I stopped eliciting and started teaching them the phonemic alphabet designed for Mam by Terrence Kaufman and used here. When we resumed elicitation everyone was happier. When I advanced to inflection, which I assumed would be straightforward, I was less happy. Mam speakers do not like simple transitives (see 6, 7, 8) and would mix in intransitive forms wherever possible, or even impossible. But after some months I got past that obstacle too.

During 1972 and 1973 the major task we were all engaged

in was compiling the dictionary. Work on it proceeded from translating a 2500 word list into Mam, to testing all possible monosyllabic roots in inflectional and derivational frames, to listing vocabulary by semantic domain. The result is a good dictionary of over 6,000 main entries which should be published soon (Maldonado, Ordóñez, Ortiz, in press). It has served me as a substantial data source in writing this grammar. Juan Maldonado and Juan Ordóñez also collected a large number of texts during this time which they transcribed and translated and several of which I analyzed. One of them is appended here.

I returned to graduate study at the University of Florida in January 1974, put in another three months of research on Mam grammar in June - August, 1974, and pulled together what I knew about Mam at that point in my dissertation (England 1975). Since then I have made four additional trips to Guatemala for fieldwork. The next was in July, 1977, when I edited the entire dictionary for what was to have been the last, but was actually the antepenultimate, time. Then in June and July of 1978 I worked with Juan Ortiz on Mam syntax and the dictionary, as I also did in June and July of 1979 and 1980. All three of these last periods of research were supported by University of Iowa Old Gold Summer Fellowships.

The data used and cited here consists of the dictionary, the text collection, and my notes. While this grammar is based in part on my dissertation, it has a number of corrections and substantial new material.

3. PERSONNEL

The research for this grammar depended on the assistance of three linguistically sophisticated Mam speakers, Juan Maldonado Andrés, Juan Ordóñez Domingo, and Juan Ortiz Domingo. All are from Ixtahuacán, all are bilingual in Spanish and Mam, and all received linguistic training at the PLFM. I began working with Juan Maldonado and Juan Ordóñez in 1971, and with Juan Ortiz in 1977. All have been magnificent to work with and also have complementary skills which have been very helpful. All are excellent speakers, readers, and writers of Mam. Juan Maldonado has incredible patience for even the most boring tasks, and in dictionary making there is considerable tedium. He also was very interested in and good at recording stories, myths, and all sorts of oral tradition among the older people in town, including an occasional shaman. Juan Ordóñez has an exceptional linguistic ability and was also interested in folk medicine. Consequently the dictionary is replete with cures and preventatives. Juan Ortiz has a highly developed sense of grammar and was able to explain to me minute differences between similar sentences. He also was unusually consistent in his judgments.

Juan Maldonado was born in 1950 and lives in the <u>aldea</u> of Acal in Ixtahuacán. Both his parents are from Ixtahuacán; his father is bilingual in Spanish and Mam and his mother is monolingual in Mam. When I met him he had nine years of formal education, but has recently completed secondary school in accounting. He has farmed, has participated in a number of community development programs, and currently works for the municipal government of Ixtahuacán.

Juan Ordóñez was born in 1953 and lives in the <u>caserio</u> of Chupil in Ixtahuacán. His father is bilingual in Spanish and Mam, his mother is monolingual in Mam; both are from Ixtahuacán. He completed six years of formal education in his town and then participated in a two-year agricultural course in Chiantla, Huehuetenango. He has given classes in Spanish and Mam literacy and is currently a <u>promotor bilingüe</u> in Ixtahuacán.

18 INTRODUCTION

Juan Ortiz was born in 1952 and lives in Chejoj, Ixtahuacán. His parents are also from Ixtahuacán. He has completed six years of formal education, has participated in a course in cooperative promotion in Panama, and has been active in community development work. He currently works for the PLFM, where much of his time is devoted to teaching literacy.

Many other people of Ixtahuacán contributed to our work by recording folklore, helping with data verification or working with us in elicitation sessions. A list of these people follows; others made informal but significant contributions also.

	aldea
Eustaquio García Ortiz	Granadillo
José Ordóñez Méndez	Chupil
Andrés Maldonado Morales	Acal
Juana Maldonado Andrés	Acal
Juan Morales Ordóñez	Acal
Miguel Velásquez Morales	Acal
Sebastián Morales Maldonado	La Cumbre
Diego Ramírez Maldonado	Laguneta
María Maldonado	Chejoj
Pedro Ordóñez Ortiz	Chejoj
Alonso Ortiz Maldonado	Vega San Miguel
Francisco Maldonado Felipe	Vega San Miguel
José Maldonado Vásquez	Chiquililá
Rafael Maldonado Vasquez	Chiquililá
Diego Domingo Felipe	Papal
José Pérez Ordóñez	Papal
Miguel Morales Ortiz	Papal
Pablo Felipe Gómez	Polojá

4. PREVIOUS STUDIES

Early works on Mam are scarce--only a few vocabulary lists and grammatical sketches exist. For a review of the grammatical sketches see Peck (1951), and bibliographies of early works on Mam can be found in The Handbook of Middle American Indians, volume 5, or in Campbell et al. (1978).

In recent years several grammatical studies have been made. The first of these is a master's thesis by Edward Sywulka (1948) in which he briefly describes the phonology and morphology of the Mam of San Juan Ostuncalco, a Southern Mam town. Sywulka studied linguistics with Pike, Nida, and Trager, and wrote his grammar according to a modified tagmemic/descriptive framework. He lists and briefly describes the phonemes and morphemes which he found for Southern Mam. Sywulka's later sketch of Mam (1966) uses the same framework but describes the Mam of San Ildefonso Ixtahuacán (Northern Mam). The latter sketch does not include phonology (although the phonemes are listed in a footnote and Sywulka has by now decided that vowel length is phonemic in Mam), but does include sections on clause structure as well as morphology. It is quite a brief description of Mam which contains a list of some morphemes, notes on sentence structure, and a spot/filler analysis of the verb clause. A sample text is appended.

Dorothy Peck's master's thesis (1951) continues the analysis begun by Sywulka and for data uses recordings made by Manuel Andrade. Peck is concerned with the syntax of Southern Mam. She includes an inventory of syntactic units, a section on the distribution of clauses which is essentially a list of sentences or clauses containing different elements, and a section on features of arrangement of sentences. Sample texts are included. Peck also makes her analysis according to a descriptive/tagmemic framework.

Among the most complete of the recent Mam grammars is that by Una Canger (1969). This work is an analysis of the Mam spoken in Todos Santos (Northern Mam, but quite different from other Northern Mam dialects) according to a glossematic theoretical framework. It gives phonological, morphological, and syntactic information and is extensive and accurate. Of particular interest are Canger's treatments of underlying phonological shapes and verb structure. If one can get beyond the glossematic model it is quite useful.

There is also a modern teaching course in Mam (Robertson, Hawkins, and Maldonado, n.d.) which includes lessons, texts, and a Mam-Spanish-English/Spanish-Mam-English glossary. This is based on the Mam of San Ildefonso Ixtahuacán. The principal author, Robertson, has recently published a monograph on pronoun incorporation in Mayan languages, including Mam (Robertson 1980).

I have written a descriptive grammar of the Mam of San Ildefonso Ixtahuacán on which this study is based (England 1975), have written a grammatical introduction to the Ixtahuacán dictionary (Maldonado, Ordóñez, Ortiz, in press), and have published several articles on Mam (England 1976a, b, c, d, 1978, 1980). The present grammar up-dates previous work and adds substantial new information on syntax. My purpose in writing it has been to provide an adequate description of Mam for anyone who wishes to learn the language, for other Mayan linguists who need comparative material, and for the purposes of theoretical linguistics in addressing issues which data from Mam can complement, particularly issues regarding verb initial languages and ergativity. Not enough is known about Mayan languages outside the small group of linguists who work with them, so hopefully this grammar will help fill the gap.

5. OVERVIEW OF THE GRAMMAR

The organization of the grammar is based on two sometimes complementary and sometimes conflicting principles: to give a coherent analysis of Mam following more or less traditional levels of grammatical description, and to present material in a fashion such that the necessary information for understanding an issue under discussion has already been given in a previous section. For these reasons I in general proceed from analysis of sounds to morphemes to phrases to sentences.

The first two chapters cover phonology. Mam, like other Mayan languages, has a series of plain stops and affricates which is paralleled by a series of glottalized stops and affricates, some ejective and others implosive. It has consonants at several points of articulation not shared with other Mayan languages, due to a tendency toward phonological innovation. It has both long and short vowels at five cardinal positions, and heavy syllable stress. Morphophonemically Mam is characterized by neutralization or dropping of unstressed vowels. The second of these tendencies results in a characteristic consonant clustering, which along with the salience of a retroflexed voiceless fricative and "creaky voice" on vowels near glottals gives Mam a distinctive and readily identifiable "sound" among the Mayan languages. Mam also partly preserves the remnants of historical harmonic and disharmonic processes. Appendices I and II give supplementary data on these processes.

Chapters 3 and 4 address morphology. Chapter 3 discusses the characteristics of root classes and inflectional morphology while chapter 4 is basically an index of derivational morphology. Like other Mayan languages Mam has a special root class (positionals) which refers to physical characteristics and spatial orientation, and makes a clear distinction between

transitive and intransitive verbs. It also has a restricted
class of possessed nouns (relational nouns) which indicate
case and locative relationships. Inflectionally Mam cross-
references NPs on verbs ergatively: one set of affixes is
used to cross-reference the agents of transitive verbs and
the possessors of nouns while another set of affixes cross-
references the patients of transitive verbs and the subjects
of intransitive verbs. The person affixes are innovative
among Mayan languages in indicating only four different persons rather than six; enclitics accompany the affixes to
complete a seven way person system. Although not as synthetic
as many other indigenous American languages Mam does have a
rich and varied morphology. Derivational morphemes perform
lexical, syntactic, and semantic functions.

Chapters 5 and 6 treat the noun phrase and verb phrase
respectively. In the interests of parallel terminology I have
used "verb phrase" to refer to only the verb with its auxiliaries and inflections. Although nonstandard this should not
add greatly to existing confusion since "verb phrase" is
already used in a number of different ways. Noteworthy in
these chapters is, first, that Mam has a noun classifier
system with pronominal functions and, second, that there are
possibilities for noun phrase focus through the use of double
person marking on verbs and double possesssion on nouns and
relational nouns. Additionally, verbs have auxiliaries which
indicate direction of movement and define certain semantic
classes among the verbs.

The last two chapters describe sentence structure and consequently contain the bulk of the syntactic analysis. Topics
covered include constituent structure, typology, voice, focus,
clause structure, and subordination. Mam is a verb initial
language with a syntax which is in general consistent with

that characteristic. Ergativity, introduced previously as a morphological category, has syntactic consequences as well, especially with regard to the structure of focused constituents. Voice is complex, including as "antipassive" with several different functions in addition to a number of different passives. Subordination is indicated in two different ways with a rather complicated distribution: certain subordinate clauses are marked by the use of dependent aspects and others by a shift in which set of person affixes cross-references nouns on the verb. Mam has been syntactically innovative with regard to the last, and the data have bearing on the phenomenon known as "split ergativity".

Finally a text with morphene-by-morpheme glosses is appended. It illustrates, through formal narrative, a number of the grammatical characteristics of Mam.

1. PHONOLOGY

1. PHONEMIC INVENTORY

The phonemic symbols used here and throughout are a practical orthography designed for Mam by Terrence Kaufman and used at the PLFM.

<u>Consonants:</u>

	bilabial	alveolar	alveo-fricated	alveopalatal	retroflex	palatal	velar	uvular	glottal
Occlusive:	p	t	tz	ch	tx	ky	k	q	7
Glottalized:	b'	t'	tz'	ch'	tx'	ky'	k'	q'	
Fricative:		s		xh	x		j		
Nasal:	m	n							
Flap:		r							
Resonant:	w	l				y			
Spanish loans:	b	d					g		

<u>Vowels:</u>

	front	back			front	back
	i	u	High		ii	uu
	e	o			ee	oo
	a		Low		aa	
	Short				Long	

2. PHONEMIC DESCRIPTION

2.1 Consonants

The occlusives are a series of eight simple or affricated voiceless stops each having a different point of articulation. The glottal stop is discussed below in section 2.3. All the stops occur initially, medially, or finally and all require release in final position. /tz, ch, tx, ky, q/ are released with affrication, while /p, t, k/ are released with aspiration. Such affrication or aspiration also occurs optionally before other consonants in clusters. The palatalized stop /ky/ and the velar stop /k/ have restricted and partially complementary distribution (see below) but contrast in some environments and are separate phonemes. The occlusives with their allophones and examples are:

/p/	[pʰ]	/_#	[siːpʰ]	/siip/	'tick'
	[p]	/_ _ _	[puːx]	/puuj/	'dust'
/t/	[tʰ]	/_#	[ɻɪʔtʰ]	/ri7t/	'solid'
	[t]	/_ _ _	[taʔw]	/ta7w/	'pain'
/tz/	[ƛ]		[wɪƛ]	/witz/	'hill, mountain'
/ch/	[č]		[kʊč]	/kuch/	'pig'
/tx/	[č̣]		[ɓuːč̣]	/b'uutx/	'boiled corn'
/ky/	[kʸ]		[kʸaqˣ]	/kyaq/	'hot'
/k/	[kʰ]	/_#	[kʊʔkʰ]	/ku7k/	'squirrel'
	[k]	/_ _ _	[ʂkóːɬyə]	/xkoo7ya/	'tomato'[1]
/q/	[qˣ]	/_#	[ᵍwuːqˣ]	/wuuq/	'seven'
	[q]	/_ _ _	[qɛʔŋ]	/qe7n/	'tortilla holder'

The glottalized occlusives are unit phonemes which contrast with plain occlusives plus glottal stop. Phonetically /tz', ch', tx', ky', k'/ are ejectives, with glottal closure occurring simultaneously or preceding the onset of oral closure. /b', q'/ are implosives. /t'/ varies between ejective and implosive, depending on the speaker. The imploded bilabial /b'/ is always voiced in initial or medial position but is devoiced finally; /t'/ is voiced initially and medially if implosive, and devoiced finally; /q'/ is partially voiced initially and medially and also devoiced finally.[2] The distribution of /ky', k'/ is similar to that of /ky, k/ and is discussed in greater detail immediately following the examples below. The glottalized phonemes with their allophones are:

/b'/	[ɓ̥]	/_#	[sɩɓ̥]	/sib'/	'smoke'
	[ɓ]	/_ _ _	[ɓaˆ:]	/b'aa/	'mole'
/t'/	[ɗ̥]∿[t$^?$]	/_#	[šxɛɗ̥]∿[šxɛt$^?$]	/xhjet'/	'stomach of animals'
	[ɗ]∿[t$^?$]	/_ _ _	[ɗʊ́dən]∿[t$^?$ʊ́t$^?$ən]	/t'ut'an/	'watery'
/tz'/	[ƛ$^?$]		[ƛ$^?$uƛ$^?$]	/tz'utz'/	'coati'
/ch'/	[č$^?$]		[poč$^?$]	/poch'/	'bedbug'
/tx'/	[ǯ$^?$]		[ǯ$^?$ɔǯ$^?$]	/tx'otx'/	'earth, land'
/ky'/	[k$^{y?}$]		[k$^{y?}$aq^x]	/ky'aq/	'flea'
/k'/	[k$^?$]		[k$^?$aˆ:]	/k'aa/	'bitter'
/q'/	[q̥]	/_#	[šlaˆ:q̥]	/xhlaaq'/	'young man, boy'
	[q̬]	/_ _ _	[q̬ɛʔŋ]	/q'e7n/	'booze'

Because /ky, ky'/ are relatively recent innovations, they still show partially complementary distribution with /k, k'/, respectively. In general, /ky, ky'/ are found next to front vowels and before /a/ when followed by a uvular stop or velar fricative, while /k, k'/ occur next to back vowels and before /a/ not followed by a uvular stop or velar fricative. Thus the conditioning factors once included both assimilation and dissimilation. Examples are:

ky, ky'		k, k'	
chikyl	'vertical'	ku7k	'squirrel'
iky'	'pass by'	xkoo7ya	'tomato'
kyixh	'fish'	uk'	'bedbug'
eky'	'chicken'	k'ooj	'mask'
le7ky	'jaw'	kuukxh	'lightning bug'
kyaq	'hot'	kaab'	'brown sugar'
ky'aj	'corn flour'	k'aay-	'to sell'
kyaq'	'guava'	ka7ch	'burst grain'

Now, however, the two sounds contrast. First, the third person plural ergative marker (see 5, 6) is an invariant ky- no matter what the following vowel is:

    kyawal 'their plant'   kyoonb'il 'their help'
    kyeelq' 'their robbery' kyuutz 'their crib'
    kyitzaaj 'their vegetables'

Second, Spanish loan words which contain a /k/ often maintain it next to /i, e/:

    chiikl 'gum (< chicle)'   kees 'cheese (< queso)'

Finally, a small number of words do not show the previous patterning but are neither possessed nor Spanish loans. For instance:

    ky'il 'pot'   k'il 'clay pot'

This pair clearly has a semantic relationship. Two possible explanations occur: that k'il was borrowed from a neighboring Mayan language after the differentiation of the separate palatal and velar occlusives had already occurred in Mam, or that Mam speakers took advantage of the new sound for semantic differentiation.

    Fricatives occur in all positions. /j/ is uvular in the environment of uvular consonants, and is velar elsewhere. The fricatives with their allophones are:

28 PHONOLOGY

/s/ [s]   [si:ɬ]   /sii7/   'firewood'
/xh/ [š]   [ša^:l]   /xhaal/   'frog'
/x/ [ṣ̌]   [ṣ̌xa^:l]   /xjaal/   'person'
/j/ [ẋ] /{_uvular} [qxa^:]   /qjaa/   'our house'
          {uvular_}
     [x] /_ _ _   [xo:x]   /jooj/   'crow'

Nasals occur in all positions. /m/ has [m] as an allophone:

/m/ [m]   [mo:g̃]   /moox/   'junebug'

The allophonic conditioning of /n/ is complex. Generally, it is velar in syllable final position after a vowel, and assimilates to the point of articulation of a following consonant. The rules are:

1. /n/ → [n] /_ {-b'il}   [ɗa^:nɓɩl]   /q'aanb'il/   'medicine'
2. /n/ → [m] /_b'   [qámɓex]   /qamb'aj/   'foot and lower leg'
                          [tqaŋ]   /tqan/   'his/her foot'
3. /n/ → [ŋ] /V _ $ [pɛt'ʔɔŋ]   /ptz'on/   'sugarcane'
                          [šɗaŋpɩt'ʔ]   /xq'anpitz'/ 'type of bird'
4. /n/ → [n] /C _ #   [ʔa^:t'ʔn]   /aatz'n/   'salt'
5. /nn#/ → [n#]   [taxɓlá^:n]   /tajb'laann/ 'it's useful'
6. /n/ → homorganic N /_ {Occlusive}
                         {y}

   [mpá^:yə]   /mpaaya/   'my bag' (</n-/ '1s' + /paa/ 'bag')
   [sxɛñkʸ]   /sjenky/   'guitar'
   [ɗañy]   /q'any/   'you, familiar (males)'
   [ʔá^:nɗɓɩl]   /aanq'b'il/ 'life'
   [ɓɔŋkʰ]   /b'onk/   'fat'
   [ʔʊntʰ]   /unt/   'brains'

7. /n/ → [n] /_ _ _   [nmó:xə]   /nmooja/   'my double thread'
                      [nɛʔl]   /ne7l/   'sheep'
                      [ʔanúpʰ]   /anup/   'silk-cotton tree'

Vowel dropping rules apply after nasalization, so that a
nasal does not assimilate to the point of articulation of
a following occlusive if a vowel has been dropped between
them:
  [wáˆ:nɓə] /waanb'a/ 'sister (of a male)' //waanVb'a//
  [čeːnɗ̥] /cheenq'/ 'beans' //cheenaq'//

As can be seen in the example under 2) and the first
example in 6), /n/ and /m/ are neutralized before a following
/b'/ or a /p/ in the same syllable. In the case of qamb'aj
'foot' the underlying form can be discovered through the
possessed form tqan 'his/her foot'. If, however, there is
no form in which the nasal occurs without a following
bilabial occlusive, the underlying phoneme cannot be
recovered, for example: xkumb'uul 'dove'.

The flap is a very infrequent sound in Mam, occurring
mostly in loans (from other Mayan languages or Spanish)
and sound imitative words. A bilingual speaker might trill
the /r/ in Spanish loans which contain the trill, but a
monolingual speaker never distinguishes between the
flap and the trill.
/r/ [ɾ]   [xoɾáˆ:tʰ] /joraat/ 'quickly'
                 [ɾɪʔtʰ]   /ri7t/   'solid'

Resonants occur in all positions. /w/ is velarized before
back vowels and after /n/. The resonants are:
/w/ [ᵍw] / {_u,o} [ᵍwoːɬ]   /woo7/   'toad'
          {n_   }   [ŋᵍwíːšə] /nwiixha/ 'my cat'
    [w]   /_ _ _   [waˆːɬx] /waa7j/   'tortilla'
/l/ [l]   [laˆː]   /laa/   'chichicaste (type of
                                          nettle)'
/y/ [y]   [yaˆːβ]   /yaab'/   'sick'

30 PHONOLOGY

In Spanish loans three additional consonants are found: /b, d, g/. /b/ also occurs in one native Mam word, baqa 'scarcely'. In old loans or in the speech of monolinguals the voiced stops from Spanish may be changed to a native Mam sound, usually the voiceless stop at the same point of articulation, but the Spanish sounds occur in many words. Examples:

/b/ [b] [baˆ:r̃kʰ] /baark/ 'boat (< barco)'
/d/ [d] [mú:ndə] /muunda/ 'world (< mundo)'
/g/ [g] [gáˆ:nə] /gaana/ 'in vain (< gana 'desire')'

One spelling convention needs to be mentioned. /t/ can be followed by /x/ over morpheme boundaries. This combination is pronounced differently from the occlusive /tx/ and so is written with a hyphen separating the two sounds (t-x).

Since Mam has a large number of minimal pairs, it is easy to find contrasting environments for the separate phonemes. A number of these pairs are listed here:

p ≠ b'
paa 'bag'
b'aa 'mole'

t ≠ t'
taal 'her son (of a woman)'
t'aal 'liquid'

tz ≠ tz'
tzankl 'bunch of hair or thread without order, lying there'
tz'ankl 'something smooth like an orange, lying there'

ch ≠ ch'
chi7l 'basket'
ch'i7l 'edible grasshopper'

tx ≠ tx'
txuutxan 'blister-like'
tx'utx' 'granary'

ky ≠ ky'
kyaq 'hot'
ky'aq 'flea'

k ≠ k'
uk 'a bug like a bedbug'
uk' 'louse'

q ≠ q'
qe7n 'tortilla holder'
q'e7n 'booze'

t ≠ tz
teet 'toy to divert children'
tzeet 'laugh'

tz ≠ ch
tzaak' 'toothy'
chaak' 'tall and skinny'

ch ≠ tx
chil 'rattle'
txil 'quetzal tail'

ch ≠ ky
tchiixh 'its dirt'
tkyiixh 'its fish'

ky ≠ k
ch'ikyl 'vertical'
chiikl 'gum'

ky ≠ k'
kyaa 'grinding stone'
k'aa 'bitter'

k' ≠ q'
k'ooj 'mask'
q'ooj 'anger'

xh ≠ ch
xhiky 'rabbit'
chiky' 'blood'

j ≠ k
joox 'first weeding of corn'
koox 'lame'

t' ≠ tz'
t'ut'an 'watery'
tz'utz' 'coati'

tz' ≠ ch'
tz'ook 'he/she came in'
ch'ook 'plow'

ch' ≠ tx'
ch'ak 'mud'
tx'a7k 'grain'

ch' ≠ ky'
ich' 'mouse'
iky' 'passed by'

ky' ≠ k
nchmeeky'a 'my turkey'
nchmeeka 'my brown wax'

k ≠ q
kuukxh 'lightning bug'
quuq 'sandy farmland'

s ≠ t ≠ tz
seet 'put firewood in fire'
teet 'toy to divert children'
tzeet 'laugh'

x ≠ tx
xiin 'spider'
txiin 'little girl'

m ≠ n
mooj 'double thread'
nooj 'fill up'

PHONOLOGY 31

s ≠ xh ≠ x

poos 'peanut shell without seed'
pooxh 'scarecrow'
poox 'single grub of a kind of large ant'

2.2 Vowels

There are ten vowels in Mam distinguished as to position (front, mid, back), tongue height (high, mid, low), and length (short, long). Long vowels tend to be higher than short vowels. Vowels are also higher before /n/ and lower before /7/. In the environment of glottal stops or glottalized consonants vowels are laryngealized (creaky voice or vocal fry) and long vowels before glottal stop have a long low off-glide accompanied by a drop in pitch. Low and mid vowels have a high off-glide before palatals. The vowel phonemes are:

/i/	[ɪ]	[ʔɪč^{ʔ}]	/ich'/	'mouse'
/e/	[ɛ]	[čɛʔw]	/che7w/	'cold'
/a/	[a]	[čap^h]	/chap/	'crab'
/o/	[ɔ]	[pɔč^{ʔ}]	/poch'/	'bedbug'
/u/	[ʋ]	[kʋƛ^{ʔ}]	/kutz'/	'humming bird'
/ii/	[i:]	[ʔi:č]	/iich/	'chili'
/ee/	[e:]	[ɓe:]	/b'ee/	'road'
/aa/	[aˆ:]	[k^{y}aˆ:]	/kyaa/	'grindstone'
/oo/	[o:]	[xo:x]	/jooj/	'crow'
/uu/	[u:]	[ʔu:ƛ]	/uutz/	'cradle'

Short unstressed vowels which follow the stressed vowel in a word tend to be neutralized to [ə] (see section 4 for a discussion of stress). The underlying form of these vowels is recoverable only if the word undergoes some morphophonemic change which shifts stress to the neutralized vowel. It creates an inconsistency in the practical

orthography because native speakers neither hear the
neutralized vowel as only one of the short vowels, nor as
a sixth short vowel. It is most commonly written as a
by native speakers, but also is written as either of the
other front vowels, e or i, or occasionally as nothing. I
have never seen it written as o or u even though these
vowels are possible underlying forms. As an example of
the variation in writing, I have seen the enclitic [ȼəŋ]
written as tzan, tzen, tzin, or tzn by the same person
transcribing a single text. Undoubtedly the spelling of
words with the neutralized vowel will become standard with
increased use of the alphabet. Here it will be written a.

In roots and stems a short unstressed vowel preceding the
stressed vowel and following a consonant tends to be dropped.
Again, the dropped vowel is unrecoverable unless it appears
in another form which undergoes appropriate morphophonemic
changes. For instance, the forms

    ma waq'naaya 'I worked'

    aq'uuntl 'work'

show that a u has been dropped between the q' and n in
the verb stem. Similarly,

    ptz'on 'sugarcane'

    npaatz'ana 'my sugarcane'

show a dropped a between the p and tz' in the root. The
second pair is also a good example of vowel neutralization
after a stressed vowel (in the possessed form) which is
recoverable when stress shifts to the otherwise neutral
vowel (in the unpossessed form). Vowel dropping leaves
many consonant clusters, which are a distinctive phonological
characteristic of Mam.

There are no vowel clusters of dissimilar vowels. Although long vowels are written as double vowels, they are

not analyzed as geminate clusters. Only one long vowel is
permitted in a word. Vowel minimal pairs are:

i ≠ e
iky'   'passed by'
eky'   'chicken'

e ≠ a
me7xh 'just developing corn'
ma7xh 'tobacco'

a ≠ o
ch'ak 'mud'
ch'ok 'magpie'

o ≠ u
ko7k   'cacaxte (wooden back pack)'
ku7k   'squirrel'

ii ≠ ee
nb'iiya 'my name'
nb'eeya 'my road'

ee ≠ aa
b'ee 'road'
b'aa 'mole'

aa ≠ oo ≠ uu
q'aaq' 'fire'
q'ooq' 'chilacayote squash'
q'uuq' 'quetzal (archaic)'

i ≠ ii
ch'im   'straw'
ch'iim 'pancreas'

e ≠ ee
b'ech   'sprout'
b'eech 'flower'

a ≠ aa
awal   'plant'
awaal 'planter'

o ≠ oo
ch'ok   'magpie'
ch'ook 'plow'

u ≠ uu
us   'fly'
uutz 'crib'

2.3 Glottal Stop

The glottal stop is noncontrastive initially in a word--
all vowel initial words have a glottal onset. In medial
and final position, however, it contrasts with its absence
and is distinctive. Medially after a consonant it definitely
follows the consonant and so is quite clearly not glottalization. There is only one example of glottal stop finally

after a consonant, and in this example it occurs during or even slightly before onset of the consonant. The example is in the enclitic -a 'first person singular', which has the variant -y7 after vowels.

[ŋxaˆːy̨] /njaay7/ 'my house'

Glottal stop after long vowels is realized as falling pitch without actual closure [↓]. Examples are:

/7/ [ʔ] [ʔi̥ʔȼəl] /i7tzal/ 'Ixtahuacán'

[↓] [siː↓] /sii7/ 'firewood'

Glottal stop has structural characteristics of both consonants and vowels. The first person possessive prefix for nouns is n- before consonants and w- before vowels. Generally, vowel initial nouns lose the noncontrastive glottal stop onset under possession and prefix w-. A few nouns, however, do not lose the glottal stop, in which case they prefix n-, just like a consonant initial noun. In the unpossessed form these words have no initial contrast with the other vowel initial words, so the 7 is still not phonemic initially. It must be inserted after possession for those words that maintain it. All Spanish loans, unlike most Mam words, maintain glottal stop under possession.[3]

anup 'silk-cotton tree'

n7anupa 'my silk-cotton tree'

Furthermore, glottal stop can separate vowels, as can any consonant:

pe7eet 'put within a fenced area'

After vowels and before consonants or finally, glottal stop is more like a vowel feature. Vowel initial suffixes or enclitics which follow a vowel either insert a y glide between the vowels or synthesize the vowels. This rule holds for a vowel followed by a glottal stop.

y glide: njaaya 'my house'   <n- + jaa + -a
          nsii7ya 'my firewood'   <n- + sii7 + -a
Synthesis: aq'neet 'to work'   <aq'naa- + -eet
          chee7t 'grind corn'   <chee7- + -eet

Stress (1.4) falls on vowels followed by glottal stop if there is no long vowel in the word. Since stress rules in general are conditioned by vowel features such as length, and other consonants do not have this effect on stress, glottal stop here seems to be a vowel feature rather than a consonant. Minimal pairs are:

7 ≠ absence   7 ≠ q'
ch'o7k 'rooster's comb'   taa7 'his water'
ch'ok   'magpie'   taaq' 'his vine'

C7 ≠ C'
t7anup 'his silk-cotton tree'
t'aal 'liquid'

3. SUMMARY OF PHONOLOGICAL PROCESSES

Briefly, Mam consonants show phonological variation in response to boundary phenomena and internal structure, and Mam vowels show variation in response to stress and length. Boundary effects on consonants include aspirated or affricated release of the occlusives, devoicing (b', t' for those who implode it, and possibly q'), and velarization of n. Internally there is nasal assimilation to a following consonant and assimilation of x to a uvular. Previously there was palatalization of k next to front vowels and dissimilation of k before a plus a uvular or velar fricative, but this process no longer applies since k and ky are now separate phonemes.

Vowels are raised with length, laryngealized near glottalization, and short vowels are neutralized or dropped in unstressed syllables. They are not permitted to cluster, while consonants are.

In general, phonological processes in Mam are not unusual. The most interesting process is undoubtedly the distribution of implosive versus ejective stops. b' and q' are always implosive while t' varies between ejective and implosive and occlusives at all other positions are ejective (tz', ch', tx', ky', k'). Pinkerton (1980) explains this pattern as a universal tendency in voicing: "front articulations favor voicing and back articulations favor devoicing." To adequately test this hypothesis for Mam we would need some precise articulatory data on whether the uvular implosives are in fact voiceless, data which is so far unavailable. At any rate, the hypothesis implies that a voiced (implosive) articulation for the bilabial and alveolar "glottalized" stops is expectable, but that the uvular stop, whether implosive or ejective, should be voiceless if any other more fronted glottalized occlusives are.

4. STRESS

Stress is predictable in Mam. Every word has one stress, according to the following rules:

1. Stress falls on a long vowel in the word.
    [ʔaqʼúːntl] /aqʼuuntl/ 'work'
    [waqʼnáˆːyə] /waqʼnaaya/ 'I worked'

2. If there is no long vowel, stress falls on the vowel preceding the last glottal stop in the word.
    [puʔláʔ] /pu7la7/ 'dipper'

38 PHONOLOGY

3. If there is no long vowel and no glottal stop, stress falls on the vowel preceding the last consonant in the root.

[spík^{y?}ə]   /spiky'a/   'clear'

[špɪčáq̓]   /xpichaq'/   'raccoon'

Thus stress is conditioned by long vowels and glottal stop and is a type of "heavy syllable" stress. It does not fall on suffixes or enclitics unless they contain long vowels or a glottal stop.

5. THE SYLLABLE

Syllabic peaks occur on vowels, which may be long or short, with or without a following glottal stop. Final short unstressed vowels plus a nasal can be reduced to a syllabic nasal. Consonants can cluster up to four in any position, usually due to vowel dropping and morpheme addition. The only consonant clusters which occur in root morphemes where no vowel dropping has occurred are of the shape nC (see 3.10).

Syllables can end or begin with either a consonant or vowel, but there is a tendency to close syllables at both ends where possible. One piece of evidence for this tendency is that all vowel initial words phonetically begin with a glottal onset. Another piece of evidence is the release behavior of occlusives. They are optionally released with affrication or aspiration in word final position or internally when followed by another consonant. Since this is basically a boundary phenomenon, it suggests that words with internal consonant clusters split the consonants between two syllables:

CVC $ CVC

and therefore the first consonant of such a cluster can be aspirated if it is an occlusive. Furthermore, nasals in this position (CVNCVC) do not show complete assimilation, but are velarized unless the following consonant is b', in which case they are bilabial. That is, nasals here do not assimilate to a following nonvelar except b'. Since the other position in which nasals are velarized is word finally, this also suggests that it is syllable boundary rather than word boundary which controls the variation, and that two internal consonants are split between the preceding and following vowels. There are not as clear suggestions as to how more than two consonants in an internal cluster would be split between syllables. I suspect that if two of those consonants are occlusives, the split would occur between them, and that if the first of such clusters is a nasal the split would occur after the second consonant, but I have no evidence to prove it or account for other instances.

6. JUNCTURE

Word juncture, which is here indicated by a space, is defined both phonologically and grammatically. Words have one and only one stress and no more than one long vowel. Therefore juncture must occur between two stresses or two long vowels in a segment. The aspirated or affricated release of simple occlusives in final position indicates juncture, as does the devoicing of implosives. Furthermore, a pause can occur at juncture, although in rapid speech it usually does not. In addition to these phonological criteria, morphological structure of words determines word boundaries.

   Morphemes consist of prefixes, roots, suffixes, and clitics. Clitics are almost always postposed to a word due to phonological or immediate constituent criteria (the major exception being <u>qa</u> 'plural', which can be either preposed or postposed to a word). Juncture therefore occurs before roots or prefixes or after roots, suffixes, or clitics. The only real problem in juncture analysis is in the verb phrase: Are aspects prefixes or words? Are directionals roots or affixes? Are absolutive person markers prefixes or words? Since decisions about the status of these elements have practical implications for writing, they are briefly considered here and solutions, perhaps arbitrary, are offered.

Some aspects are phonologically bound (those that have no vowels) and some are independent (those that have a vowel). The phonologically free aspects can take enclitics, while the bound ones cannot. Therefore I consider that the free aspects are separated from the rest of the verb by juncture, and they are written here with a space.

Directionals are derived from free roots and are preposed to the main verb in the verb phrase. Pause can occur after directionals, and they can also receive stress, although in connected speech they usually do not. For these reasons, directionals are written as separate words. For other syntactic reasons (see chapter 8) it seems that Mam speakers are somewhat ambivalent as to whether directionals are free roots or not. Thus, while they shorten any long vowel in the roots from which they are derived, native speakers will often write an incorrect long vowel in a directional.

Ergative person markers are phonologically bound (they contain no vowels) and are therefore written together with what follows. Absolutive person markers are phonologically independent in the first person singular or plural and in the nonfirst person plural (they do contain vowels).

They are written separately, except when they occur with the
verb 'go' to which they are in fact phonologically bound:

Absolutive	'Go' Form	
chin-	ma chiinxa	'I went'
(bound)	ma txi	'he/she went'
qo-	ma qo7x	'we went'
chi-	ma che7x	'they went'

The vowels of qo- and chi- also synthesize with several
vowel initial directionals (at least on occasion) and are
written together with these directionals. The major
elements of the verb phrase are therefore written as follows:

Unbound Aspect # Absolutives # Directional #
Bound Aspect - Bound Absolutives -

Ergatives - Stem - Enclitics

NOTES
1. [ˊ] is used here to indicate stress; [↓] indicates the
   allophone of glottal stop which consists of falling
   pitch without actual closure.
2. Judgments of voicing have been made impressionistically;
   if sonographs of these implosives are made it might be
   found that q' is voiceless throughout. b' is undoubtedly
   voiced except in final position.
3. The fact that Spanish loans predictably maintain glottal
   stop under possession, even though these words in
   Spanish do not have a glottal onset, is an instance of
   generalization, in which the most common of the possessive
   prefixes, n-, is used for all new words. The few Mam
   stems which have a firm glottal stop are not predictable.
   They are also not the same ones as those in other Mayan
   languages, so a clear historical pattern does not emerge.

In teaching literacy it is necessary to teach writing initial glottal stop by rote, implying that it is nondistinctive for the native speaker. Mam speakers at the PLFM thought it unnecessary.

2. MORPHOPHONEMICS

Morphophonemic processes primarily involve vowels. The various changes which occur are principally due to tendencies which involve unstressed vowels, constraints against vowel clusters, and historical tendencies towards harmony and disharmony. Vowels have been much less stable than consonants in Mam. Other alternations have to do with glottals and nasals.

1. VOWELS

1.1 Vowel Dropping
Short unstressed vowels occurring before the stressed vowel in a root have a tendency to be dropped. This is a "tendency" in that it does not occur in all instances. It is possible that it might be predictable when such vowels are dropped and when they are not on the basis of constraints against consonant clusters, but so far I have not found any completely consistent pattern in consonant clustering and there are at least a few counter examples to the obvious hypotheses. Kaufman states that Mam loses a "first short vowel in two-syllable morphemes if the first syllable begins or closes with s̱, ṣ [x], c [tz], or č̣ [tz']" (1969: 161). The examples below show vowel dropping between other consonants as well, and there are a few instances where vowels next to s, x, tz, and tz' are not dropped, although the rule does account for many examples of vowel dropping. The data need to be subjected to a detailed historical analysis. If the root in which a vowel has been dropped occurs in another form in which

stress is shifted to where the dropped vowel should be, it reappears. If no such form appears, the dropped vowel is not synchronically recoverable.

Examples:

xjab'	'shoe'	tzyuul	'to grab'
nxaajb'aya	'my shoe'	tzuyb'il	'instrument for grabbing'
k'lab	'sisle cord'	chmeet	'is woven'
k'aloo-	'tie'	chemb'il	'loom'
sniky	'ant'	txjup	'animal'
tnom	'town'(from Nahuatl)	b'luk	'ankle'
kyq'iiq'	'fart'	kjo7n	'corn field'

Exceptions:

chinab'	'marimba'	wanoj	'type of cactus'
ch'ejeem	'type of bird'	ky'ijaaj	'string'
saqach	'game'	ch'ixaaw	'fear, anxiety'

Vowels are also always dropped between two y's. For example, xkoo7ya 'tomato' adds the enclitic -ya when possessed, and the resultant form is nxkoo7yya 'my tomato'.

1.2 Vowel Neutralization

Short unstressed vowels which follow the stressed vowel in a word tend to be neutralized to [ə](/a/). If there is a form in which the neutralized vowel receives stress it can be recovered; if such a form does not exist it is unrecoverable synchronically.

Examples:

tpaatz'an	'his/her sugarcane'	nchookaxha	'my thread'
ptz'on	'sugarcane'	chekoxh	'thread'
nchuulala	'my zapote'		
chulil	'zapote'		

Again, there are some exceptions:
 naapixh 'turnip'(<Sp. nabos)   chaapil 'nance (a type of
                                                 fruit)'
Further, in a few instances a short unstressed vowel following
a stressed vowel is dropped rather than neutralized:
 eelq' 'robbery'   waakxh   'cattle'
 eleq' 'thief'   nwaakaxha 'my cattle'
This is more often optional:
 q'ootaj or q'ootj 'corn gruel'
 aatz'an or aatz'n 'salt'

1.3 Vowel + Vowel Phenomena

Since Mam does not permit two vowels to cluster, and since morphemes can begin or end with vowels, there must be some mechanism to separate vowels which occur next to each other across morpheme boundaries. There are two ways to do this: through vowel synthesis and y insertion.

If a vowel final prefix occurs before a vowel initial root, the two vowels are synthesized or, in a few instances, the root maintains a firm glottal stop. The only vowel final prefixes are two of the absolutive person markers, qo- 'first person plural' and chi- 'non-first person plural'. These usually synthesize with the following vowel:
 ma qook-a 'we entered' from qo- + -ook
 ma chook   'they entered' from chi- + -ook
The prefixes can be separated from the vowel initial root by a glottal stop, although this is less common:
 ma chi7ook 'they entered'
The latter option preserves the separate status of the prefix to a greater extent (see the discussion of juncture, 1.6).

If a vowel initial suffix or enclitic follows a vowel final stem, either the vowels are synthesized or a y is inserted between the two vowels. Whether the strategy used is synthesization or _y_ insertion is morphologically conditioned. The suffix -_eet_ 'passive' requires synthesization:

   aq'neet 'work (passive)' from aq'naa- + -eet

Which vowel will be suppressed in synthesization seems to depend in part on a morphological hierarchy and in part on lexical factors. For example, the vowel of the passive suffix -_eet_ suppresses a different stem vowel, as in the above example, but is in turn suppressed by the vowel of a causative suffix which it follows:

   tunkpiit 'chop down trees (passive)' from tunk- + -pi +
                                                             -eet

On occasion different lexemes with the same root will be distinguished in the passive by one of them retaining the stem final vowel and the other not:

   pajeet 'hammer' from pajoo- + -eet
   pajoot 'choke' from pajoo- + -eet

An example of an instance in which _y_ insertion rather than vowel synthesis is required is the person enclitic -_a_:

   jaa 'house'
   njaa_y_a 'my house'

1.4 Vowel Variation

Vowel variation is caused by a number of processes, some of which operate synchronically and some of which are historical processes which are no longer productive. They include harmony, disharmony, variation due to stress, metathesis, and vowel length effects.

1.4.1 _Harmony_. Vowel harmony is probably only semi-productive synchronically. Two suffixes show vowel harmony. The first is -_Vi_ (4.6 #74), which forms measure words. The vowel of the suffix is any one of the five short vowels, in agreement with the root vowel:

    tx'anaj   'piece of food'   tenej   'group'
    potzoja- 'package (verb)'   b'u7uj 'a lot'

There are a few exceptions to the harmony; for instance, the only example I have found for -ij follows a root with a: xhqanij 'double thread'. There are also a few words derived through this suffix in which the root vowel has been dropped, so we can only assume that it was in fact the same as the suffix vowel:

    k'laj 'load of firewood'
    k'loj 'group'

Furthermore, several words with -uj have a as the root vowel, but this can be explained by the more general process of metathesis (see below):

    b'a7uj or b'u7uj 'a lot'
    katxuj 'roll'
    taquj 'piece of something long'

The transitive stem formative vowel (4.1 #3) also shows partial vowel harmony. The underlying form of this suffix is -oo, but it changes to -uu following a u root vowel:

    b'ujuu- 'degrain'
    muquu- 'bury'

Other variation in this particular suffix is not due to harmony.

1.4.2 **Disharmony**. A group of nonproductive suffixes shows the vestiges of an earlier system of vowel disharmony. The suffixes all consist of a consonant plus a vowel, and they form transitive verbs from positional, affect, and transitive roots. They can be loosely classified as "causatives;" some simply form a verb, some form a verb which causes the quality

Table 1. Vowel Disharmonic Suffixes

Preceding Vowel:

(# of examples)	i	e	a	o	u
Suffixes:					
-pii	1		1	7	7
-puu	8	10	7		1
-q'ii					1
-q'uu	4	1	2		
-chaa				3	2
-chii					1
-chuu	1		3		
-tz'aa				1	
-tz'ii			1	1	
-tz'uu		2	4		1
-tzii			1		1
-tx'ii					1
-lee	2			1	
-lii			2		
-luu		1			
-k'uu			2		
-b'aa		1	3		1
-b'ee			3	2	2
-naa	2		1		
-nee			1		
-maa	1				
-muu			2		
-wee			1		
-wii					1

described by the root, and some form a verb which indicates that the quality described by the root arises through the application of force. Specific examples of all of these suffixes are contained in chapter 4, #8, 9, 10, 11, 12, 13, 14, 15, 17, 18, 19, and 20. The most common of the suffixes is -pV, which shows almost perfect disharmony. It has the form -pii after back vowels and -puu after nonback vowels. -q'V also shows the same pattern of disharmony, but other suffixes either have too few examples to see as clear a pattern, or there are too many exceptions to the disharmonic tendencies. Table 1 shows each suffix and the number of times it occurs after each possible root vowel, using the Ixtahuacán dictionary as a data base. Appendix I lists each form found with its meaning.

1.4.3 <u>Stress Effects</u>. Three suffixes which contain a vowel change that vowel to -ii when the suffix follows a nonstressed syllable in the stem. Since most Mayan roots are of the shape CVC (see chapter 3), this rule usually applies to derived stems in which the nonfinal vowel is long or has a glottal stop and is stressed, so that the final vowel or the stem is unstressed. The three suffixes which have this pattern are the stem formative vowel (4.1 #3), the abstract noun suffix -al (4.2 #47), and the intransitivizing suffix -ax (4.1.2 #26). Examples:

iyajii- 'harden young plants or seeds' from iiyaj 'seed'
xb'alamii- 'dress' from xb'aalan 'clothing'
t-xaqaniil 'stoniness' from xaqan 'rocky'
ttx'attx'ajiil 'dirtiness' from tx'attx'aj 'dirty'
a7lajiix 'become green, tender' from a7laj 'young, tender'
chichaniix 'become humid' from chiichan 'humid'

1.4.4 <u>Metathesis</u>. The shifting of stress to long vowels and the neutralization of vowels following the stressed syllable often results in what looks like metathesis. For instance, <u>q'apooj</u> 'young woman' has stress on the last syllable. If an abstract noun is made from this stem, stress shifts to the suffix (-<u>iil</u> in this word, even though the suffix follows a stressed syllable) and the form is <u>tq'opajiil</u> 'youth (of women)'.

Other examples look more like true metathesis, where the stressed vowel maintains the same quality, even when it falls in a different syllable. Example:

   chek<u>o</u>xh 'fine thread'

   nch<u>oo</u>kaxha 'my fine thread'

Another common type of metathesis, or perhaps just vowel neutralization, occurs with the vowel harmonic variant of the stem formative. As was seen above, the form of the stem formative after roots which contain a <u>u</u> is -<u>uu</u>; after the suffix is added the root vowel in many examples changes to <u>a</u>:

   jaquu- 'scratch, scrape'

   maluu- 'paint'

   aluu- 'dissolve'

The reason for analyzing these forms as having an underlying <u>u</u> is that the <u>u</u> reappears in other forms on occasion, and some forms even have two variants of the transitive stem, one with <u>a</u> and one with <u>u</u>:

   jak'uu- <u>or</u> juk'uu- 'pull'

   k'axuu- <u>or</u> k'uxuu- 'eat munchies'

1.4.5 <u>Vowel Length Effects</u>. Since Mam of Ixtahuacán has a constraint against more than one long vowel in a word, several processes operate to shorten one of the vowels when a suffix with a long vowel is added to a stem with a long vowel.

Either the stem vowel or the suffix vowel is shortened; which one shortens is morphologically conditioned. The stem formative vowel, which is an underlying -oo, shortens (and neutralizes to a) after a stem which has a long vowel or a vowel plus glottal stop in the final syllable. Examples:

  b'iitza- 'sing'

  ma7la- 'measure'

The three examples of ii which were seen above in suffixes when they follow unstressed syllables (1.4.3) shorten a preceding stem vowel, however. This means that if a stem has a long vowel in the final syllable, then the stem formative vowel is short, while if a stem has a long vowel in a nonfinal syllable the stem formative vowel is -ii and the preceding long vowel shortens. Examples:

  atz'amii- 'give salt to cattle' from aatz'an 'salt'

  tq'ulaniil 'warmth' from q'uulan 'warm'

  q'ulaniix 'become warm'

Other suffixes either are short after a preceding long vowel in the stem, or shorten a preceding stem vowel. The productive causative suffix -saa has a short vowel after a long stem vowel. A number of suffixes shorten preceding stem vowels, and several of them do not even have long vowels themselves. A list of these suffixes is: -najee7 'repetitive' (4.1.1 #21), -b'een 'resultant locative' (4.2 #45), -ab'iil 'abstract noun' (4.2 #48), -le7n 'abstract noun' (4.2 #50), -na 'participle' (4.4 #60), -naj 'participle' (4.4 #61), -b'aajal 'facility' (4.4 #63), -$V_1C_2V_1V_1$n 'facility' (4.4 #64), and -nax 'direction' (4.7 #75).

2. GLOTTALS

Glottal stops also show some morphophonemic alternation which may reflect less stability than is shown by other consonants in Mayan languages. This includes alternation with glottalized consonants and movement toward long vowels.

2.1 Glottal Stop/Glottalized Consonant Alternation

Glottal stop often alternates with glottalized consonants in final position, usually freely. Examples of such free variation are:

   weeky'a ∿ weey7 'it's mine'
   kub' ∿ ku7 'down (directional)'
   tjaq' ∿ tja7 'underneath it'

There is additionally one suffix in which this variation is obligatory. It is the suffix -eeb', which derives intransitive verbs from positional roots, and which in stem final position has the form -ee7. Note that by stem final I mean that either word finally or before enclitics it is -ee7, and the only time it appears as -eeb' is before other suffixes:

   txul- 'quiet (P)'
   ma txulee7 'he/she became quiet' (final)
   ma chin txulee7ya 'I became quiet' (+ enclitic)
   ktxuleeb'al 'he/she will become quiet' (+ suffix)

A few verbs that begin with glottalized consonants lose the consonant in some forms, which is similar to the above variation except that the initial glottal stop can then drop after prefixes.

   q'oot 'give'
   q'oontza ∿ antz 'give me!'
   q'iit 'take/bring'
   ma txi wii7na 'I took it'

Glottal stops which occur before glottalized consonants usually disappear:

ku7 'down' + b'aj 'finish' → kub'aj 'finish down'

There are exceptions to this tendency, however:

-b'ji7b'il 'nominalizing suffix (#52)'

txa7q' 'the action of crunching a flea'

2.2 Glottal Stops and Long Vowels

There is a constraint against a glottal stop following a short vowel if there is a long vowel in the word. Suffixes with glottal stops which might follow short vowels, either because they follow short vowels in the suffix or because they might occur after a short stem formative or other stem vowel either: 1) shorten a preceding long vowel, or 2) move toward a preceding long vowel. Suffixes which shorten a preceding long vowel include -le7n 'abstract noun (#50)', and -bji7b'il 'nominalizer (#52)'.

q'ooj 'anger' + -le7n → q'ojle7n 'state of fighting'
b'eeyb'il 'poverty' + -b'ji7b'il → b'eyb'ji7b'il 'poverty'

Suffixes which move toward a long vowel are -7n 'participle', -7kj 'processive', -7tz 'processive imperative', and -7...al 'specific termination'. The last of these has a slightly different pattern from the first three, so I will discuss the others first. The participle, processive, and processive imperative suffixes pattern according to the following rules:

1. If the root has a long vowel followed by a resonant (m, n, r, l, w, y), the glottal stop moves to that long vowel.
2. If the root has a long vowel followed by a nonresonant consonant, the glottal stop is deleted.
3. If the root has a short vowel, the glottal stop follows the stem formative vowel, which is short.

Examples:
    sjoora-   'snore'; sjoo7ran 'snoring'; sjoo7rakj- 'go and snore'; sjoo7ratz 'go snore!'
    liipa-   'fly'; liipan 'flying'; liipakj- 'go and fly'; liipatz 'go fly!'
    b'iyoo- 'kill'; b'iyo7n 'killing'; b'iyo7kj- 'go and kill'; b'iyo7tz 'go kill!'

The glottal stop of -7...al 'specific termination', however, always moves toward the stem vowel, no matter what consonant intervenes:
    eel- 'go out'; ee7lal- 'go out to a specific point'
    aaj- 'return'; aa7jal- 'return from a specific point'
    ook- 'go in'; oo7kal- 'go in to a specific point'
    kub'- 'go down'; kub'al- 'go down to a specific point'
    (here the glottal stop precedes a glottalized consonant and consequently disappears)

3. NASAL ALTERNATION

Although words can end in m, a number of words change a base form m in final position to n. If a suffix is added to these words the m reappears. This may reflect an earlier rule whereby all m became n finally. Examples:

    poon   'incense'   aatz'an   'salt'
    poomal   'burn incense'   atzamii- 'give salt to cattle'

    xb'aalan 'clothing'   qiinan   'rich'
    xb'alamii- 'dress'   tq'inamiil 'richness'

Final n plus l is reduced to l, even over an intervening vowel (which is dropped). Examples:
    poon- 'arrive there' + -al 'potential' → pool
    taan- 'sleep' + -al 'potential' → taal

3. ROOTS AND WORDS

This chapter describes the classes of roots which exist in Mam, and their special characteristics. Word classes correspond to root classes with the exception that positionals are a root class only. The necessary inflection for forming words from bound roots is also described, but derivational stem forming processes are discussed in the next chapter. They are mentioned here only to the extent that certain root classes are partially defined by special derivational properties. Inflection, derivation, and syntactic properties all help define root and word classes.

1. VERBS

Verb roots are bound forms which must be inflected for person and for aspect or mode. Depending on the type of inflection they take, verb roots are either intransitive or transitive. Two major sets of allomorphs cross-reference the arguments of a verb. These have been called Set A and Set B by Mayan linguists. Set A cross-references the agent of a transitive verb and is the ergative set of person markers, while Set B cross-references the patient of transitive verbs or the subject of intransitive verbs and is the absolutive set of person markers. I will use the terms 'agent', 'patient', and 'subject' throughout to refer to the three different arguments of verbs (see chapter 7 for a more thorough discussion of this terminology). In certain types of subordinate constructions (see 8.1) ergative markers replace absolutive markers to cross-reference the subject of an intransitive verb or the patient of a transitive verb, but the distribution pattern described above applies in all independent clauses and defines Mam verb/argument morphology as ergative (see also chapter 6). Ergativity has syntactic consequences as well (see chapters 7 and 8).

Accompanying the sets of person prefixes are person enclitics. Together the prefixes and enclitics comprise the full person system, as follows:

		Set A	Set B	Enclitics
1	singular	n- ∿ w-	chin-	-a ∿ -ya
2	singular	t-	∅- ∿ tz- ∿ tz'- ∿ k-	-a ∿ -ya
3	singular	t-	∅- ∿ tz- ∿ tz'- ∿ k-	
1	plural exclusive	q-	qo-	-a ∿ -ya
1	plural inclusive	q-	qo-	
2	plural	ky-	chi-	-a ∿ -ya
3	plural	ky-	chi-	

The allomorphs are mostly phonologically conditioned.

    n- ∿ w-:   n- /__C
                  w- /__V
    ∅- ∿ tz- ∿ tz'- ∿ k-:
                  k- /potential
                  tz'- /__V initial root, nonpotential
                  tz- /__ uul 'arrive here' and iky' 'pass by', nonpotential
                  ∅- /__C, nonpotential
    -a ∿ -ya: -ya /V__
                  -a /C__
                  After vowels, -ya varies freely with the forms -ky'a and -y7 in the first person only.

While I will gloss the combination of person prefixes and

enclitics as 1, 2, 3 singular and plural, the prefixes in fact only indicate four different persons--the presence or absence of first person in the singular and plural. Historically the prefixes once indicated all the basic person distinctions (England 1976a), and the enclitics something else, but today the two types of morphemes act together to make all the possible distinctions. First person plural forms refer to us (a group) as opposed to you (another group), so the enclitic on the first person forms excludes second person. The enclitic used with second person forms clearly has a different function; that of marking the presence of second person[1]. Absence of an enclitic implies its opposite. The functions of the prefixes and enclitics can be analyzed as follows:

	Prefixes			Enclitics
A.	+1s	(n- ∿ w-, chin)	A.	-2s (-a ∿ -ya)
B.	-1s	(t-, ∅- ∿ tz- ∿ tz'- ∿ k-)	B.	+2s (-a ∿ -ya)
C.	+1p	(q-, qo-)	C.	-2p (-a ∿ -ya)
D.	-1p	(ky-, chi)	D.	+2p (-a ∿ -ya)

```
PreA + EncA:   1s (+1s, -2s)
PreB + EncB:   2s (-1s, +2s)
PreB:          3s (-1s, -2s)
PreC + EncC:   1p excl (+1p, -2p)
PreC:          1p incl (+1p, +2p)
PreD + EncD:   2p (-1p, +2p)
PreD:          3p (-1p, -2p)
```

PreA is always accompanied by EncA. The singularity of PreA demands exclusion of second person. Some dialects of Mam simply do not mark first person singular with an enclitic, because there is no possible contrast between an exclusive and an inclusive first person singular.

An example of a transitive verb using Set A (ergative)

prefixes and their accompanying enclitics to mark the agent follows. The patient is the unmarked third person singular, the aspect is <u>ma</u> 'recent past', and the verb stem is <u>tzeeq'a-</u> 'hit'.

ma ∅-n-tzeeq'a-ya	'I hit it'
ma ∅-t-tzeeq'a-ya	'you hit it'
ma ∅-t-tzeeq'a	'he/she hit it'
ma ∅-q-tzeeq'a-ya	'we (not you) hit it'
ma ∅-q-tzeeq'a	'we-all hit it'
ma ∅-ky-tzeeq'a-ya	'you-all hit it'
ma ∅-ky-tzeeq'a	'they hit it'

See below, 1.1, for a full explanation of how the two sets of person markers combine on transitive verbs. An example of an intransitive verb with Set B (absolutive) markers for subject follows. The stem is <u>b'eet-</u> 'walk'.

ma chin b'eet-a	'I walked'
ma ∅-b'eet-a	'you walked'
ma ∅-b'eet	'he/she walked'
ma qo b'eet-a	'we (not you) walked'
ma qo b'eet	'we walked'
ma chi b'eet-a	'you-all walked'
ma chi b'eet	'they walked'

Aspect markers are preposed to the verb. They are:

ma	'recent past'
o	'past'
n-	'progressive'
ok	'potential'
x-	'recent past dependent'
∅-	'past dependent'

All but <u>ok</u> are obligatory. The aspects with vowels are phonologically independent and at times are separated from the verb or combine with enclitics. The other aspects are phonologically dependent and are never separated from the verb. x- synthesizes with certain of the absolutive person markers:

    x- + chin- → xhin-
    x- + tz-, tz'- → s-
    x- + chi- → xhi-

In other environments it is realized as x-. ∅- synthesizes with the first consonant of the absolutive prefixes, resulting in the deletion of that consonant:

    ∅- + chin → in
    ∅- + tz-, tz'- → ∅
    ∅- + qo → o
    ∅- + chi → i

The synthesis only affects absolutive markers, and never directionals or anything else which might follow the aspect.

There are two modes, potential and imperative, which are indicated by suffixes on the verb stem. The suffixes are different for transitive and intransitive verbs:

	Potential	Imperative
Transitive:	-a7	-m (→ -n / __directionals)
Intransitive:	-1	--

-1 follows the stem formative vowel (4.1 #3) and lengthens the vowel of a root which ends in a short vowel. It also synthesizes with the compounding directionals -x 'away' and -tz 'toward':

keelax	'he will go out'	k- (3sA) + eela- (go out)
		+ -1 (pot) + -x (away)
keelatz	'he will come out'	k- + eela- + -1 + -tz
kookax	'he will go in'	k- + ooka- + -1 + -x
kookatz	'he will come in'	k- + ooka- + -1 + -tz
kjaawax	'he will go up'	k- + jaawa- + -1 + -x
kjaawatz	'he will come up'	k- + jaawa- + -1 + -tz

    kb'elax   'he will go down'   k- + kub'a- + -l + -x
    kb'elatz   'he will come down'   k- + kub'a- + -l + -tz
    kaajatz   'he will come back'   k- + aaja- + -l + -tz
    kiky'ax   'he will go to the   k- + iky'a- + -l + -x
                other side'
    kiky'atz   'he will come to   k- + iky'a- + -l + -tz
                this side'

The imperative mode precludes the use of any aspect marker, but the potential aspect marker can optionally co-occur with the potential mode. This leads to considerable redundancy, since potential is marked by the mode suffix, by the person marker for third person singular absolutive (k-) and then optionally by the aspect ok. If a construction is neither potential nor imperative, aspect is obligatory. The potential mode suffix for transitive verbs occurs very rarely, since it only accompanies transitive verbs without directionals, and most transitives are used with directionals.

1.1 Transitive Verbs

Transitive roots are bound forms which can be inflected to form transitive verbs without derivation. Most roots are clearly transitive or not on the basis of whether they can be inflected immediately as transitive verbs; very few bivalent roots exist in Mam. Example:

    tzuy- 'grab'

    ma   Ø-t-tzuy   'he grabbed it'
    rec 3sA-3sE-GRAB

Transitive verbs cross-reference their patients with absolutive prefixes, cross-reference their agents with ergative markers, and use the transitive forms of the suffixes of mode^2. The agent can be omitted entirely to express an unknown or indefinite agent (see 7.1.3.1). Person marking is deleted for second person singular of imperatives, as the unmarked imperative. The patient is never deleted, although it is frequently indicated by the prefix for third person singular (∅-) where it is unmarked.

Although there are two sets of prefixes to indicate the agent and patient of a transitive verb, there is only one set of enclitics, which refers to either the agent or both the agent and the patient. If the agent does not require an enclitic, then the patient cannot have an enclitic[3]. If the agent does require an enclitic, then the patient may or may not be indicated by the enclitic. Consequently agent involvement and first person involvement are clear, but patients can be ambiguous, as can nonfirst person involvement. Disambiguation is possible through specification of third person arguments in noun phrases and through use of the antipassive (7.1.3.2). Table 2 shows the logically possible combinations of agent and patient incorporated into the verb, and the actually realized combinations. Marginal forms are indicated by a ?. The analysis of the verb is: ma (recent past) + absolutives + ok (directional) + ergatives + tzeeq'an- (stem, 'hit') + enclitic.

Table 2 shows that the pairs:

1s → 2s, 1s → 3s
1s → 2p, 1s → 3p
1p excl → 2s, 1p excl → 3s
1p excl → 2p, 1p excl → 3p

are not distinct and are therefore ambiguous because there is no way to differentiate the patient when the agent requires an enclitic, unless the third person is indicated in a noun phrase.

Furthermore, the combinations:

Table 2. Agent and Patient Incorporation

Logically Possible:	Actual Forms:	Gloss:
1s → 2s	ma tz'-ok n-tzeeq'an-a	'I hit you/him/her/it'
1s → 3s		
1s → 2p	ma ch-ok n-tzeeq'an-a	'I hit you-all/them'
1s → 3p		
2s → 1s	ma chin ok t-tzeeq'an-a	'you hit me'
2s → 3s	ma tz'-ok t-tzeeq'an-a	'you hit him/her/it'
2s → 1p excl	ma qo ok t-tzeeq'an-a	'you hit us'
2s → 3p	ma ch-ok t-tzeeq'an-a	'you hit them'
3s → 1s	? ma chin ok t-tzeeq'an[3]	'he/she/it hit me'
3s → 2s	? ma tz'-ok t-tzeeq'an[3]	'he/she/it hit you'
3s → 3s	ma tz'-ok t-tzeeq'an	'he/she/it hit him/her/it'
3s → 1p excl	*	
3s → 1p incl	ma qo ok t-tzeeq'an	'he/she/it hit us-all'
3s → 2p	*	
3s → 3p	ma ch-ok t-tzeeq'an	'he/she/it hit them'

Table 2 continued

Logically Possible:	Actual Forms:	Gloss:
1p excl → 2s	ma tz'-ok q-tzeeq'an-a	'we hit you/him/her/it'
1p excl → 3s		
1p excl → 2p	ma ch-ok q-tzeeq'an-a	'we hit you-all/them'
1p excl → 3p		
1p incl → 3s	ma tz'-ok q-tzeeq'an	'we-all hit him/her/it'
1p incl → 3p	ma ch-ok q-tzeeq'an	'we-all hit them'
2p → 1s	ma chin ok ky-tzeeq'an-a	'you-all hit me'
2p → 3s	ma tz'-ok ky-tzeeq'an-a	'you-all hit him/her/it'
2p → 1p excl	ma qo ok ky-tzeeq'an-a	'you-all hit us'
2p → 3p	ma ch-ok ky-tzeeq'an-a	'you-all hit them'
3p → 1s	*	
3p → 2s	*	
3p → 3s	ma tz'-ok ky-tzeeq'an	'they hit him/her/it'
3p → 1p excl	*	
3p → 1p incl	ma qo ok ky-tzeeq'an	'they hit us-all'
3p → 2p	*	
3p → 3p	*	

ROOTS AND WORDS 63

3s → 1p excl
3s → 2p
3p → 1s
3p → 2s
3p → 1p excl
3p → 2p

are ungrammatical because the agent does not take an enclitic and the patient therefore cannot. The combinations:

3s → 1s
3s → 2s

should be subject to the same constraint but there is native speaker disagreement as to acceptability of these forms.

The combination 3p → 3p seems to be impossible for some other reason, perhaps "confusion". This, and the other ungrammatical combinations, can be expressed instead by using the antipassive and indicating the patient in an oblique phrase.

One transitive verb, se7- 'do', is defective and only occurs with the interrogative particle tii 'what?':

    tii q-se7   'what are we going to do?'

All other transitive verbs are perfectly regular with regard to inflection.

1.2 Intransitive Verbs

Intransitive verb roots are also bound and form verbs without derivation. Example:

    kyim- 'die'

    ma   Ø-kyim 'he died'
    rec 3sA-DIE

They cross-reference the subject with the absolutive prefixes, and use the intransitive forms of the suffixes of mode[4]. There is a subclass of intransitive verbs which has been called affect verbs. Morphologically they are like other intransitive verbs, but have a distinctive derivation (4.1.2 #25), and are also distinctive syntactically (8.1.3) and semantically. They usually describe the manner in which an action is performed, and therefore combine verbal and adverbial functions. Examples:

leqeqeen 'walk stooped over'
wit'it'iin 'go running'
lach'ach'aan 'go on all fours'

Intransitive verbs of motion also form a subclass. It is from them that directionals are derived (chapter 6), and they also require equivalent noun phrase deletion in complement clauses (8.4.1). The verbs in this class are:

xi7	'go'	tzaaj	'come'
uul	'arrive here'	poon	'arrive there'
kub'	'go up'	jaaw	'go down'
eel	'go out'	ook	'go in'
kyaj	'remain'	aaj	'return'
iky'	'pass by'	b'aj	'finish'

The forms of one intransitive verb cannot be predicted. The verb is xi7- 'go', and it takes the following forms in the nonpotential:

ma chiin-x-a 'I went'
ma t-xi7 'he/she went'
ma qo-7x 'we went'
ma che-7x 'they went'

The forms of the potential are:

chin xee-l-a 'I will go'
k-xee-l 'he/she will go'
etc.

2. NOUNS

Most noun roots are free forms which can be used with no further derivation or inflection. They are inflected for possession, using a set of prefixes and accompanying enclitics which are identical to the ergative markers used on verbs (Set A). Example of a possessed noun:

    jaa   'house'
    n-jaa-ya   'my house'
    t-jaa-ya   'your house'
    t-jaa   'his/her house'
    q-jaa-ya   'our (not your) house'
    q-jaa   'our (everyone's) house'
    ky-jaa-ya   'you-all's house'
    ky-jaa   'their house'

Several subclasses of noun roots are defined by changes which the root undergoes in the possessed form or in the absolute form. These are described below, and are identified according to the classification used in the Ixtahuacán dictionary prepared at the PLFM and currently in press (Maldonado, Ordóñez, Ortiz). A few additional classes of nouns are defined according to semantic or syntactic properties.

Nouns function as the head of a noun phrase (see chapter 5), and can be modified by adjectives, determiners, measure phrases or plurals, and relative clauses.

2.1 S1

These are noun roots which do not change under possession. The root is a free form. Example:
   k'ooj 'mask'
   n-k'ooj-a 'my mask'

2.2 S1A

The root is a free form and the last vowel of the root lengthens under possession. Nouns which fall into this class show partial phonological conditioning in that all nouns of the shape CV7C belong to it, but there are also a large number of roots whose membership in the class cannot be predicted on phonological grounds. Examples:

    xaq 'rock'
    n-xaaq-a 'my rock'

    ne71 'sheep'
    n-nee71-a 'my sheep'

2.3 S1B

The penultimate vowel of the root is lengthened under possession and the root is a free form. Because unstressed vowels which precede stressed vowels are often dropped (2.1.1), it may seem that a long vowel is inserted where there was no vowel previously, and it is also necessary to know both the possessed and unpossessed forms to know the base form of the root. Example:

    tz'lom 'plank'
    n-tz'aalma-ya 'my plank'
    //tz'alom// base form

2.4 S2

The root is a free form but adds a suffix -V(V)1 for the possessed from. The suffix is basically the same as that which forms abstract nouns (4.2 #47). Only five roots now belong to this class in Ixtahuacán Mam, which suggests that the class may be disappearing. Furthermore, all of them can be possessed without the suffix, although this sometimes involves a change in meaning. Examples:

chiky' 'blood'   xjaal 'person'
n-chiky'-eel-a 'my blood'   n-xjaal-al-a 'my people'

xiinaq 'man'   xu7j 'woman'
n-xinaq-iil-a 'my man'   n-xu7j-al-a 'my wife'

b'aaq 'bone'
n-b'aaq-al-a 'my bone (of my body)'

2.5 S3

The root is a bound form. In the absolute form it adds a suffix -b'aj or -j, while in the possessed form it drops the suffix. All the roots in this class are objects which are normally, or expected to be, possessed by humans. Most of the roots that take -b'aj are body parts and relatives, while most of the roots that take -j are articles of clothing. General food terms fall into both categories. Not all body parts, relatives, foods, and clothing are in the class, and the semantic distinction between the two suffixes is not perfect.

The food terms which belong to this category are terms which describe a general class of food, and each one is matched by a special verb by which the class of food is eaten. The verb stem and noun root are closely related (England, 1980). The food terms are:

chi-b'aj 'meat, beans, vegetables, etc.'
    cho- 'eat meat'
lo-j 'fruit'
    lo- 'eat fruit'
k'ux-b'aj 'roasting ear'
    k'ux- 'eat crunchy foods'
waa7-j 'corn and corn products'
    waa7- 'eat corn'

k'a7-j 'beverage'
    k'a- 'drink'

Examples in possessed and unpossessed forms are:

-b'aj
    qam-b'aj 'foot'
    n-qan-a 'my foot'

    yaa-b'aj 'grandmother'
    n-yaa7-ya 'my grandmother'

-j
    aam-j 'skirt'
    w-aam-a 'my skirt'

    lo7-j 'fruit'
    n-lo7-ya 'my fruit'

Exceptions to the semantic categories:
    txo7w-b'aj 'blanket'
    xmuuj-b'aj 'shawl'
    ky'itz-b'aj 'belt'
    iim-j 'breast'

One word, paasb'il, falls into this class although the suffix in the absolute form is not -b'aj or -j. The suffix is -b'il, an instrumental (4.2 #44), but under possession it is dropped, just like other articles of clothing: n-paas-a 'my hat'.

2.6 Never Possessed Nouns

There is a class of free noun roots which are never possessed because their referents are not considered possessable. The common nouns in the class usually refer to natural phenomena. Examples:

    kya7j 'sky'
    che7w 'star'

2.7 Always Possessed Nouns

These are bound forms which are always possessed, usually and sometimes exclusively by a third person possessor. Most of these nouns refer to parts of objects (non-human, and usually inanimate). Some roots belong to class S3 when they refer to humans (e.g. body parts) and to this class when they refer to objects. All relational nouns (2.10) belong to the class on morphological grounds but are here considered separately for syntactic reasons. Examples:

   t-lok'   'its root'
   t-b'aq'   'its seed'

2.8 Compound Nouns

Compound nouns are nouns which contain two roots, one of them a noun root and the other a noun or adjective root, where the entire minimal phrase refers to a single lexeme. If it is possible to possess a compound noun, it is possessed as a unit; that is, the prefix precedes the compound and the enclitic follows it. Examples:

   saqb'aaq   'rope' (from saq 'white' and b'aaq 'bone')
   n-saqb'aaq'a   'my rope'
   saq ch'i7x^5 'white thorn tree' (from saq and ch'i7x 'thorn')
   nsaq ch'i7xa   'my white thorn tree'

2.9 Complex Nouns

Another class of compounds is formed from two noun roots where the first is possessed by the second. Again the phrase refers to a single lexeme, but if it can be possessed, it is only the second root which receives the possessive affixes. Examples:

t-qul klo7j   'huipil neckline' (from qul 'neck and klo7j
                                                  'huipil')
t-qul n-koolb'a   'my huipil's neckline'
t-q'ab' a7   'branch of a river' (from q'ab'- 'hand' and
                                       a7 'water')
t-q'ab' w-aa7-ya   'my river branch'

2.10 Relational Nouns

A small set of always possessed noun roots indicates grammatical relations in a sentence. Thus while morphologically the nouns are like other always possessed nouns, they have a special syntactic function. That function is to indicate case or locative relationships. A number of the relational nouns are related to common nouns, usually ones that refer to body parts. The only time when a relational noun is not possessed is when it is preceded by the interrogative particle al and the entire phrase functions in an information question (7.4.2). The relationals, possessed by third person singular, and the common nouns to which they are related follow. The parts given in parentheses are the phrase final forms for those relational nouns which have a different phrase final form.

Location:	Relational Noun:		Common Noun:	
	t-witz	'on'	witz-b'aj	'face'
	t'xeel	'instead of'	xeel-b'aj	'replacement'
	t-xool	'between'	xool-b'aj	'interval'
	t-txlaj	'beside'		
	t-iib'(aj)	'over'		
	t-jaq'	'below'	jaq'-b'aj	'cushion'
	t-xe	'under'	t-xee7	'its root'
	t-uj	'in'		
	t-wi7	'above'	wi7-b'aj	'head'
	t-txa7n	'at the edge'	txa7m-b'aj	'nose'

72 ROOTS AND WORDS

    t-b'utx' 'at the corner'
    t-tzii7 'at the entrance'   tzii-b'aj 'mouth'

<u>Case</u>:
    t-i7j 'about'
        (patient, thematic)
    t-uuk'(al) 'with'   t-uuk'al 'his/her companion'
        (instrument, comitative)
    t-u7n 'by, because of, with'
        (agent, causative, instrument)
    t-e(e) 'to, of, at, for'
        (dative, possessive, benefactive, patient)
    t-iib'(aj) 'reflexive'

Examples:

<u>Location</u>:

(3-1)   at-∅   jun el jun woo7 at-∅
        LOC PRED-3sA ONE TIME ONE TOAD LOC PRED-3sA

        t-aal   <u>t-uj</u>   jun a7
        3s-OFFSPRING 3s-RN/in ONE WATER

        'Once upon a time there was a toad that had its offspring <u>in</u> the water.'

(3-2)   ∅-jaw-lee-t   jun xaq kyee7yax <u>t-jaq'</u>
        3sA-GO UP-caus-pas ONE ROCK PRECIOUS 3s-RN/below

        yooxh tx'otx' t-kub'
        RED   EARTH   3sE-GO DOWN

        'A precious stone appeared <u>below</u> the red earth.'

(3-3)   maax-tzan k-tzaaja-l   asta   maax   <u>t-wi7</u>
        UP TO-well 3sA-COME-pot UP TO TO THERE 3s-RN/above

        witz
        HILL

'Well, it has to come from there <u>above</u> the hill.'

Case:

(3-4)   Thematic

juun t-xileen   <u>t-i7j</u>   axi7n ojtxa
ONE 3s-EXPLANATION 3s-RN/thematic CORN BEFORE

'an explanation <u>about</u> corn in the old days'

(3-5)   Comitative

n-qo-ok-ka   teen-a   yoola-1 <u>t-uuk'</u>   matii
prog-1pA-dir-but BE-1p ex TALK-inf 3s-RN/com INTENS

Liixh Peels
Andrés Pérez

'And we started to talk <u>with</u> Andrés Pérez.'

(3-6)   Agent

ax   leq'-ch   ma ∅-tzaaj a7   <u>ky-u7n-a</u>
ALSO FAR-pos adj rec 3sA-COME WATER 2p-RN/agt-2p

'Also <u>you-all</u> brought the water from far away.'

(3-7)   Causative

t-ok   b'aj   tzii7 ch'el t-u7n   nim-aal xaq
3sE-dir FINISH BEAK PARROT 3s-RN/caus DEM   ROCK

'The beak of the parrot was finished <u>because of</u> the rock.'

(3-8)   Instrument

ma ∅-aq'naa-n Kyeel   <u>t-u7n</u>   asdoon
rec 3sA-WORK-ap Miguel 3s-RN/inst HOE

'Miguel worked <u>with</u> a hoe.'

(3-9)   Dative

74 ROOTS AND WORDS

> b'isan ky-ee-tzan-ma   ma   ∅-txi7
> SOON   3p-RN/dat-well-cl/man rec 3sA-dir
>
> q-q'o-7n-a   kyaqiil-ka-x oon-b'il
> 1pE-GIVE-ds-1p ex   ALL-but-encl HELP-inst
>
> 'Soon we gave them all the help.'

(3-10) Possessive

> per enteer jun w-ee-ky'   k-tzaja-l
> BUT WHOLE ONE 1s-RN/pos-1s 3sA-dir-pot
>
> ky-q'o-7n-a
> 2pE-GIVE-ds-2p
>
> 'But you're going to give me mine whole.'

(3-11) Benefactive

> ma chi tzy-eet   cheej t-ee   ky-ajw-iil
> rec 3pA GRAB-pas   HORSE 3s-RN/ben   3p-OWNER-abs n
>
> 'The horses were rounded up for their owner.'

(3-12) Patient

> t-neej-al   ∅-ul   aaj   qo7-ya
> 3s-FIRST-ord num 3sA-dir RETURN   STATIVE/1pA-1p ex
>
> awtorisaa7ra-l t-e   komitee
> AUTHORIZE-inf   3s-RN/pat COMMITTEE
>
> 'First we came to authorize the committee.'

(3-13) Reflexive

> ma kub' t-b'iyoo-n   t-iib'   xiinaq
> rec dir   3sE-KILL-ap 3s-RN/refl MAN
>
> 'The man killed himself.'

2.11 Names

Names include given names, surnames, and toponyms. Given names and surnames are usually borrowed from Spanish and transliterated into Mam, since only a very few older Mam names remain in use. Toponyms name places, and are often descriptive compounds. Relational nouns indicating a specific location are common in the compounds. Examples:

Given Names		Surnames		Toponyms	
Liixh	'Andrés'	Peels	'Pérez'	Chna7jal	'Huehuetenango'
Looxh	'Alonso'	Tmiink	'Domingo'	I7tzal	'Ixtahuacán'
Cheep	'José'	Toontz	'Ordóñez'	Tuj Ch'yaq	'Tuchiac'
Waana	'Juana'	Tis	'Ortiz'	Jlajxa	'Mexico'
Mal	'María'	Mnaal	'Maldonado'	Meq'maja7	'Quezaltenango'
Xwaan	'Juan'	Miintz	'Méndez'		
Liina	'Catarina'				
Wiit	'Natividad'				

3. NON-VERBAL PREDICATES

There are two different sets of non-verbal predicates--one which has stative functions and the other which has locative or existential functions. There are no independent pronouns in Mam; on occasion the stative predicates look like independent pronouns, but they are only used pronominally in focus constructions where they are better analyzed as statives followed by embedded clauses (see 7.2 and 8.2). The structure of the two sets of non-verbal predicates is similar. Each has a base which signals its type, to which is then added person markers which closely resemble the absolutive (Set B) person prefixes, and enclitics. The two sets are:

	Stative 'this is X'	Locative/Existential 'X is (in a place)'
1s	(aa) qiin-a	(a)t-iin-a
2s	aa-ya	(a)t-(a7-y)a
3s	aa	(a)t-(a7)
1p excl	(aa) qo7-ya	(a)t-o7-ya
1p incl	(aa) qo7	(a)t-o7
2p	aa-qa-ya	(a)t-e7-ya
3p	aa-qa	(a)t-e7

The base of a stative predicate is a demonstrative such as <u>aa</u> in the above forms (the <u>aa</u> can be deleted when the rest of the stative is an independent form, i.e. not an enclitic), or a noun or an adjective. An example of a stative with a nominal base is:

	'X is a person'
1s	xjaal qiin-a
2s	xjaal-a
3s	xjaal
1p excl	xjaal qo7-ya
1p incl	xjaal qo7
2p	xjaal-qa-ya
3p	xjaal-qa

The <u>qa</u> in the second and third person plural forms is the plural clitic. An example of a stative with an adjective base follows.

	'X is tired'
1s	sikynaj qiin-a
2s	sikynaj-a
3s	sikynaj
1p excl	sikynaj qo7-ya
1p incl	sikynaj qo7
2p	sikynaj-qa-ya
3p	sikynaj-qa

The base of a locative/existential predicate is (a)t, in which the a is always optional and is actually used the most in the second and third person singular forms, usually mutually exclusively with the a7. Consequently two common forms are in variation with each other for each of second and third person singular:

    2s   ata or ta7ya

    3s   at or ta7

The enclitics which accompany these predicates are the same as those which accompany person marking on verbs and nouns. The person marking is not quite the same as any other set, but is fairly close to the absolutive markers. The second and third person stative forms include the clitic qa in the plural. A comparison of the person marking on the non-verbal predicates with the absolutive markers shows their similarity:

	Stative	Locative	Absolutive
+1s	qiin-	-iin-	chin
-1s	∅	∅ or -a7-	∅
+1p	qo7	-o7-	qo
-1p	∅ (+ qa)	-e7-	chi

Examples of the non-verbal predicates in sentences follow.

(3-14)   t-a7   maax jaa
             LOC PRED-3sA UP TO HOUSE

             'He is in the house.'

(3-15)   noq-tzan pwaq at-∅
             ONLY-well MONEY LOC PRED-3sA

             'Well, only the money is there.'

(3-16)   t-neej-al   ∅-ul   aaj   qo7-ya
             3s-FIRST-ord num 3sA-dir RETURN 1pA-1p ex

             awtorisaa7ra-l t-e   komitee
             AUTHORIZE-inf 3s-RN/pat COMMITTEE

'First we came to authorize the committee.'

4. SUMMARY OF INFLECTION

The three types of words which have been covered so far are those which take inflection. Verbs are inflected for aspect, mode, and person; nouns are inflected for the person of a possessor, and non-verbal predicates are inflected for person. If we consider that the person inflections on non-verbal predicates are variants of the absolutive person markers, then we can summarize the distribution of person markers as follows:

Ergative Marker Functions:	Absolutive Marker Functions:
Agent of Transitive Verb	Patient of Transitive Verb
Possessor of Noun	Subject of Intransitive Verb
	Subject of Stative or Existential/Locative Predicate

5. POSITIONALS

Positionals are a unique root class in Mayan languages. In Mam they are a root class only; the root must be derived to form a stem, which is usually an adjective or verb stem. Several derivational suffixes are specific to this root class. The roots have a distinctive lexical and semantic role, and words derived from positionals have a distinctive syntactic role (see 7.1.5.2 and 8.1.3). Positional roots furthermore have characteristic phonological properties.

Positional roots are overwhelmingly of the shape CVC. Of over 250 positional roots which have been found in Ixtahuacán Mam, only a handful deviate from this pattern. One root has the shape VC (or perhaps this should be considered to be 7VC, since the glottal stop is firm after prefixes): uch'- 'quiet, of a crybaby; wilted, plant'. Three roots have the shape

CCVC[6]: xpret- 'lying there, a thick and large tortilla or something similar'; xhpreq'- 'sitting or standing, of a short, chubby person'; tz'link- 'naked, peeled'. Fifteen roots have the shape CVnC, where the second C is k, ky, or ch:

(x)b'onk-	'standing or sitting, a fat person'
(ch)renky-	'standing or sitting, a person with fat legs'
chank-	'thrown down, a spool or a leafless branch'
(ch)jenky-	'standing, a fat person'
(x)lanch-	'sprawling, an animal, person, or trunk'
(x)lank-	'standing or sitting, a person without shoes'
(x)lenky-	'standing, sitting, lying, of a fat person'
slinky-	'standing, sitting, lying, of a naked person'
xhlunk-	'without branches, of a standing tree'
(xh)tunk-	'sitting or standing, a one-armed or one-legged person'
tzank-	'thrown down, a lightweight substance'
tz'ank-	'thrown down, of a round or spherical object'
tz'link-	'naked, peeled'
(x)wank-	'thrown down, a load'
(x)wink-	'thrown down, something knotted; lying there, a ball of something; badly planted'

Positional roots usually describe a combination of physical characteristics and position of an object, but also sometimes describe either physical characteristics or position. A few roots do not participate in either of these semantic roles. Examples of roots falling into the different semantic categories are:

Physical characteristics plus position:

b'at'-	'thrown down, of a light object'
tzak'-	'thrown down, a dead person or animal with teeth bared'
lej-	'sitting or standing, of a bald person'

b'otz'-   'wrapped up and placed somewhere'
b'oq'-   'thrown down, of a cylindrical object'

Physical characteristics primarily:
letx'-   'broken'
patx-   'uncombed, unkempt'
tow-   'empty'

Position primarily:
koxh-   'lying down'
mej-   'kneeling'
mok'-   'crouched'

Neither physical characteristics nor position:
k'otz-   'quiet'
naq'-   'accustomed'
num-   'tranquil'

Three derivational suffixes have the specific and restricted function of deriving stems from positional roots. One, -$\underline{l}$ ∿ -$\underline{ch}$, derives the positional adjective with the meaning 'placed in the position, form, or state described by the root'. Examples:

b'etzl   'placed in the position of a toad'
jilch   'stretched out, of an animal; unoccupied, of a person who does no community work'

Intransitive verbs with the meaning 'be or be placed in the position, form, or state described by the root' are derived through the suffix -$\underline{ee7}$ ∿ -$\underline{eeb}$'. Examples:

paq-   'lying down'   paqee7-   'lie down'
tutz'- 'sitting'   tutz'ee7-   'sit down'
txal-   'to one side'   txalee7-   'go or place one's self to one side'

Transitive verbs are derived from positionals through the

suffix -b'aa 'place or leave something in the position, state, or form described by the root'. Examples:

mutz-	'upside down'	mutzb'aa-	'place upside down'
wank-	'thrown down, load or lump'	wankb'aa-	'place in form of a lump'

Additionally, adjectives, verbs, affect words, nouns, and measure words can be derived from positionals through a number of other suffixes which are not unique to the root class (see chapter 4), or through lengthening the root vowel or adding a glottal stop after the root vowel. All the derived forms take the meaning of the root as their main semantic source.

A number of positional roots are bivalent with transitive and adjective roots (and a few are bivalent with noun, affect, or measure word roots). Transitive verb roots which have the same form as positional roots add a verbal meaning to the basic meaning of the root:

Positional:		Transitive:	
b'aq-	'wilted'	b'aq-	'pull up (plants)'
chit-	'broadcast'	chit-	'sow broadcast'
jaq-	'open, divided'	jaq-	'uncap, open'
jet'-	'placed, small load'	jet'-	'carry small loads'
pak'-	'face up'	pak'-	'carry face up'

There are not as many adjective roots which are the same as positional roots as there are bivalent transitive/positional roots, and the semantics are a little different. Instead of adding some further meaning to the basic positional sense, as the transitive roots do, the adjectives remove the positional meaning from the basic semantics and instead refer to the physical characteristics alone. Further, among all possible adjectives, there are a number of semantic classes which are never found shared with a positional root. These include colors, flavors, odors, abstract qualities, temperatures, sounds, and personalities. Examples of roots which are both positional and adjectival are:

Positional:
b'at'- 'thrown down, light object'
b'ej- 'lying with full stomach'
tuk- 'thrown, short thing'

Adjective:
b'at' 'unkempt'
b'ej 'very full, animal's stomach'
tuk 'short'

Perhaps it makes sense to say that positional roots are semantically somewhere between adjectives and transitive verbs. They describe the characteristics of an object which can be described adjectivally, but they add to a purely adjectival description the meaning of being placed in a position somewhere and having those characteristics. A transitive verb adds to this a verbal meaning, of carrying something with such characteristics, or doing something which results in an object having such characteristics.

Positionals, however, have another function which is not adequately covered by this description of the similarities and differences between them and adjectives and transitive verbs. The positional adjective form (that derived with -$\underline{1}$), is used to <u>focus</u> on position, rather than to merely describe some physical characteristic of an object. They necessarily occur preverbally, in focus position (see 7.1.5):

(3-17)   b'onk-1   t-kub'   t-witz   tx'otx'
         FAT-pos adj 3sE-GO DOWN 3s-RN/on GROUND

'It is placed (something fat) on the ground.'

(3-17) focuses on position, or placing, of the object which has the characteristic of being fat. If a related adjective is used instead, the structure of the sentence is different

and the meaning changes to be descriptive of the quality of
the object rather than its position:
(3-18)   t-kub' b'onk tx'yaan t-witz tx'otx'
                 DOG

'The fat dog is on the ground.'

The positional adjective can be sentence initial, to look
structurally more like (3-17), but the sentence now focuses
on the entire noun phrase and still not on position:
(3-19)   b'onk tx'yaan aj t-kub' t-witz tx'otx'
                        rel

'It is the fat dog which is on the ground.'

(3-19) is now a complex sentence (see chapters 7 and 8).
Thus in addition to the special characteristics of positionals
as a root class and their unique derivation, there is semantic and syntactic evidence for considering them a separate
class in Mam, and not a subclass of verbs or adjectives.

6. ADJECTIVES

Adjective roots are free forms which take no inflection or
derivation to form words. Adjectives modify nouns in noun
phrases (see chapter 5), and several derivational suffixes
apply to them as a class, including the suffix -ax (4.1.2 #26)
which derives intransitive stems and the abstract noun suffix
-al (4.2 #47). Examples of adjectives are:

cha7x	'green, blue'	b'a7n	'good'
yooxh	'red'	nach	'bad'
ky'aaj	'lazy'	la7m	'toasted'

Numbers are a subclass of adjectives which have a somewhat
different position in the noun phrase (chapter 5). The number one functions as an indefinite article, and the number

two functions as an indefinite plural. The numbers in Mam are:

juun	1	junlaaj	11	wiinqan juun	21
kab'	2	kab'laaj	12	wiinqan kab'	22
oox	3	oxlaaj	13	wiinqan oox	23
kyaaj	4	kyajlaaj	14	etc.	
jwe7	5	olaaj	15		
qaq	6	qaqlaaj	16		
wuuq	7	wuqlaaj	17		
wajxaq	8	wajxaqlaaj	18		
b'elaj	9	b'elajlaaj	19		
laaj	10	wiinqan	20		

winaq laaj	30
kya7wnaq	40
oxk'aal	60
junmutx'	80

The numbers above twenty are only rarely used in Ixtahuacán, and are not usually known by any but very old speakers. Instead, Spanish numbers have been borrowed. I was not able to elicit more than the numbers given here. While the number system is undoubtedly derived from the old base twenty Mayan system in which each interval over twenty was counted on the way to the next twenty (that is, twenty-one was one toward forty), it has changed and disappeared so that the only remnants are the original numbers from one to nineteen and the numbers for twenty, forty, sixty, and eighty. To all intents and purposes the number system is now decimal.

7. AFFECT WORDS

Affect words describe an action, a movement, the moment of doing something, or a sound or noise. There are a number of roots which function as affect words with no derivation or inflection; other affect words are derived from positional and verb roots (see chapter 4). Affect words precede a verb and require either dependent person or dependent aspect marking (see 7.1.5.2, 8.1, and 8.2). They are not onomatopoeic, or only minimally so, but there are certain phonological conventions which go with certain types of actions. Momentaneous or abrupt actions are described by affect words which usually terminate in a single consonant. Longer actions may reduplicate the entire word, reduplicate part of the word, reduplicate the final consonant, or may lengthen the vowel. In other words, while the form of the root is not onomatopoeic, the root or stem may be phonologically (and paralinguistically) manipulated to be more onomatopoeic. Examples:

(3-20) ni7m s-ee-x   xjaal t-u7n   cheej
              x-tz'-eel-x
        UMPH rec dep-3sA-GO OUT-dir PERSON 3s-RN/agt HORSE

        'Umph! the horse pushed the man.'

(3-21) am   jaq s-ook-x   t-lam-eel
                   x-tz'-ook-x
        SUDDENLY BANG rec dep-3sA-GO IN-dir 3s-CLOSE-abs n

        kamuun
        OUTHOUSE

        'Suddenly, bang! the outhouse door slammed.'

jejejeey 'the sound of laughter' (partial reduplication)
ch'aw ch'aw 'the sound of a hammer on metal' (complete
             reduplication)
matz matz 'the action of scissors cutting hair' (complete
           reduplication)
kall 'the movement of a flea walking beneath the body

hair' (final consonant reduplication)

tzii7r 'the action of shooting' (lengthened vowel)

8. MEASURE WORDS

Measure words quantify mass nouns so that they can be counted. Mam has a great many measure words which are quite specific in reference. Many of them are roots, often identical to common noun roots or to positional roots, and there is also at least one way in which measure words are derived from other roots (4.6 #74). Morphologically measure words are like never possessed noun roots, but they have a special function in the noun phrase (5.1.6). They are obligatorily preceded by a number or the interrogative particle <u>jte7</u> 'how many?'. Examples:

Measure Word		Common Noun	
baas	'glassful (Sp)'	baas	'glass'
ma7l	'shot of liquor'		
laq	'plateful'	laq	'plate'
pixh	'piece'		
txut	'drop'	txut	'drop'
ba7uj	'a lot'		

9. PARTICLES

Particles are words which are never subject to inflection or derivation. A very large number of words, (mostly having syntactic or adverbial functions), belong to this catch-all category in Mam. Particles can be compounded and can add enclitics. Lists, not entirely exhaustive, of the various classes of particles follow. Classes are distinguished by function in the sentence.

9.1 Interrogatives

Interrogatives function to introduce information questions and indirect questions (see 7.4).

    alkyee   'who (question human noun in direct constituency to the verb)'

    al   'who, what (the base of a question of a noun in an oblique phrase)'

    al i7j   'about whom, what' (questions patient, thematic)

    al uuk'al   'with whom' (questions instrument, comitative)

    al u7n   'by, because of, with whom or what' (questions agent, causative, instrument)

    al ee   'to, of, at, for whom or what' (questions dative, possessive, benefactive, patient)

    al iib'aj   'over what'

    al uj   'in what'

(I do not have the other locatives attested in question formations, but assume that they can appear.)

    jtoj   'when'

    jatu(u)ma   'where'

    jaa   'where'

    jte7   'how much, how many'

    tza7n   'how'

    tii   'what'

    tii tqal   'what'

    ti tiil   'what'

    tii qu7n   'why'

    jniky'   'what time'

    niky'puun   'what size'

    je7ky   'how are you'

    kwaanto   'when (Sp)'

9.2 Negatives

Most negatives are formed from a negative root <u>mii</u>. See 7.3 for negative construction.

 mii7n 'no; negates verbs in potential and imperative'
 nlaay ∽ milaay 'it's not possible'
 mijuun 'no one'
 mi7aal 'negates human locative or existential predicates'
 tz'iinan 'no one/nothing is here'
 nti7 ∽ miti7 'negates non-human locatives and existentials; verbs in the nonpotential, nonimperative'
 nyaa7 ∽ miyaa7 'negates statives, direct agents or patients'
 njaa7 'it isn't'
 na7x 'still not'
 mii ∽ miix 'no'
 mixti7 'there isn't'
 ky'eenan 'no one'
 miiky' 'not like that'
 miwtla 'hope not'
 ii ∽ iichaq 'it doesn't matter'
 qamii 'if not'

9.3 Affirmatives

 ja7ka 'it's possible'
 ok 'yes'
 kii 'it's okay'
 joo7 'yes'
 baay 'okay (Sp)'
 byeen 'good, okay (Sp)'
 weena 'good, okay (Sp)'

9.4 Conjunctions

```
b'ix      'and'
mo        'or'
ii        'and (Sp)'
pera      'but (Sp)'
entoons   'then (Sp)'
pwees     'then, well (Sp)'
yajtzan   'and then'
ax        'also'
sineke    'but rather (Sp)'
b'ala     'maybe'
qapa      'maybe'
qa(ma)    'if'
kee       'that (Sp) (subordinator)'
el(a7)    'when (subordinator)'
aj        'when (subordinator)'
ok        'when (subordinator)'
porkee    'because (Sp)'
komo      'like, as if (Sp)'
ii        'that (subordinator)'
```

9.5 Locatives

```
(ma)chii7w  'there'
tzluu7      'here'
jlaj        'on the other side'
luu7        'it's here'
maax(a)     'up to, over there'
asta        'up to (a point) (Sp)'
```

9.6 Temporals

```
ja7la   'now'
yajxa   'later'
```

maaky' 'just now'
qaa7la 'afternoon'
maa yiin 'a little while ago'
nchi7j 'tomorrow'
eew 'yesterday'
ch'ix 'right now'
ojtxa 'before'
yaa 'now (Sp)'
aatxax 'a long time ago'
b'isan 'soon'
despwees 'after (Sp)'
kukx 'still'
k'itxqee 'a little while ago'
priimx 'early (Sp)'
kuxi7 'every little while'
alpiin 'at last (Sp)'
naaj 'soon'

9.7 <u>Manner Adverbs</u>
kyja7 'like this'
iky 'like this'
joraat 'quickly'
cheeb'a 'slowly'
jongaana 'strongly (Sp)'
tx'u7jb'an 'at full speed'
jona7wax 'instantly'
junyaa7 'quickly'
e7lakyim 'as quickly as possible'
b'aaka 'little by little'
chiix 'suddenly'
qit 'at times'
teemb'ix 'always'

yalnax 'usually, simply'
kabaal 'completely (Sp)'
kaasi 'almost (Sp)'
b'i7x 'all at once'
lijeer 'rapidly (Sp)'
q'ab'aal 'by accident'
kix 'like this'
gaana 'in vain (Sp)'
jomajx 'always'
mes 'unintentionally'

9.8 Demonstratives

jluu7 'this one/that one'
aj 'this, that'
ajaj 'this, that'
aqaj 'these, those'
aa 'this, that (stative base)'
naq 'that'

9.9 Exclamations

a 'don't bother me!'
ajuu 'fear of cold water'
ak 'fear of hot water'
aay 'oh!'
a7n 'don't bother me!'
a7ny 'what a shame!'
enaan 'exclamation of fright'
eeq'a 'not a chance! (between men)'
kye7 'not a chance! (between women)'
i7y 'how filthy!'
yii 'what's happening!'
ye 'how nice'

    ooy   'not a chance!'
    kyii7ra 'ridiculous!'

9.10 Vocatives
    oom   'you (familiar between men)'
    q'any 'you (familiar between men)'
    q'oy7 'you (familiar between women)'
    yaa7   'you (familiar between women)'
    oow   'you (familiar between spouses)'
    naan   'mom, ma'am'
    taat   'dad, sir'

9.11 Others
    o7kx   'only'
    noq   'only'
    soolo 'only (Sp)'
    puro   'very (Sp)'
    maas   'more (Sp)'
    ch'iin 'a little'
    yiin   'a little'
    ni7xa 'a few'
    mejoor 'better (Sp)'
    pyoor 'worse (Sp)'
    kuna   'goodbye (first speaker)'
    kuu   'goodbye (second speaker)'
    aax   'the same'
    par   'for (Sp)'
    baseer 'it will be (Sp)'
    mas byeen 'but rather (Sp)'
    dyaay 'what's up (Sp)'
    jodiida 'what a mess (Sp)'
    elj   'in case'

kisan   'right'
maj   'time (vez)'
el   'time (vez)'
jee7kyala   'who knows'
kuuya   'who knows'
sabeer   'who knows (Sp)'
baqa   'scarcely'
kyee7yax   'good, beautiful, excellent'
nemaas   'everyone else (Sp)'
iil   'necessary'

10. CANONICAL SHAPE OF ROOTS

Most Mam roots are of the shape CVC, and in fact only noun, adjective, and particle roots can have more than one vowel, and that rarely. Verbs, positionals, and affect roots are quite restricted as to shape. The only root final consonant cluster that is possible is -nC. Root initial consonant clusters occur, but always as a reduction of CVC to CC through vowel dropping rules. In the shapes that follow for each type of root, the first C is optional, since vowel initial roots of the same shapes occur. (Note however that only one positional root with an initial vowel has been found.)

10.1 Transitive Roots

CV	se-	'burn up firewood'
CV7	se7-	'do'
CVC	tyuy-	'grab'
CV7C	ch'i7l-	'singe'

10.2 Intransitive Roots

| CV7 | xi7- | 'go' |
| CVV7 | kyee7- | 'reach, last' |

CVC	b'aj-	'finish'
CV7C	tz'e7y-	'burn'
CVVC	ch'iiy-	'grow'

10.3 Positional Roots

CVC	pew-	'discoid'
CVnC	wank-	'in form of a ball'
CCVC[7]	xhpreq'-	'sitting, standing, a short chubby person'

10.4 Noun Roots

CVV	b'aa	'mole'
CVV7	kyaa7	'type of caterpillar'
CVC	jos	'egg'
CV7C	ch'i7x	'thorn'
CVVC	b'aaq	'bone'
CVV7C	muu7n	'seedling'
CVnC	chank	'instrument for rolling thread'
CVVnC	peenky'	'type of flower'
CV7VVC	sa7aan	'part of a loom'
CVVCV	q'eeb'a	'type of tree'
CVCVC	chinab'	'marimba'
CVCVVC	ky'ijaaj	'twine'
CV7CVC	wi7tan	'cypress'
CVVCVC	siik'al	'oak'
CCVC	b'laq	'corn cob'
CCVVC	jb'aal	'rain'

10.5 Adjective Roots

CV7	chi7	'sweet'
CVV	k'aa	'bitter'
CVV7	nee7	'small'

CVC	ch'ul	'squishy'
CV7C	b'a7n	'good'
CVVC	juuch'	'narrow'
CVnC	b'onk	'fat'
CV7nC	ri7nk	'like tiny birds without feathers'
CVCVV7	neqaa7	'near'
CVVCV	meeb'a	'poor'
CVCVC	pak'at	'subsoil-like'
CVCVVC	matiij	'big'
CCVC	jyom	'hollow stick'
CCV7C	tx'le7j	'hairless'

10.6 Affect Roots

CVC	quy	'movement of a worm'
CV7C	txa7q'	'crunch (sound)'
CVV	pii	'a call for turkeys'
CVV7	kee7	'song of chickens'
CVVC	kuuw	'song of doves'
CVV7C	tzii7r	'action of shooting'

10.7 Particle Roots

CV	qa	'if'
CV7	kye7	'not a chance!'
CVV	tii	'what'
CVV7	joo7	'okay'
CVC	ch'ix	'now'
CV7C	tza7n	'how'
CVVC	naaj	'soon'
CVV7C	mii7n	'no'
CVCV	baqa	'scarcely'
CVVCV	maaxa	'up to'
CV7CV	ja7la	'now'

CVnC	q'any	'you (familiar between men)'
CVCVC	b'isan	'soon'
CVCVVC	joraat	'quickly'
CCV7	kyja7	'like this'

NOTES

1. It may seem contrived and over-analytical to analyze at least two different enclitics, and in fact four enclitics (see below in text), from an invariable form. Other dialects of Mam, however, have variation in the enclitic used with different persons, so there is historical as well as synchronic evidence for such an analysis. Ixtahuacán Mam has simply applied vowel neutralization rules to the enclitics. Tacaná (Western Mam) has preserved the maximum distinction:
   A. -2s ∅
   B. +2s -a(7)
   C. -2p -o7
   D. +2p -e7

   (Data from the PLFM dialect surveys.)

2. Ergative markers replace absolutive markers in certain subordinate clauses (8.1), and complex transitive verbs with directionals take intransitive mode suffixes on the directional (chapter 6).

3. There is apparently native speaker disagreement about this. Some people I worked with would not accept forms in which the agent does not require an enclitic but the patient does, others accepted at least several of these forms, such as 3s → 1s, 3s → 2s. These forms, where acceptable, do not have an enclitic.

4. Again, ergative markers replace absolutive markers in certain subordinate clauses (8.1).

5. A space is left between the two roots in this example but not in the previous example. This follows the writing conventions of native speakers, and perhaps indicates that some compounds are more singly lexemic than others.
6. An initial x-, xh-, s-, or ch- is most likely a prefix if it precedes another consonant (4, #1). This is the only prefix which can be added to a positional root. The r in two of the forms is an anomaly anyway since r is not a native Mam sound.
7. The initial xh- is a prefix. This particular consonant cluster must not have come from the reduction of CVC to CC because no positional roots have two vowels.

4. STEM FORMATION

Stems are formed from roots or other stems through the addition of one of a large class of derivational affixes which have the functions of changing the class or the meaning of the root or stem to which they are added, or both. This chapter is basically an index of all of the derivational affixes which have been identified in Ixtahuacán Mam. It is arranged according to the class of the derived stem, and a chart at the end reviews derivation from the opposite point of view by showing which classes of roots and stems can take which affixes. Each affix is numbered for ease in cross-referencing elsewhere in the grammar, and each includes the following information:
1. affix and gloss
2. morphophonemic variation
3. productivity
4. function and examples

Where the primary function of the affix is lexical, words are given as examples, but where the function is more syntactic, sentences are used to illustrate the process.

1) 1. S- 'lexical derivation'
    2. s-, xh-, x-, ch-. Lexically determined.
    3. Productive
    4. These prefixes derive stems of any class from roots or stems of any class, usually with no change in class. They create new lexemes which are similar to, or at times identical to, the meaning of the underived stem. This is an extremely productive way to derive new vocabulary as needed. Examples:

```
q'an    'ripe' (A)              xhq'an   'yellow' (a)
k'aa    'bitter' (A)            xk'aa    'bile' (n)
juk     'short and fat' (A)     chjuk    'potbellied' (a)
toq'    'frog' (N)              xtoq'    'frog' (n)
wit'-   'jump' (T)              xwit'-   'jump' (t)
che7w   'cold' (A)              sche7w   'shivering' (a)
```

2) 1. Reduplication
   2. various
   3. Nonproductive
   4. There are a number of different examples of reduplication which create stems of several classes and for which there are not enough examples to generalize.
      Examples:

```
k'uxk'ub'       'a type of high grass' (n)
saqtz'utz'ub'   'partly dry' (a)
pixhixhii7      'a water bird' (n)
waqlaq          'type of bird' (n)
xko7j   'brown' (A)     xkojkojtee7   'spiny plant, yellow
                                       in color' (n)
jet-    'uneven' (P)    jetetjee7     'uneven'
```

1. VERB STEMS

3) 1. -VV 'stem formative'
   2. The morphophonemics of this suffix are complex. Its basic form is -oo. Morphophonemic rules are:
      a. → a / {VV} C__   b'iitza-   'sing'
                {V7}
                                 ma7la-   'measure'
      b. → uu /CuC__   b'ujuu-   'degrain'
                                 muquu-   'bury'
      b'. at times, and often in free variation, a u in the root → a /__uu (stem formative), for

example:

s̲akuu- ∿ s̲ukuu- 'tie up badly'

c. → ii /V___C___
   [- stress]

    iyaj̲i̲i̲- 'toughen plants and seeds' (from i̲i̲yaj̲ 'seed')

    xb'alam̲i̲i̲- 'dress' (from xb'aala̲n 'clothes')

d. → vowel length with transitive roots which terminate in a vowel or vowel plus glottal stop.

    b'i̲i̲- 'hear'
    tx'a̲a̲7 'bark, bite'

e. a y̲ glide is inserted between nontransitive stems which terminate in a vowel and the stem formative.

    b'eey̲a- 'make a road' (from b'e̲e̲ 'road')

    meb'ay̲ii- 'adopt' (from meeb'a 'orphan')

f. VV → V /___(y)ii

    meb'ayii- 'adopt' (from me̲e̲b'a)

g. → oo /___ ___ (That is, after a CVC root in which the vowel is any vowel but u̲.)

    b'iyoo- 'kill, hit'
    jaqoo- 'open'
    jekoo- 'hang'
    k'ochoo- 'shave'

There are a fairly large number of exceptions to these rules, which are detailed in Appendix II. Briefly, they are that a number of roots or stems take -aa, unpredictably, a few take -ii unpredictably, one root takes -ee, and a number of CVC roots take -a̱. Perhaps the rules are synchronically unproductive and the exceptions have arisen recently.

3. Productive
4. The stem formative vowel is obligatory in the formation of certain verb words:
   a. It occurs before the infinitive suffix -l and the agentive suffix -l, for both transitive and intransitive stems and roots.

b'iy- 'kill, hit' b'iyool 'assassin'
                   b'iyool 'to kill'

   b. It occurs before the antipassive suffix -ṉ, the participle suffix -7ṉ, the processive suffixes -7kj̱ and -7tẕ, and the passive suffix -n̲j̲t̲z̲.

                   b'iyoon- 'kill' (antipassive)
                   b'iyo7n 'killed' (participle)
                   b'iyo7kj- 'go and kill' (processive)
                   b'iyo7tz- 'go and kill!' (processive imperative)
                   b'iyoonjtz- 'be killed' (passive)

   c. It occurs optionally in the nonpotential for transitive roots of the shape CVC, and obligatorily for stems of other shapes.

ma t-b'iy ∿ ma t-b'iyo̱o̱ 'he killed it'
ma t-b'iitẕa̱ 'he sang' (*ma t-b'iitz)

   d. It occurs before the transitive imperative -m and the intransitive potential suffix -l.

tzuy- 'grab'   tzyu̱u̱-m-a 'grab it!'
b'eet- 'walk'   k-b'eeṯa̱-1 'he will walk'

The stem formative vowel also derives transitive stems from other classes of roots or stems.

102 STEM FORMATION

Examples:

b'iitz 'song' (N)   b'iitza- 'sing'
muq- 'buried' (P)   muquu- 'bury'
iil 'fault, sin' (N)   iila- 'scold'
jiip 'tight' (A)   jiipa- 'make clothing tight'

1.1 Transitive Stems

4) 1. -b'aa 'transitivizer'
   2. No variation
   3. Productive
   4. Derives transitive stems from positional roots, with the meaning 'put or leave in the position described by the root'.

mutz- 'upside down'   mutzb'aa- 'put upside down'
txal- 'to one side'   txalb'aa- 'put to one side'
wank- 'in form of ball' wankb'aa- 'put in form of ball'

5) 1. Vowel Length 'transitivizer'
   2. No variation
   3. Productive
   4. Derives transitive stems from positional and affect roots, with the meaning 'do something so that the position or quality described by the root results'.

mok'- 'crouched' (P)   mook'- 'crouch'
b'otz- 'wrapped up' (P)   b'ootz- 'wrap up'
qin- 'stretched' (P)   qiin- 'stretch'
lach' 'a big stem' (AF)   laach'- 'walk with big steps'
pis 'action of breaking something thin and dry' (AF)   piis- 'break something thin and dry'
qech 'noise of grinding' (AF)   qeech- 'grind'

6) 1. -laa 'applicative'

2. -la / V7__
   Shortens a preceding long vowel.
3. Nonproductive
4. Derives transitive stems from noun roots and stems, with the meaning 'use the noun specified by the stem'.

a7	'water' (N)	a7la-	'water'
aam-	'skirt' (N)	amlaa-	'use a skirt'
paasb'il	'hat' (n)	pasb'laa-	'use a hat'
maakb'il	'tool' (n)	makb'laa-	'use tools'
uuw-	'necklace' (N)	uwlaa-	'use a necklace'

7) 1. -wa 'applicative'
   2. No variation
   3. Nonproductive
   4. Derives transitive stems from noun roots. Example:

   si7 'firewood' (N)   si7wa- 'gather firewood'

8) 1. -b'V 'causative'
   2. Varies between -b'aa and -b'ee. See Appendix I for all examples found. While a number of verb 'causative' suffixes show vowel disharmony, this is one of the weakest in terms of showing a consistent distribution.
   3. Nonproductive
   4. Derives transitive stems from transitive, intransitive and unidentified roots. Examples:

aj-	'want' (T)	ajb'ee-	'want'
oq-	'flee' (I)	oqb'ee-	'abandon'
*sas-		sasb'ee-	'feel pulse, touch, weigh'
*k'aal-		k'alb'aa-	'begin a job'
laj-	'drive animals' (T)	lajb'aa-	'retire, move away'

9) 1. -chV 'causative'
   2. Varies between -chaa, -chii, -chuu, with imperfect

vowel disharmony: a /o, u__
i /u__
u /i, a__

See Appendix I for distribution.
3. Nonproductive
4. Derives transitive stems from positional, affect, and unidentified roots. With positional roots the action often involves applying force to something in the position described by the root or so that the position will result. Examples:

b'ow-   'swollen part' (P)   b'owchaa-   'cause to fall'
*ch'up-   ch'upchii- 'wash head'
q'am-   'sound of brea-   q'amchuu-   'break branches'
        king cane' (AF)

10) 1. -k'uu 'causative'
    2. No variation
    3. Nonproductive
    4. Derives transitive stems from affect and unidentified roots. Examples:

jas   'speech in a soft   jask'uu-   'say softly'
      voice' (AF)
*taq-   taqk'uu-   'cut wood'

11) 1. -lV 'causative'
    2. Varies between -<u>lee</u>, -<u>lii</u>, and -<u>luu</u>, more or less disharmonically. See Appendix I for distribution.
    3. Nonproductive
    4. Derives transitive stems from intransitive, noun, and unidentified roots. Examples:

iky'-   'pass by' (I)   iky'lee-   'insult'
q'ooj   'anger' (N)   q'ojlee-   'fight'
*xpap-   xpaplii-   'criticize, blaspheme'

12) 1. -mV 'causative'

2. Varies between -maa (after a root with i) and -muu (after roots with a). There are so few examples that no reliance can be put on the apparent disharmony.
3. Nonproductive
4. Derives transitive stems. Examples:

*siq-   siqmaa-   'blow the nose'
*taq-   taqmuu-   'cut sticks into many equal pieces; fold tortillas'
*yaq-   yaqmuu-   'cut sticks in pieces'

13) 1. -nV 'causative'
2. Varies between -naa and -nee with too few examples to be sure of conditioning. All examples are in Appendix I.
3. Nonproductive
4. Derives transitive stems. Examples:

*tz'iy-   tz'iynaa-   'line up'
*q'ax-   q'axnee-   'warm oneself by fire'

14) 1. -pV 'causative'
2. Varies between -pii and -puu with near consistent vowel disharmony: i /u, o__
                                                                       u /i, e, a__

There are some exceptions. A complete list is found in Appendix I.
3. Nonproductive
4. Derives transitive stems from positional, affect, transitive, and unidentified roots. With positional roots at least the derived verb implies that an action was done suddenly or forcefully to something in the position described by the root. Examples:

b'onk- 'fat' (P)   b'onkpii- 'knock over a fat person'
tuch'- 'work land badly' (T)   tuch'pii- 'work land badly'

106 STEM FORMATION

    *seky'-   seky'puu-   'frighten'
  jas 'single blow' (AF)   jaspuu-   'cut with one blow'

15) 1. -q'V 'causative'
    2. Varies between -q'ii (one example) and -q'uu. Examples are in Appendix I.
    3. Nonproductive
    4. Derives transitive stems from positional, affect, and unidentified roots. Again, force is sometimes implied. Examples:

  *mul-   mulq'ii-   'sink'
  pich'- 'head down' (P)   pich'q'uu- 'let fall head down'
  tzib'   'moment of spil-   tzib'q'uu- 'spill'
            ling' (AF)

16) 1. -saa 'causative'
    2. -sa / $\left\{\begin{array}{l}VV\\V7\end{array}\right\}$ C__; -saa /CVC__
    3. Semiproductive
    4. This is the only somewhat productive causative suffix. It derives transitive stems from adjective and intransitive roots and stems with the meaning 'cause the quality or action specified by the root'. Examples:

  nim   'a lot' (A)   nimsaa-   'make big'
  nooj 'fill' (I)   nojsaa-   'fill it'
  tx'e7l 'toasted' (A)   tx'e7lsa- 'toast'

17) 1. -tzii 'causative'
    2. No variation
    3. Nonproductive
    4. Derives transitive stems from unidentified roots. There are only two examples:

  *ab'-   ab'tzii- 'place an order'
  *ub'-   ub'tzii- 'cure pots'

18) 1. -tz'V 'causative'

2. Varies between -tz'aa, -tz'ii, and -tz'uu with some disharmonic tendencies. Full examples are in Appendix I.
3. Nonproductive
4. Derives transitive stems from affect, transitive, and unidentified roots. Examples:

paq- 'baste, hem' (T) paqtz'uu- 'fold (cloth)'
*b'al- b'altz'ii- 'roll up string'

19) 1. -tx'ii 'causative'
2. No variation
3. Nonproductive
4. Derives a transitive stem. There is only one example:

*kum- kumtx'ii- 'make something return'

20) 1. -wV 'causative'
2. One example has -wee and one has -wii. These are the only examples encountered.
3. Nonproductive
4. Derives transitive stems. Examples:

suk- 'net, wrap' (T) sukwii- 'glean after the harvest'
*tzaq'- tzaq'wee- 'answer'

21) 1. -najee7 'repetitive'
2. No variation; preceding long vowels shorten.
3. Nonproductive
4. Derives transitive stems from transitive roots and stems, and positional roots, adding the meaning 'repetitive' to the action. Examples:

qej- 'lie down' (P) qejnajee7- 'lie down every little while'
qeel- 'run' (t) qelnajee7- 'run every little while'

22) 1. -7kj 'processive'
2. This suffix requires the stem formative vowel. It

has several variants depending on root or stem shape:
    a. CVC + -7kj → CVC + stem formative (shortened) + -7kj

    b. CV$\begin{Bmatrix}V\\7\end{Bmatrix}$C + -7kj → CV$\begin{Bmatrix}V\\7\end{Bmatrix}$C + stem formative + -kj

    c. CVVC   + -7kj → CVV7C + stem formative + [+sonorant] -kj

3. Productive

4. Derives transitive stems from transitive and intransitive stems, adding the meaning 'go and do it'. There are several other ways to add 'go' to the meaning of the verb, and this strategy is slightly different. It is possible to use the verb <u>xi7</u> 'go' followed by a conjoined main verb or by an infinitive (see 8.4.1), and it is possible to add the directional derived from <u>xi7</u> in the verb phrase, which then adds the element of 'movement away'. There are two other processive suffixes, an imperative (#23) and a passive (#31). Examples:

b'iitza-	'sing' (t)	b'iitzakj-	'go and sing'
ma-	'say' (T)	ma7kj	'go and say'
b'eeta-	'walk' (i)	b'eetakj	'go and walk'
qeela-	'run' (t)	qee7lakj-	'go and run'

(4-1) a. conjoined 'go' and verb:

    ma Ø-txi7 b'ix ma Ø-t-il   axi7n t-uj
    rec 3sA-GO AND rec 3sA-3sE-SEE CORN 3s-RN/in

    plaas
    MARKET

    'He went and he saw the corn in the market.'

b. 'go' plus infinitive:

ma   ∅-txi7 kii-l[1]   axi7n t-uj plaas
rec 3sA-GO SEE-inf

'He went to see the corn in the market.'

c. directional plus transitive:

ma   ∅-txi7 t-ki-7n   axi7n t-uj plaas
rec 3sA-dir 3sE-SEE-ds

'He saw (away) the corn in the market.'

d. processive:

ma   ∅-txi7 t-la-7kj   axi7n t-uj plaas
rec 3sA-dir 3sE-SEE-proc

'He went and saw the corn in the market.'

23) 1. -7tz 'processive imperative'
    2. The suffix requires the stem formative and has the same types of variants and distribution that -7kj does:
       a. CVC + -7tz → CVC + stem formative (shortened) + -7tz
       b. CV{V/7}C + -7tz → CV{V/7}C + stem formative + -tz
       c. CVVC   + -7tz → CVV7C + stem formative
          [+ sonorant]
          + -tz
    3. Productive
    4. Derives transitive stems from transitive and intransitive stems, adding 'go' and the imperative to the meaning. Examples:

    ila-   'see' (t)   la7tz-   'go and see!'
    qeela- 'run' (t)   qee7latz- 'go and run!'

tzeeq'a- 'hit' (t)   tzeeq'atz- 'go and hit!'
(4-2) Ø-Ø-la-7tz-a   axi7n t-uj
       3sA-2sE (imp)-SEE-proc imp-2s CORN 3s-RN/in

       plaas
       MARKET

       'Go and see the corn in the market!'

1.2 <u>Intransitive Stems</u>
24) 1. -n 'antipassive'
    2. No variation; requires the stem formative.
    3. Productive
    4. This suffix has the syntactic function of deriving an intransitive verb from a transitive stem whereby the original agent (only) is cross-referenced by the absolutive markers on the verb and the original patient, if it appears, is in an oblique phrase. The antipassive is used for various functions, including unknown or unmentioned patient, agent promotion, object (patient) incorporation into the verb, and lexical functions. See 7.1.3.2 for an analysis of the antipassive. Example:
(4-3) a. transitive

      ma Ø-b'aj w-aq'na-7n-a
      rec 3sA-dir 1sE-WORK-ds-1s

      'I worked it.'

      b. antipassive

      ma chin aq'naa-n-a
      rec 1sA WORK-ap-1s

      'I worked.'

25) 1. -Vn 'affect'
   2. Lengthens the last vowel and adds n̲.
   3. Productive
   4. Derives affect verb stems from affect stems (#72). This may be the stem formative vowel plus the antipassive, added to affect stems. Examples:

wit'it'i 'action of running' (af)   wit'it'iin- 'go running'
palala 'action of floating' (af)   palalaan 'go floating'

26) 1. -ax 'versive'
   2. → -iix / V ___ C
              [-stress]
      VV(7) → V / ___iix
   3. Productive
   4. Derives intransitive stems from adjectives, with the meaning 'become or take on the quality of the adjective'. Examples:

saq 'white' (A)   saqax- 'become white'
xq'iilan 'green' (a)   xqilaniix- 'become green'
niiw 'dirty' (A)   niiwax 'become dirty'
ch'ikych'aj 'rough' (a) ch'ikych'ajiix- 'become rough'

27) 1. -ee7 'versive'
   2. → -eeb' /___V (in suffix, not enclitic)
   3. Productive
   4. Derives intransitive stems from positional roots, with the meaning place in or assume the position specified by the root. Examples:

paq- 'lying down' (P)   paqee7- 'lie down'
tutz'- 'sitting' (P)   tutz'ee7- 'sit'
txal- 'to one side' (P)   txalee7- 'go or put to one side'

28) 1. -eet 'passive'

112 STEM FORMATION

2. Varies according to the shape of the root or stem:

   → -at / CV $\begin{Bmatrix} V \\ 7 \end{Bmatrix}$ C__

   → -t / ...VV(7)__

   → -eet / CVC__

3. Productive

4. Derives a syntactic passive from transitive stems and roots. The verb cross-references the original patient with absolutive markers and agents, if expressed, appear in oblique phrases. Most derived verb stems passivized through -<u>eet</u> do not permit an oblique agent. See 7.1.3.1 for an analysis of passives. Example:

(4-4) a. transitive

    ma   ∅-kub'   ky-tzeeq'a-n   qa-xu7j   xiinaq
    rec   3sA-dir   3pE-HIT-ds   pl-WOMAN   MAN

'The women hit the man.'

b. passive

    ma   ∅-tzeeq'-at   xiinaq   (ky-u7n   xu7j)
    rec   3sA-HIT-pas   MAN   3p-RN/agt   WOMAN

'The man was hit (by the women).'

29) 1. -j 'passive'

   2. → -1 / CVC__

       → -j / CVVC__

   3. Productive

   4. Derives a lexical passive from transitive stems with the implication that the agent has lost control of the action. An agent of any person is permitted in an oblique phrase. See 7.1.3.1 for a discussion of passives and comparisons between this passive and the

syntactic passive. Example:

(4-5) a. transitive

    ma   ∅-ku7-x   t-yuupa-n   Cheep q'aaq'
rec 3sA-dir-dir 3sE-PUT OUT-ds José FIRE

'José put out the fire.'

    b. passive

    ma   ∅-ku7-x   yuup-j   q'aaq' (t-u7n
rec 3sA-dir-dir PUT OUT-pas FIRE   3s-RN/agt

Cheep)
José

'The fire was put out (by José).' (By accident)

30) 1. -njtz 'passive'
    2. No variants; requires the stem formative.
    3. Semiproductive
    4. Derives another lexical passive with the same implication of loss of agent control. Only underived transitives can take this passive, and only third person agents are permitted in oblique phrases. Some stems take both the -njtz passive and the -j passive, some take one or the other, and some take neither. See 7.1.3.1 for further examples and discussion. Example:

(4-6) a. transitive

    ma   chin tzaj t-tzyu-7n-a   Kyel
rec 1sA   dir   3sE-GRAB-ds-1s Miguel

'Miguel grabbed me.'

    b. passive

    ma   chin tzyuu-njtz-a (t-u7n   Kyel)
rec 1sA   GRAB-pas-1s   3s-RN/agt Miguel

114 STEM FORMATION

'I was grabbed (by Miguel).' (By accident)

31) 1. -b'aj 'processive passive'
    2. No variation
    3. Productive
    4. This forms the processive passive which corresponds to the processive (#22) and the processive imperative (#23). The action happens to the patient because the agent goes to do it. A directional is required with this passive and a third person agent only is permitted in an oblique phrase. See 7.1.3.1 for more on passives. Example:

(4-7) a. transitive

ma Ø-txi7 t-la-7kj   Cheep axi7n t-uj
rec 3sA-dir 3sE-SEE-proc José CORN 3s-RN/in

plaas
MARKET

'José went and saw the corn in the market.'

b. passive

ma Ø-txi7 il-b'aj   axi7n t-u7n   Cheep
rec 3sA-dir SEE-proc imp CORN 3s-RN/agt

t-uj plaas

'The corn was seen in the market by José (because he went to do it).'

c. *ma Ø-txi7 il-b'aj axi7n w-u7n-a
                              1s-RN/agt-1s

32) 1. -b'a 'intransitivizer'
    2. No variation
    3. Nonproductive
    4. Derives intransitive stems from a few adjective and

unidentified roots. Examples:

 *ky'ix   ky'ixb'a- 'be wounded'

 kyaq 'red' (A) kyaqb'a- 'be angry'

33) 1. -ch 'intransitivizer'
 2. No variation
 3. Nonproductive
 4. This is found with one transitive stem; it forms an intransitive stem and shortens the preceding long vowel. Example:

 yuuk- 'move it' (T) yukch- 'move'

34) 1. -chaj 'intransitivizer'
 2. No variation, but note that this suffix as well as #35 and #37 begin with the same consonant that some of the transitivizing 'causative' suffixes have, and end with a -j. These suffixes may be composed of the same suffix as the transitive causatives plus the passive -j; because there are few forms and the process is not productive there is no way to be sure. If so, then the passive -j can be used with derived transitive stems as well as underived ones.
 3. Nonproductive
 4. Derives intransitive stems from positional and unidentified roots. Examples:

 b'ow- 'swollen place'(P) b'owchaj- 'fall' (i)

 *q'ip-   q'ipchaj- 'slip (the hand)'

35) 1. -paj 'intransitivizer'
 2. No variation, see discussion in #34.
 3. Nonproductive
 4. Derives intransitive stems from positional and unidentified roots. Examples:

 wit'- 'standing' (P) wit'paj- 'jump'

 lit'- 'stretched' (P) lit'paj- 'stretch'

116 STEM FORMATION

    qin- 'stretched' (P)   qinpaj- 'stretch'
    *tzoq-   tzoqpaj- 'escape'
    *seky-   sekypaj- 'be frightened'
    *loq-   loqpaj- 'wilt'

36) 1. -t 'intransitivizer'
    2. No variation
    3. Nonproductive
    4. Derives intransitive stems from adjective and unidentified roots. Examples:

    b'a7n 'good' (A)   b'ant- 'be well; known'
    *meq'-   meq't- 'be hot'
    *lab'-   lab't- 'bother'
    *q'aj-   q'ajt- 'call, say'
    *siky-   sikyt- 'be tired'
    *tx'uj-   tx'ujt- 'flee'

37) 1. -tz'aj 'intransitivizer'
    2. No variation
    3. Nonproductive
    4. Derives intransitive stems from positional roots. Example:

    jom- 'empty stomach' (P) jomtz'aj- 'be empty'

38) 1. -tz'aq 'intransitivizer'
    2. No variation
    3. Nonproductive
    4. Derives intransitive stems from unidentified roots. Example:

    *kutz-   kutztz'aq- 'fall'

39) 1. -7...al 'specific termination'
    2. The 7 follows the root vowel.
    3. Nonproductive
    4. Derives intransitive stems from intransitive verbs of motion, adding specificity of end point of the action.

Examples:

eel-	'go out' (I)	ee7lal-	'go out to a specific point'
aaj-	'return' (I)	aa7jal-	'return from a specific point'
jaaw-	'go up' (I)	jaa7wal-	'go up to a specific point'
ook-	'go in' (I)	oo7kal-	'go in to a specific point'
kub'-	'go down' (I)	kub'al-	'go down to a specific point'

2. NOUN STEMS

40) 1. aj- 'agent'
   2. No variation
   3. Productive
   4. Derives noun stems from noun roots, with the meaning that the stem indicates a person who uses or is associated with the noun indicated by the root. Examples:

q'iij	'day' (N)	ajq'iij	'diviner'
mees	'table' (N)	ajmees	'shaman'
cheej	'mule, horse' (N)	ajcheej	'mule driver'
miis	'mass' (N)	ajmiis	'Catholic'
poon	'incense' (N)	ajpoon	'person of traditional beliefs'
b'iitz	'song' (N)	ajb'iitz	'singer'

41) 1. aj- 'native'
   2. No variation
   3. Productive
   4. Derives nouns referring to the inhabitants of a place from toponyms. Examples:

Xhniil	'Colotenango'	ajxhniil	'person from Colotenango'

Chna7jal 'Huehuetenango' ajchna7jal 'person from Huehue-
                                        tenango'
I7tzal 'Ixtahuacán'   aji7tzal   'person from Ixtahuacán'

42) 1. -l 'agentive'
    2. Requires the stem formative.
    3. Productive
    4. Derives nouns referring to the agent of an action from
       transitive and some intransitive stems. Examples:

   yoola-   'speak' (t)   yoolal   'speaker'
   aq'naa- 'work' (t)   aq'naal 'worker'
   waa7-   'eat' (t)   waa7l   'eater of tortillas'
   b'eeta- 'walk' (i)   b'eetal 'walker'

43) 1. -eenj 'patient'
    2. No variation; shortens preceding long vowel.
    3. Productive
    4. Derives noun referring to the semantic patient of an
       action from transitive verbs. Examples:

   b'iy-   'kill' (T)   b'iyeenj   'killed person'
   txik-   'cook' (T)   txikeenj   'something cooked'
   chem-   'weave' (T)   chemeenj   'weaving'

44) 1. -b'il 'instrumental'
    2. No variation
    3. Productive
    4. Derives nouns from transitive and intransitive verbs,
       positional and unidentified roots. The noun refers
       to an instrument for doing the action or, less com-
       monly, the place where an action occurs. Examples:

   luk-   'pull up' (T)   lukb'il   'instrument for pulling
                                         up'
   ooq'-   'cry' (I)   ooq'b'il   'something which causes
                                         crying'
   tutz'- 'sitting' (P)   tutz'b'il 'bench or chair'

STEM FORMATION   119

    poom- 'perform rites'   poomb'il 'place for performing
     (t)   rites'

45) 1. -b'een 'resultant locative'
   2. No variation, shortens a preceding long vowel.
   3. Productive
   4. Derives nouns from transitive verbs and positional roots, referring to the place where an action has occurred. Examples:

    juus- 'burn' (t)   jusb'een   'burned place'
    aq'n- 'work' (t)   aq'anb'een 'worked place'
    qej- 'lying down' (P) qejb'een   'place where one has lain down'

46) 1. -b'an 'remainder'
   2. No variation
   3. Semiproductive
   4. Derives noun stems from transitive verbs and positional roots, referring to whatever remains after the action is complete. Examples:

    waa7- 'eat' (t)   waab'an   'remains of food'
    tx'a- 'chew' (T)   tx'ab'an 'something chewed once'
    sjiil- 'slip' (t)   sjiilb'an 'where something has slipped once'
    xpe71- 'plane wood' (t)   xpe71b'an 'wood shavings'
    lo-   'eat fruit' (T)   lob'an   'bits of fruit'
    qej-   'lying down' (P)   qejb'an   'where someone has lain down'

47) 1. -al 'abstract noun'
   2. → iil / V _____ C__
         [- stress]

     VV(7) → V /__iil

     ∅ → y / V__ {al, iil}

There are a large number of exceptions to these rules which are listed in Appendix II. The rules are probably historical and no longer operate synchronically. Interestingly, the suffix -ax (#26) has the same variants and conditioning factors with no exceptions.

3. Productive
4. Derives abstract nouns from any class of root except particles and affect roots, and usually from adjectives. Most abstract nouns are obligatorily possessed. Examples:

lak'	'sticky' (A)	tlak'al	'stickiness'
yooxh	'red' (A)	tyooxhal	'redness'
q'aynaj	'rotten' (a)	tq'aynajiil	'rottenness'
q'uulan	'warm' (a)	tq'ulaniil	'warmth'

Some abstract nouns are not possessed, however. Common exceptions are:

yaab'	'sick' (A)	yaab'il	'sickness'
jb'aal	'rain' (N)	jb'aalil	'rainy season'
nim	'a lot' (A)	nimaal	'big, important'
q'iij	'sun' (N)	q'iijal	'dry season'

There are also some words which apparently add the suffix twice and reduce it to -laal or -liil:

q'iij	'sun' (N)	q'ijliil	'dry spell in the rainy season'
-iib'	'reflexive relational noun'	tib'laal	'form, appearance'

48) 1. -ab'iil 'abstract noun'
   2. Shortens preceding long vowels.
   3. Productive
   4. Derives abstract nouns from adjective roots. The derived noun is always possessed. This suffix has the same function as the -al abstract noun suffix,

and often varies freely with it. Some roots require -ab'iil rather than -al to form an abstract noun, however. Examples:

la7j 'lying' (A)   tlajab'iil 'lies, falsehoods'
look 'crazy' (A)   tlokab'iil 'craziness'

49) 1. -leen 'abstract noun'
    2. Preceding long vowels are shortened.
    3. Productive
    4. Derives abstract nouns from transitive and intransitive roots and stems. The nouns are usually, but not always, possessed. Examples:

kyaaj- 'remain' (I)   tkyajleen 'lateness'
ookx- 'enter' (I)   tokxleen 'entrance'
b'iitz- 'sing' (t)   b'itzleen 'his singing'
tooq- 'break' (t)   toqleen 'fracture'

50) 1. -le7n 'abstract noun'
    2. Preceding long vowels are shortened.
    3. Productive
    4. Derives nouns from any class of root or stem except particles and affect words. The noun indicates the state specified by the root or stem. Examples:

q'ooj 'anger' (N)   q'ojle7n 'state of fighting'
sikyt- 'be tired' (i)   sikytle7n 'tiredness'
matiij 'big' (A)   tijle7n 'old age'
kab'- 'wound' (T)   kab'le7n 'wound'

51) 1. -an 'ordinal'
    2. -al with the root neej- 'first'; -an with all other numerals.
    3. Productive
    4. Derives ordinal numbers from cardinal numbers. The ordinal numbers are always possessed, hence this suffix forms noun stems. Examples:

122 STEM FORMATION

    tneejal 'first'
    tkab'an 'second'
    tooxan 'third'
    etc.

52) 1. -b'ji7b'il 'nominalizer'
    2. No variation
    3. Nonproductive
    4. Derives noun stems from adjective stems which usually have the suffix -b'aajal (#63), without a change in meaning. The suffix appears to be composed of -baajal plus some other suffix, but the forms are now frozen and unanalyzable. Examples:

kib'b'aajal 'visible' (a) kib'ji7b'il 'ease of seeing'
achb'aajal 'happy' (a)   achb'aji7b'il 'happiness'
b'eeyb'il 'poor' (a)   b'eyb'ji7b'il 'poverty'
moyb'aajal 'easy to do- moyb'ji7b'il 'domination'
  minate' (a)

53) 1. -b'al 'nominalizer'
    2. No variation
    3. Nonproductive
    4. Derives noun stems from transitive stems. Example:

b'iinch- 'arrange, do' b'iinchb'al 'arrangement'
  (t)

54) 1. -b'atz 'nominalizer'
    2. No variation
    3. Nonproductive
    4. Derives noun stems from transitive stems. Example:

xiim- 'think' (t)   xiimb'atz 'thought'

55) 1. -l 'nominalizer'
    2. No variation
    3. Nonproductive
    4. Derives nouns from intransitive verbs of motion.

Examples:

jaaw- 'go up' (I)   jaawl 'ascent'
kub'- 'go down' (I) kub'l 'descent'

56) 1. -tl 'nominalizer'
    2. No variation
    3. Nonproductive
    4. Derives a noun stem from an unidentified root.

*aq'un-   aq'uuntl 'work'

57) 1. -tz 'nominalizer'
    2. No variation
    3. Nonproductive
    4. Derives nouns from transitive and intransitive roots.
    Examples:

iq- 'carry' (T)   iqtz 'load'
q'a7j- 'ride a horse'   q'a7jtz 'mounting block'
  (T)
ook- 'enter' (I)   nooktz 'entrance'

3. THE INFINITIVE STEM
58) 1. -l 'infinitive'
    2. Requires the stem formative.
    3. Productive
    4. Derives the infinitive from transitive and intransitive verbs. I am including this in a separate section because the infinitive is of course a verbal form which does not take inflection for person or aspect, and because there is no evidence to suppose that it is a verbal noun in Mam. That is, the infinitive is not, as far as I know, ever possessed. Infinitives function in the complements of intransitive verbs of motion and certain causative (transitive) verbs, where the absolutive constituent in the main

clause controls equivalent noun phrase deletion (see
8.4.1). Examples:

(4-8) a. ma <u>chin</u> uul-a
          rec 1sA COME-1s

          'I came.'

      b. ma Ø-b'aj   <u>n</u>-yoo7la-n-a
          rec 3sA-dir 1sE-TALK-ds-1s

          'I talked.'

      c. ma <u>chin</u> uul-a yoola-1
                                    inf

          '<u>I</u> came to talk.'

(4-9) a. ma <u>tz'</u>-ok   n-lajo-7n-a
          rec 2sA-dir 1sE-OBLIGATE-ds-1s

          'I obligated you.'

      b. ma Ø-b'aj   <u>t</u>-aq'na-7n-a
          rec 3sA-dir 2sE-WORK-ds-2s

          'You worked (it).'

      c. ma <u>tz'</u>-ok n-lajo-7n-a aq'naa-1   t-ee
                                           -inf   3s-RN/pat

          'I obliged <u>you</u> to work (it).'

4. ADJECTIVE STEMS

59) 1. -7n 'participal'

    2. This suffix requires the stem formative vowel. It
        has the same type of variation as do -7kj and -7tz
        (#22 and #23):

        a. CVC + -7n → CVC + stem formative (shortened)
            + -7n

b. CV $\begin{Bmatrix} V \\ 7 \end{Bmatrix}$ C + -7n → CV $\begin{Bmatrix} V \\ 7 \end{Bmatrix}$ C + stem formative + -n

c. CVVC   + -7n → CVV7C + stem formative
    [+ sonorant]
    + -n

3. Productive
4. Derives the past participle from transitive stems. The suffix is required on the main verb when a transitive verb is accompanied by a directional. This may be evidence that transitive verbs with directionals are actually nominalized forms of verbs (since they take ergative markers, which could also be possessive markers). Other uses of the participle are adjectival; they appear in noun phrases or in statives. Examples:

(4-10) iiqa-n̲   nu7xh kyaqiil q'iij t-u7n   t-txuu7
       CARRY-part BABY EVERY DAY 3s-RN/agt 3s-MOTHER

   'The baby is carried every day by her mother.'

(4-11) jaqo-7n̲   ∅-∅-jaaw   tzi   n-k'a7-ya
       OPEN-past past dep-3sA-GO UP MOUTH 1s-DRINK-1s

   gasyoosa
   CARBONATED

   'My soda is opened.' (Lit: 'Opened, the mouth of my drink went up.')

(4-12) baqa   nti7 nn-∅-el   t-sjoo7̲ma-n̲-a
       SCARCELY NEG prog-3sA-dir 3sE-UNDRESS-ds-2s

   t-i7j-a   ok   t-puuntz'a-n-a
   2s-RN/pat-2s WHEN 2sE-SWIM-ap-2s

   'Don't you at least undress yourself when you swim?'

126 STEM FORMATION

60) 1. -na 'participle'
   2. Shortens a preceding long vowel.
   3. Productive
   4. Derives the past participle from some transitive and intransitive verbs. The participle thus derived is used adjectivally. Examples:

   yuup- 'put out fire' (t)   yupna 'put out'
   tooq- 'break' (t)   toqna 'broken'
   kyim- 'die' (I)   kyimna 'dead'
   nooj- 'fill' (I)   nojna 'full'

61) 1. -naj 'participle'
   2. Shortens preceding long vowels.
   3. Nonproductive
   4. Derives participles from verb stems and unknown roots. How this participle is different from productively derived participles in unclear. Examples:

   *mal-   chmalnaj 'humid'
   yuup- 'put out fire' (t)   yupnaj   'put out'
   xoop- 'perforate' (t)   xopnaj   'perforated'
   q'aay- 'rot' (I)   q'aynaj   'rotten'

62) 1. -l 'positional adjective'
   2. → -ch / l__
      A few roots which begin with l also take -ch to form the positional adjective.
   3. Productive
   4. Derives the positional adjective from positional roots. This adjective is used to emphasize the position described by the root, and as an emphatic is sentence initial (see 3.5 and 7.1.5.2 for more on positionals and syntactic characteristics). Examples:

   tutz'l 'seated'   koxhl 'lying down'
   txulch 'quiet'   molch 'crouching'

lach'l 'standing with   leq'ch 'far'
  feet apart'
63) 1. -b'aajal 'facility'
    2. Shortens preceding long vowels.
    3. Productive
    4. Derives adjective stems from positional roots and transitive verbs meaning easily able to be acted upon in the way specified by the root or stem. Examples:
  txik-   'cook' (T)   txikb'aajal   'easy to cook'
  b'iinch- 'do' (t)   b'inchb'aajal 'easy to do'
  tutz'- 'sitting' (P)   tutz'b'aajal   'easy to seat'
64) 1. $-V_1C_2V_1V_1n$ 'facility'
    2. Shortens preceding long vowels.
    3. Productive
    4. Derives adjective stems from transitive roots or stems with the meaning '(easily) able to be acted upon in the way specified by the root or stem'. Examples:
  tooq-   'break' (t)   toqoqoon   'breakable'
  liich'- 'break' (t)   lich'ich'iin   'breakable'
  mool-   'burn' (t)   mololoon   'easily wilted'
65) 1. -chaq 'distributive'
    2. -chaq on all numbers and some quantity words
       -kaj optionally with <u>kab'</u> '2', <u>ox-</u> '3'
       -kyaj optionally with <u>kyaj</u> '4'
       -7ix optionally with <u>ox-</u> '3'
    3. Productive
    4. Derives distributive adjectives from numbers and some other quantity words. Several senses of distribution are covered by this one suffix. Examples:
  jwe7chaq 'five to each', 'five for one', 'five by five', 'five each'

128   STEM FORMATION

(4-13) <u>qaq-chaq</u> s-ee-tz   k'um   w-u7n-a
              x-tz'-eel-tz
       SIX-dist rec dep-3sA-GO OUT-dir SQUASH 1s-RN/agt-1s

       'I bought the squash for <u>six cents each</u>.' (Lit:
       'Six each went out the squash by me.')

(4-14) <u>kab'-kaj</u> t-teen   ∅-q'oo-n-ka-x-a
       TWO-dist 3sE-EXIST 2s imp-GIVE-imp-dir-dir-2s

       t-uj   k'il
       3s-RN/in POT

       'Put it in the pot <u>two by two</u>.'

(4-15) <u>jwe7-chaq</u> s-e-tz   q'o-7n-∅
              x-tz'-el-tz
       FIVE-dist rec dep-3sA-dir-dir GIVE-ds-pas?

       q'iinan t-ee
       HOG PLUM 3s-RN/dat

       'They gave him the hog plums at <u>five for one cent</u>.'

66) 1. -ka 'atenuator'
    2. No variation
    3. Productive
    4. Adds the meaning 'a little of the quality' to adjec-
       tives and noun phrases. Examples:
   neqaa7 'close' (A)   neqaa7ka 'a little close'
   b'a7n   'good' (A)   ba7nka   'a little good'
   spiiky'an 'clear' (A)   spiiky'anka 'a little clear'
   chib'aj 'meat' (n)   noqax chib'ajka 'meat that's
                                             so-so'

67) 1. -maj 'emphatic'
    2. No variation
    3. Productive

STEM FORMATION 129

4. This can be added to the participle formed by -7n to give emphasis, without change in class or other change in meaning. Examples:

tx'ee7man   'cut'   tx'ee7manmaj   'cut'
aq'na7n   'worked'   aq'na7nmaj   'worked'
sb'iit'an   'ripped'   sb'iit'anmaj   'ripped'

68) 1. -an 'adjectivizer'
    2. No variation
    3. Productive
    4. Derives adjective stems from noun roots. Examples:

xaq   'stone' (N)   xaqan   'made of stone'
tz'iis 'garbage' (N)   tz'iisan 'clean'
tx'otx' 'earth' (N)   tx'otx'an 'made of earth'
looq' 'adobe' (N)   looq'an   'made of adobe'

69) 1. -an 'adjectivizer'
    2. No variation
    3. Nonproductive
    4. Derives adjective stems from transitive verbs and unidentified roots. Examples:

*t'ut'-   t'ut'an   'squishy'
juuk- 'burn' (t)   juukan   'burnable'
*b'uun-   b'uunan   'soft ground'
*luub'-   luub'an   'stretchy'

70) 1. $-C_1 aj$ 'adjectivizer'
    2. No other variation
    3. Nonproductive
    4. Derives adjectives from positional and unidentified roots. Examples:

*chap-   chapchaj   'tasteless'
lin-   'laid out' (P) linlaj   'laid out'
*meq'-   meq'maj   'hot'
*maq-   kyaqmaqmaj 'stuttering'

```
    *txub'-              txub'txaj  'tasty'
    *k'at-               xhk'atk'aj 'content'
```

5. AFFECT STEMS

71) 1. -an 'affect'
    2. No variation
    3. Semiproductive?
    4. Derives affect stems from positional roots, transitive roots and stems, and affect roots. Examples:

```
    qit-   'untied' (P)       qitan   'the action of coming
                                       loose'
    qor-   'turkey gobble'    qoran   'turkey gobble'
           (AF)
    qitz'- 'squeak'           qitz'an 'the squeak that the bed
                                       makes (e.g.) when it is moved'
```

72) 1. $-V_1C_2V_1$ 'affect'
    2. No other variation
    3. Semiproductive
    4. Derives affect stems from positional, affect, and unidentified roots. These forms are the bases from which affect verbs (#25) are derived. Examples:

```
    txul-  'quiet' (P)         txululu  'action of walking with-
                                         out speaking'
    qitx'  'noise that pigs    qitx'itx'i 'grinding of teeth'
           make with teeth' (AF)
    wit'-  'standing' (P)      wit'it'i 'action of going run-
                                         ning'
    *wul-                      wululu   'noise of several people
                                         talking'
```

73) 1. -ch 'affect'
    2. No variation
    3. Nonproductive

4. Derives affect stems from positional and unidentified roots. Examples:

qej-   'lying down' (P)   qejch 'the action of lying down'
*qom-   qomch 'the sound of water falling in a jar'

6. MEASURE STEMS
74) 1. -V₁j 'measure'
    2. No other variation
    3. Semiproductive
    4. Derives measure words from transitive, positional, and unidentified roots. Examples:

k'al-   'tie' (T)   k'laj   'load of firewood'
ch'uq- 'heaped up' (P)   ch'uquj 'heap'
*tx'an-   tx'anaj 'piece of food'

7. DERIVED ADVERBIAL STEMS
75) 1. -nax 'direction'
    2. Shortens preceding long vowel.
    3. Nonproductive
    4. Derives directions from intransitive verbs of motion. Examples:

jaaw-   'go up' (I)   jawnax   'up'
eel-   'go out' (I)   elnax   'West'
ook-   'go in' (I)   oknax   'East'
uul-   'arrive here' (I)   ulnax   'close'
kub'-   'go down' (I)   kub'nax 'down'

76) 1. 'time in future'
    2. These are frozen affixes which show some pattern. -j or -x is added to some form of a number for 'days in the future', while a number is compounded with ab'- 'year' for 'years in the future'.

132 STEM FORMATION

    3. Nonproductive

    4. Forms 'days in the future' and 'years in the future' from numbers. The following forms (only) exist:

kab'	'2'	kaa7j	'in 2 days'
oox	'3'	oxj	'in 3 days'
kyaaj	'4'	koj	'in 4 days'
wuuq	'7'	quub'x	'in a week (7 days)'
kyajlaaj	'14'	kyajlooj	'in 2 weeks (14 days)'
wiinqan	'20'	wiinq'aj	'in 3 weeks (20 days)'
juun	'1'	jnab'	'in 1 year'
kab'	'2'	kob'ab'	'in 2 years'
oox	'3'	oxab'	'in 3 years'

77) 1. 'time in the past'

    2. Again, time in the past words are formed through a frozen pattern of affixation showing some pattern. -Vjee or -xee are added to numbers for 'days in the past', and a number is compounded with aab'a- 'year' for 'years in the past'.

    3. Nonproductive

    4. The only forms for days or years in the past are:

kab'	'2'	kab'ajee	'day before yesterday'
oox	'3'	oxojee	'3 days ago'
wuuq	'7'	qub'xee	'a week ago (7 days)'
kyajpaaj	'14'	kyajlojee	'2 weeks ago (20 days)'
wiinqan	'20'	winq'ajee	'3 weeks ago (20 days)'
juun	'1'	jnaab'a	'a year ago'
kab'	'2'	kob'aab'a	'2 years ago'
oox	'3'	oxaab'a	'3 years ago'

8. STEM FORMATION THROUGH VOWEL LENGTH AND GLOTTAL STOP ADDITION

An apparently productive way to form stems of other classes

from CVC roots is through lengthening the vowel or adding a glottal stop to the vowel of the root. Since all positional and transitive roots are of the shape CVC, these are the classes of roots from which other related stems can usually be assumed to be derived. Derived stems of this type include transitive stems, noun stems, adjective stems, and affect stems. The derived stem is usually semantically unchanged from the root meaning--meaning is only affected in so far as is necessary to change the class. Examples:

 b'ow- 'swollen from a b'oow- 'strike' (t)
  blow' (P)
 joch'- 'sitting doing jooch' 'lazy' (a)
  nothing' (P)
 top- 'lying there with- to7p 'dull (of point or blade)'
  out a point or blade' (a)
  (P)
 chos- 'deflated' (P) choos 'lung' (n)
 jow- 'standing or sit- jo7w 'tunic' (n)
  ting with loose
  clothes' (P)
 chit- 'broadcast' (P) chi7t 'moment of broadcasting'
    (af)
 b'uch- 'shatter, smash, b'u7ch 'money in coins (pieces)'
  break in pieces' (T) (a)
 yuch- 'wash clothes' yuuch 'wrinkled (cloth)' (a)
  (T)

9. REVIEW OF DERIVATION

Seventy-seven derivational affixes and the process of lengthening the root vowel or adding glottal stop to the root vowel have been found in analyzing stem formation in Ixtahuacán Mam. Forty of these are productive or semiproductive.

134 STEM FORMATION

Most have rather different functions, which range from lexical derivation, to simple class change, to semantic change, to syntactic functions; a few have overlapping functions. The affixes were presented in the previous sections according to the class of the root or stem to which they are added. Each is identified by its number and by whether it is productive (p) or semiproductive (s).

Stem or Root Class	Derived Stem Class	Affix		
transitive	transitive	1)	S-	'lexical' (p)
		3)		Stem formative (p)
		8)	-b'V	'causative'
		14)	-pV	'causative'
		18)	-tz'V	'causative'
		20)	-wV	'causative'
		21)	-najee7	'repetitive'
		22)	-7kj	'processive' (p)
		23)	-7tz	'processive imperative' (p)
	intransitive	24)	-n	'antipassive' (p)
		28)	-eet	'passive' (p)
		29)	-j	'passive' (p)
		30)	-njtz	'passive' (s)
		31)	-b'aj	'processive passive' (p)
		33)	-ch	'intransitivizer'
	noun	42)	-1	'agentive' (p)
		43)	-eenj	'patient' (p)
		44)	-b'il	'instrumental' (p)
		45)	-b'een	'resultant locative' (p)
		46)	-b'an	'remainder' (s)
		49)	-leen	'abstract noun' (p)

	50) -le7n 'abstract noun' (p)
	53) -b'al 'nominalizer'
	54) -b'atz 'nominalizer'
	57) -tz 'nominalizer'
adjective	Vowel length
	Glottal insertion
	59) -7n 'participal' (p)
	60) -na 'participal' (p)
	61) -naj 'participal'
	63) -b'aajal 'facility' (p)
	64) $-V_1C_2V_1V_1n$ 'facility' (p)
	69) -an 'adjectivizer'
affect	71) -an 'affect' (s)
infinitive	58) -l 'infinitive' (p)
measure	74) $-V_1j$ 'measure' (s)
intransitive transitive	8) -b'V 'causative'
	11) -lV 'causative'
	16) -saa 'causative' (s)
	22) -7kj 'processive' (p)
	23) -7tz 'processive imperative' (p)
intransitive	1) S- 'lexical' (p)
	39) -7...l 'specific termination'
noun	42) -l 'agentive' (p)
	44) -b'il 'instrumental' (p)
	49) -leen 'abstract noun' (p)
	50) -le7n 'abstract noun' (p)
	55) -l 'nominalizer'
	57) -tz 'nominalizer'
adjective	60) -na 'participle' (p)
	61) -naj 'participle'

136 STEM FORMATION

	adverbial	75) -nax 'direction'
	infinitive	58) -1 'infinitive' (p)
positional	transitive	3) Stem formative (p)
		4) -b'aa 'transitivizer' (p)
		5) Vowel length 'transitivizer' (p)
		9) -chV 'causative'
		14) -pV 'causative'
		15) -q'V 'causative'
		21) -najee7 'repetitive'
	intransitive	27) -ee7 'versive' (p)
		34) -chaj 'intransitivizer'
		35) -paj 'intransitivizer'
		37) -tz'aj 'intransitivizer'
	noun	Vowel length
		Glottal insertion
		45) -b'een 'resultant locative'
		46) -b'an 'remainder' (s)
	adjective	Vowel length
		Glottal insertion
		62) -1 'positional adjective' (p)
		63) -b'aajal 'facility' (p)
		70) -C_1aj 'adjectivizer'
	affect	Vowel length
		Glottal insertion
		71) -an 'affect' (s)
		72) -$V_1C_2V_1$ 'affect' (s)
		73) -ch 'affect'
	measure	74) -V_1j 'measure' (s)
noun	transitive	3) Stem formative (p)

		6)	-laa	'applicative'
		7)	-wa	'applicative'
		11)	-1V	'causative'
	noun	1)	S-	'lexical' (p)
		40)	aj-	'agent' (p)
		41)	aj-	'native' (p)
		47)	-al	'abstract noun' (p)
		50)	-le7n	'abstract noun' (p)
	adjective	68)	-an	'adjectivizer' (p)
adjective	transitive	3)	Stem formative (p)	
		16)	-saa	'causative' (s)
	intransitive	26)	-ax	'versive' (p)
		32)	-b'a	'intransitivizer'
		36)	-t	'intransitivizer'
	noun	47)	-al	'abstract noun' (p)
		48)	-ab'iil	'abstract noun' (p)
		50)	-le7n	'abstract noun' (p)
		52)	-b'ji7b'il	'nominalizer'
	adjective	1)	S-	'lexical' (p)
		66)	-kà	'atenuator' (p)
		67)	-maj	'emphatic' (p)
affect	transitive	5)	Vowel length (p)	
		9)	-chV	'causative'
		10)	-k'uu	'causative'
		14)	-pV	'causative'
		15)	-q'V	'causative'
		18)	-tz'V	'causative'
	intransitive	25)	-Vn	'affect' (p)

affect   1)   S-   'lexical' (p)
              71) -an   'affect' (s)
              72) $-V_1C_2V_1$ 'affect' (s)

NOTES

1. The verb <u>il</u>- 'see' is somewhat suppletive with <u>ki</u>- 'see'. <u>Ki</u>- is used more often in the infinitive, and in the participle form (or with directionals) <u>il</u>- (<u>lo7n</u>) has the meaning 'known' rather than 'seen'; hence, the variation in stem in these examples.

5. THE NOUN PHRASE

Many relations, including case and location, are indicated by noun phrases in Mam. The only constituents of a sentence which do not consist of noun phrases are adverbs, verbs, and certain particles which indicate such things as interrogation and negation. Direct noun phrases indicate the subject, agent, or patient of the sentence, while oblique noun phrases, introduced by relational nouns, are obligatorily used to indicate all other nominal relations and under certain circumstances indicate those of subject, agent or patient also (see 7.1). All noun phrases are headed by nouns; the difference between a direct noun phrase and an oblique noun phrase is that the former has no special introducer while the latter is introduced by a relational noun and is therefore a complex noun phrase with a possessed noun plus noun structure.

Noun phrases can include, in addition to the head noun, a possessor, plural, adjectives, number, measure, demonstratives, or a relative clause. Figure 4 shows the immediate constituent structure of the noun phrase; numbers in parentheses are keyed to the discussion which follows. Adjectives precede nouns if there is no other element in the noun phrase, but follow them if other modifiers are present. A few adjectives commonly precede nouns even if there are other modifiers in the phrase; these are <u>matiij</u> 'big', <u>nim</u> 'a lot', <u>nii</u> 'small', and <u>tal</u> 'small'.

140 THE NOUN PHRASE

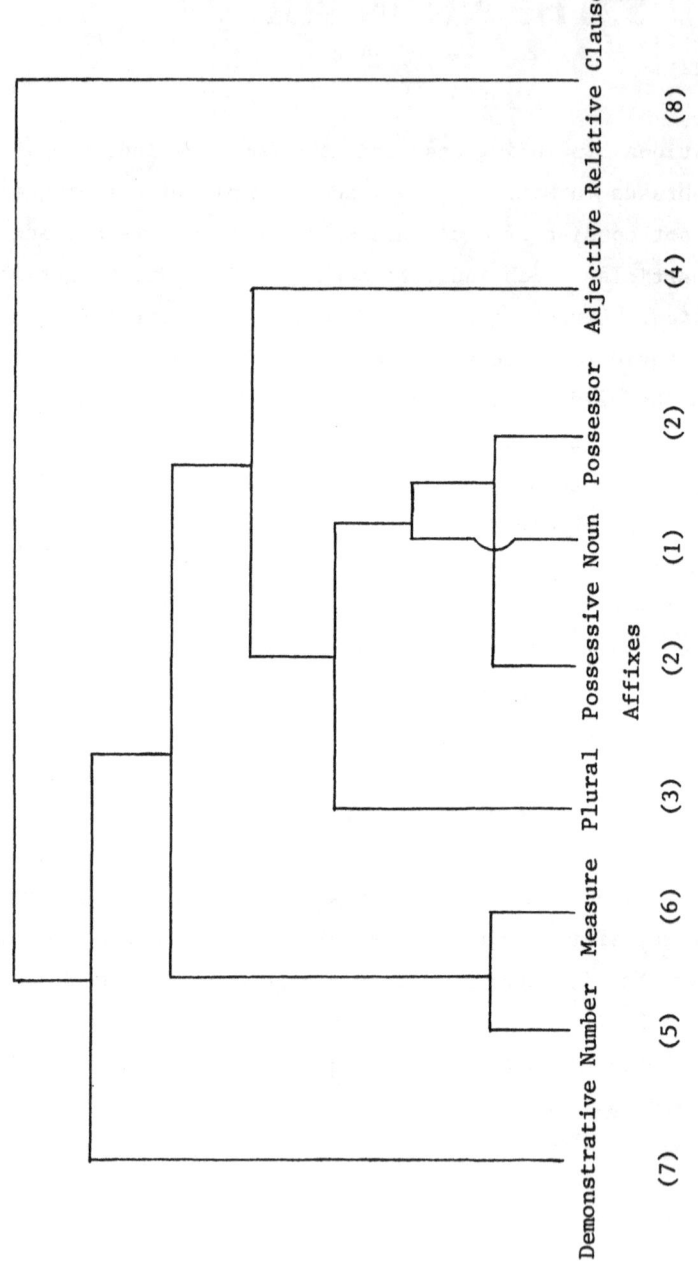

Figure 4. The Immediate Constituent Structure of the Noun Phrase

1. THE STRUCTURE OF THE NOUN PHRASE

1.1 Noun

Nouns are the heads of noun phrases and can be any simple or compound noun stem. The noun can also be the only element in a noun phrase, since it is not obligatorily accompanied by any other constituent. Nouns in direct noun phrases lexically specify a participant which is also cross-referenced by person markers on the verb or nonverbal predicate in a sentence. Nouns in relational noun phrases (see 5.3) lexically specify a participant which is cross-referenced by person markers on the relational noun. Nouns can be conjoined by b'ix 'and' or mo 'or'. Examples:

(5-1) ma   tz'-ook-x   weech
      rec 3sA-GO IN-dir   FOX

'The fox went in.'

(5-2) nti7 ∅-∅-ook   nin-q'iij
      NEG past dep-3sA-GO IN BIG-DAY
                             CELEBRATION

'There wasn't a celebration.'

(5-3) ma   chi kub' t-b'iyo-7n Xwaan xiinaq
      rec 3pA dir   3sE-HIT-ds Juan MAN

'Juan hit the men.'

(5-4) t-i7j-la   qa-witz b'ix chik'uul...
      3s-RN/behind pl-HILL AND FOREST

'Behind the hills and forests...'

1.2 Possessor

Possessed nouns are inflected for the possessor by ergative markers which cross-reference the person and number of the possessor. If the possessor is a third person noun, it can be lexically represented and follows the possessed noun. Therefore a full lexical representation of a possessed noun consists of: ergative marker-noun + possessor. Note that all relational nouns have this structure, where the possessive marker on the possessed (relational) noun cross-references the "object" (possessor). Examples:

(5-5) at-∅   t-naa-b'il
       LOC PRED-3sA 3s-THINK-inst

       'It is his thought.'

(5-6) n-∅-tzaj   t-ma-7n   n-maan-a
       prog-3sA-dir 3sE-SAY-ds 1s-FATHER-1s

       'My father said it.'

(5-7) ma ch-e7x q'ii-1   t-kamb'   meeb'a
       rec 3pA-GO TAKE/BRING-inf 3s-PRIZE ORPHAN

       'They went to bring the orphan's prize.'

(5-8) at-∅   a7   t-uj   xooch
       LOC PRED-3sA WATER 3s-RN/in WELL

       'There is water in the well.'

A possessor can also be possessed itself, which results in a string of possessed nouns. Examples:

(5-9) t-waa   t-b'an-al   axi7n
       3s-FOOD 3s-GOOD-abs n CORN

       'his food of good corn' (Lit: 'his food of corn's goodness')

(5-10) t-uj   ky-witz xjaal
       3s-RN/in 3p-HEAD PERSON

       'in the people's heads'

Contrastive emphasis of the possessor can be expressed through double possession. There are two ways to do this. Simple contrastive emphasis, or focus, uses two person prefixes before the noun, and no enclitic. As a consequence, only the four distinctions indicated by the prefixes, first and second person singular and plural, are possible. The w-variant of the first person prefix is always used for the first prefix, which implies that the forms actually have a vowel separating the two occurrences of person markers, but the vowel is usually not pronounced due to vowel dropping rules. Forms:

jaa	'house'
w-n-jaa	'<u>my</u> house'
t-t-jaa	'<u>your</u> house'
q-q-jaa	'<u>our</u> (exclusive) house'
ky-ky-jaa	'<u>you-all's</u> house'

The usual person prefixes can also be postposed to the noun in addition to being preposed to it, which again doubly possesses the noun. Postposed person markers indicate topicalization as well as focus. The vowel <u>a</u>, presumably the enclitic, must follow the postposed person marker. Here, third person focus is possible. If the form possessed by <u>t-</u> or <u>ky-</u> has no noun following it to specify a third person possessor, it is interpreted as second person. If however, there is a lexical representation of the possessor (which is either a noun (phrase) or a noun classifier, see 4.2) then it is interpreted as third person. There is still no way to focus on a first person plural inclusive possessor. The forms are:

n-jaa-wa	'<u>my</u> house'
t-jaa-ta	'<u>your</u> house'
t-jaa-ta xu7j	'the <u>woman's</u> house'
q-jaa-qa	'<u>our</u> (exclusive) house'

ky-jaa-kya   'you-all's house'
ky-jaa-kya xu7j   'the women's house'

Several contrasting examples show the difference between a simply focused noun (preposed double possession) and a focused and topicalized noun (postposed double possession):

(5-11) a. focus

    w-n-jaa   kyee7yex ∅-kii-n
    1s-1s-HOUSE NICE   3sA-SEE-ap

    'My house looks nice.'

    b. focus and topicalization

    n-jaa-wa   aj   jaa   kyee7yex ∅-kii-n
    1s-House-1s   rel HOUSE NICE   3sA-SEE-ap

    'It is my house that looks nice.'

(5-12) a. focus

    ma   ∅-kub'   tiil-j   w-n-jaa
    rec 3sA-dir   KNOCK DOWN-pas   1s-1s-HOUSE

    'My house was knocked down.'

    b. focus and topicalization

    n-jaa-wa   ma   ∅-kub'   tiil-j
    1s-HOUSE-1s   rec 3sA-dir   KNOCK DOWN-pas

    'It was my house that was knocked down.'

1.3 Plural

The noun itself does not obligatorily express number. Usually number is indicated by the person marker which cross-references a noun on a verb, nonverbal predicate, or relational noun. For example, if the verb has a prefix indicating that a nominal constituent is third person singular, then the

noun is interpreted as singular, while if the person marking
on the verb is plural, then the noun is also plural:
(5-13) a. ma ∅-beet   xu7j

  rec 3sA-WALK WOMAN

  'The woman walked.'

  b. ma chi b'eet xu7j

  3pA

  'The women walked.'

If, however, a speaker wishes to clarify the number of a noun,
the plural clitic qa can be used. It generally precedes the
noun, but can also follow it. Qa is never required except
in third person plural stative predicates. Examples:
(5-14) nti7 qa-q-pwaq

  NEG pl-1p-MONEY

  'There isn't any of our money.'

(5-15) ma chi b'eet qa-xu7j

  rec 3pA WALK pl-WOMAN

  'The women walked.'

1.4 Adjectives

Adjectives modify nouns, and precede them if there is no other
modifier, such as a number, demonstrative, negative, etc. If,
however, there is another word in the noun phrase which precedes the noun, then the adjective follows the noun. Exceptions are matiij 'big', nim 'a lot', nii 'small', and tal
'small', which can precede or follow the noun no matter what
else there is in the noun phrase. Adjectives can be conjoined by b'ix 'and' or mo 'or'. The conjunctions are never
deleted, which would result in a list of modifying adjectives,
and there are almost never more than two adjectives conjoined

to modify a noun. Examples:

(5-16) a. q'ay-na lo7j
ROT-part FRUIT

'rotten fruit'

b. *lo7j q'ay-na

(5-17) a. juun t-wiixh saq
ONE 3s-CAT WHITE

'a cat of his'

b. *juun saq t-wiixh

(5-18) a. kab' matiij   xjaal
TWO   IMPORTANT PERSON

'two important people'

b. kab' xjaal matiij

'two important people'

(5-19) a. nuch b'ix sib' tx'yaan
SMALL AND GRAY DOG

'small and gray dog'

b. *nuch sib' tx'yaan

1.5 Number

Number precedes the noun. The number <u>juun</u> 'one' is also the indefinite article, while the number <u>kab'</u> 'two' is also an indefinite plural ('some'). <u>Juun</u> has the following allomorphs:

<u>jun</u> before an unpossessed noun,

<u>juun</u> before a possessed noun or with no noun.

Examples:

(5-20) a. at-∅   juun n-jaa-ya
           LOC PRED-3sA ONE 1s-HOUSE-1s

           'It is a house of mine.'

      b. at-∅   jun jaa
          LOC PRED-3sA ONE HOUSE

          'It is a house.'

      c. at-∅   juun
          LOC PRED-3sA HOUSE

          'It is one.', 'There is one.'

It is very common to have <u>both</u> the indefinite article and a possessive prefix, unlike English where the indefinite article and possession do not co-occur. This use of the partitive or pleonastic possessive is also characteristic of sixteenth century Spanish and modern Guatemalan Spanish. The translation of (5-20a) above would be <u>Tengo una mi casa.</u> in perfectly good Guatemalan Spanish (Martin, 1978).

<u>Juu7n</u> 'each' is derived from <u>juun</u> 'one' and behaves like any other number. Ordinal numbers are possessed nouns which precede the noun they modify, but structurally are the heads of a possessed noun phrase. Examples:

(5-21) at-∅   qaq xjaal
       LOC PRED-3sA SIX PERSON

       'There are six people.'

(5-22) jun tx'yaan q'aq
       ONE DOG   BLACK

       'one black dog', 'a black dog'

(5-23) kab' xiinaq
       TWO MAN

       'two men', 'some men'

(5-24) juu7n xooch
       EACH WELL

       'each well'

(5-25) t-neej-al   jb'aal t-uj   ab'q'ii
       3s-FIRST-ord num RAIN   3s-RN/in   YEAR

       'the first rain of the year'

(5-26) t-kab'an   tx'yaan jawan
       3s-TWO-ord num   DOG   FIERCE

       'the second fierce dog'

1.6 Measure

While count nouns can be directly modified by numbers, mass nouns must first be modified by a word which designates a countable quantity of that noun. Measure words are the class of words which designate countable quantities of mass nouns. There are a rather large number of quite specific measure words in Mam. They are obligatorily preceded by a number or the interrogative particle <u>jte7</u> 'how much, how many' in the noun phrase. Examples:

(5-27) jun <u>laq</u>   kaalt
       ONE PLATEFUL   BROTH

       'a plateful of broth'

(5-28) kab' <u>ma71</u> t-k'a7-ya   q'e7n
       TWO   SHOT   2s-DRINK-2s   BOOZE

       'two shots of booze'

(5-29) jte7   <u>k'oxh</u>   cheenaq' t-aj-a
       HOW MANY   DIPPER   BEAN   2sE-WANT-2s

       'How many measures of beans do you want?'

1.7 Demonstratives

Demonstratives specify which item in a group is the item under discussion. Demonstratives in Mam do not indicate relative location or distance. Demonstratives which function in the noun phrase before a head noun (which can be deleted) are <u>aj</u> 'this, that', <u>ajaj</u> or <u>aqaj</u> 'these, those', and <u>naq</u> 'this, that'. The demonstrative <u>aa</u> 'this, that' forms the base of a stative predicate (3.3, 7.2) and several demonstratives which do specify distance are used pronominally to substitute for noun phrases. These are <u>jluu7</u> 'this', <u>ajkiina</u> 'that', and <u>aj machii7w</u> 'that (more distance)'. They are the "pointers" and cannot be used to modify nouns. Examples of the demonstratives in noun phrases are:

(5-30) aj   kab' samaan
        DEM TWO   WEEK

        'these two weeks'

(5-31) aj   matiij k'uxb'il
        DEM BIG   TOOL

        'that big tool'

(5-32) naq juu7n-qa xjaal
        DEM EACH-pl   PERSON

        'all those people'

(5-33) ajaj oox   tx'yaan saq
        DEM   THREE DOG   WHITE

        'these three white dogs'

1.8 Relative Clause

Relative clauses follow the noun they are modifying. See 8.3 for a more thorough explanation of relative clause formation. Relative clauses are introduced by the demonstrative aj which here functions as a relative particle. Aj can, however, be deleted under certain circumstances and also can metathesize with the head noun. Relative clauses which contain a verb indicating an action (rather than a state) use dependent aspect marking (8.2) in the past and recent past, but show no dependent marking in other aspects. Examples:

(5-34) a. aj xiinaq [∅-∅-ku7-x   awaa-n
         DEM MAN   past dep-3sA-dir-dir PLANT-ap

   ky-e   laanch]
   3p-RN/pat ORANGE

   ma ∅-tzaj t-q'o-7n   kab' wi7   q-ee-ky'
   rec 3sA-dir 3sE-GIVE-ds TWO   PLANT 1p-RN/dat-1p ex

   'The man [who planted oranges] gave us some plants.'

b. aj xiinaq [∅-kb'-el-ax   t-awa-7n   laanch]
              3sA-dir-pot-dir 3sE-PLANT-ds

   ma ∅-tzaj t-q'o-7n kab' wi7 q-ee-ky'

   'The man [who will plant the oranges] gave us some plants.'

Here the a) sentence has a relative clause in the past so the dependent past aspect (∅) is used, and the b) sentence has the same relative clause in the potential, so no dependent marker appears. The a) sentence also focuses the head noun (xiinaq) before the verb, but it can be said perfectly well without focusing the head noun:

   c. ma tzaj t-q'o-7n xiinaq [∅-∅-ku7-x awaa-n ky-e

   laanch] kab' wi7 q-ee-ky'

   'The man [who planted oranges] gave us some plants.'

Relatives can be formed on any noun, no matter what syntactic or semantic role it plays in the sentence (see 8.2.1 and 8.3 for more examples). If the verb in the relative clause indicates a state rather than an action (intransitive verbs of motion and the verb <u>teen-</u> 'exist' can be stative) then it is marked with dependent person marking rather than dependent aspect marking:

(5-35) aa Cheep Toontz <u>t</u>-jaa-x   t-iib'aj
       DEM José Ordóñez 3sE-GO UP-dir 3s-RN/above

       q-jaa-y7
       1p-HOUSE-1p ex

       'It is José Ordóñez who <u>is</u> above our house.'

2. DEFINITENESS

There is no definite article in Mam. The indefinite article alone marks a noun phrase as indefinite; its absence implies definiteness:

(5-36) a. ma Ø-txi7 t-k'aa7ya-n xiinaq axi7n
         rec 3sA-dir 3sE-SELL-ds MAN   CORN

       '<u>The</u> man sold <u>the</u> corn.'

   b. ma Ø-txi7 t-k'aa7ya-n <u>jun</u> xiinaq axi7n

       '<u>A</u> man sold the corn.'

The indefinite article co-occurs with possessive markers:
(5-37) ma Ø-txi7 t-k'aa7ya-n xiinaq <u>juun</u> <u>t</u>-waakxh
                                            3s-COW

      'The man sold <u>his</u> cow.' (...a cow of his)

The indefinite article cannot co-occur with demonstratives in a simple noun phrase:
(5-38) a. <u>aj</u> xiinaq ma Ø-txi7 t-k'aa7ya-n axi7n
        DEM

'<u>This</u> man sold the corn.'

 b. <u>jun</u> xiinaq ma ∅-txi7 t-k'aa7y.a-n axi7n

  '<u>A</u> man sold the corn.'

 c. *aj jun xiinaq ma ∅-txi7 t-k'aa7ya-n axi7n

If, however, <u>aj</u> is a relative marker which precedes a head noun, then <u>juun</u> can be used to indicate indefiniteness, along with <u>aj</u>:

(5-39) a. aj xiinaq lo-7n w-u7n-a   ∅-∅-ok
    rel MAN SEE-part 1s-RN/agt-1s past dep-3sA-dir

    b'iyoo-n t-e   Luuch
    HIT-ap 3s-RN/pat Pedro

   'I know the man who hit Pedro.'

 b. aj <u>jun</u> xiinaq lo-7n w-u7n-a ∅-∅-ok b'iyoo-n t-e

  Luuch

  'I know <u>a</u> man who hit Pedro.'

If a noun phrase follows a stative predicate whose base is the demonstrative <u>aa</u>, then the indefinite article marks indefiniteness while lack of an article implies definiteness, just as with any other noun phrase:

(5-40) a. aa-∅ xiinaq ∅-∅-xi   k'aaya-n t-e
    DEM-3sA MAN past dep-3sA-dir SELL-ap 3s-RN/pat

    axi7n
    CORN

   'It was <u>the</u> man who sold the corn.'

 b. aa-∅ <u>jun</u> xiinaq ∅-∅-xi k'aa7a-n axi7n

  'It was <u>a</u> man who sold the corn.'

Thus it is the indefinite which is lexically marked, while

lack of marking implies definiteness. A demonstrative includes definiteness and cannot co-occur with the indefinite article, but possession does not exclude indefinite marking.

3. RELATIONAL NOUN PHRASES

All sentence constituents except the verb, the direct agent, patient, or subject, and adverbs are indicated by relational noun phrases. This means that all nondirect cases and most locations occur in relational noun phrases. The structure of such a phrase is ergative marker-relational noun plus noun, where the ergative marker is cross-referenced to the noun (phrase) which follows the relational noun and which indicates, loosely, its "object". In fact this noun is the possessor of a relational noun, and the structure of a relational noun phrase is exactly like that of any possessed noun. I am reviewing that structure here simply because it is perhaps unusual for all case and locative relations to be expressed through possession and because relational nouns play an important role in Mam sentences. More information on relational nouns is contained in 3.2.10 and further examples of their use to indicate sentence constituents can be found in 7.1.1.2.

The relational nouns and their functions are:

    -u7n   'agent, instrument, causative'
    -ee   'dative, possessive, patient, benefactive'
    -i7j   'patient, thematic'
    -uuk'al   'instrument, comitative'
    -iib'aj   'reflexive'

All the rest are locative:

    -b'utx'   'at the corner'
    -i7jla   'around'
    -iib'aj   'over'
    -jaq'   'under'

154 THE NOUN PHRASE

    -txa7n   'at the edge of'
    -txlaj   'beside'
    -tzii7   'at the entrance of'
    -uj   'in'
    -witz   'on top of'
    -wi7   'on, at the tip of'

It is most common for relational nouns to cross-reference third person singular nouns, but all possibilities are used:

(5-41) a. ax   leq'-ch   ma   ∅-tzaaj   aj
          ALSO FAR-pos adj rec 3sA-ARRIVE HERE WATER

          'And the water came from far away.'

   b. ax leq'-ch ma ∅-tzaaj a7 <u>w-u7n-a</u>
                                        1s-RN/agt-1s

      '<u>I</u> brought the water from far away.'

   c. ax leq'-ch ma ∅-tzaaj a7 <u>t-u7n-a</u>
                                       2s-RN/agt-2s

      '<u>You</u> brought the water from far away.'

   d. ax leq'-ch ma ∅-tzaaj a7 <u>t-u7n</u>   (xiinaq)
                                      3s-RN/agt MAN

      '<u>He</u> (the man) brought the water from far away.'

And so on with <u>q-u7n-a</u> 'by us', <u>q-u7n</u> 'by all of us', <u>ky-u7n-a</u> 'by you-all', <u>ky-u7n</u> 'by them', or <u>ky-u7n qa-xiinaq</u> 'by the men'.

The possessor (or "object") of a relational noun can itself be a possessed or relational noun phrase, which then gives a possessed noun phrase embedded in a possessed noun phrase, a process which is presumably limited only by time and patience. Examples:

(5-42) toons ma-tzan tz'-ook-x   weech <u>t-uj</u>   <u>t</u>-jaa
       THEN rec-well 3sA-GO IN-dir FOX   3s-RN/in 3s-HOUSE

   <u>t</u>-oky' xaq
   3s-HOLE ROCK

   'Then the fox went <u>in</u> <u>his</u> house in the hole <u>in</u> the rock.'

(5-43) maax   t-ook-x   maa   <u>t-iib'</u>   pweent
       UP THERE   3sE-GO IN-dir THERE 3s-RN/over BRIDGE

   <u>t-uj</u>   kyqa7
   3s-RN/in HOT WATER

   'There it is <u>above</u> the bridge <u>by</u> the hot springs.'

-<u>ee</u>, the relational noun which indicates possession and the dative, and sometimes indicates the patient (see 7.1.4), appears to have other functions which are unrelated to these. It occurs in discourse before constituents which are clearly neither possessed nor datives or patients. I have not yet analyzed what this function is, but it is probably related to discourse. A similar use of -<u>ee</u> occurs in Aguacatec (Larsen 1979). Several examples of -<u>ee</u> in discourse related functions occur in the text in Appendix III.

4. PRONOMINALIZATION

There are no independent pronouns in Mam. In general, deletion of a noun phrase can be accomplished without substituting a pro-form for the deleted noun because the noun phrase is cross-referenced on the verb, nonverbal predicate, or relational noun and such cross-referencing remains when the noun phrase is deleted. Direct agents, patients, and subjects are cross-referenced on verbs:

(5-44) a. ma ∅-tzaj ky-tzyu-7n kab' xiinaq Luuch
           rec 3sA-dir 3pE-GRAB-ds TWO MAN Pedro

   'Some men grabbed Pedro.'

   b. ma ∅-tzaj ky-tzyu-7n

   'They grabbed him.'

(5-45) a. ma tz'-ook-x   Mal t-uj   jaa
           rec 3sA-GO IN-dir María 3s-RN/in HOUSE

   'María went in the house.'

   b. ma tz'-ook-x t-uj jaa

   'She went in the house.'

The subjects of stative or locative/existentials are indicated on the predicate:

(5-46) a. matiij-∅ cheej
           BIG-3sA HORSE

   'The horse is big.'

   b. matiij-∅

   'It's big.'

(5-47) a. t-e7   qa-xjaal t-uj   t-jaa   dyoos
           LOC PRED-3pA pl-PERSON 3s-RN/in 3s-HOUSE GOD

   'There are people in church.'

   b. t-e7 t-uj t-jaa dyoos

   'They are in church.'

All noun phrases but the direct agent, patient, or subject of verbs and the subjects of locative/existential or stative predicates occur in relational noun phrases and are cross-referenced on the relational noun:

(5-48) a. ma chi tzy-eet   cheej t-e   ky-ajw-iil
           rec 3pA GRAB-pas HORSE 3s-RN/ben 3p-OWNER-abs n

           'The horses were captured for their owner.'

       b. ma chi tzy-eet cheej t-ee

           'The horses were captured for him.'

       c. ma chi tzy-eet cheej ky-e ky-ajw-iil
                                3p-

           'The horses were captured for their owners.'

       d. ma chi tzy-eet cheej ky-ee

           'The horses were captured for them.'

There are occurrences of what look like independent pronouns for emphasis, which are discussed below. There are also noun classifiers, which are used pronominally to specify a deleted third person noun. This is also discussed below.

4.1 Emphatic Pronouns

The statives can be used to focus on a participant when there is no lexical representation of that participant which could indicate focus (by being preposed to the verb, see 7.1.5). Statives used for focus must precede the verb and the entire sentence can be analyzed as a main clause with a stative predicate followed by an embedded clause containing the main verb. The verb which follows an emphatic pronoun is marked dependently.

(5-49) a. aax   qo7-ya   n-q-uul   b'iincha-1
           THE SAME 1pA-1p ex   prog-1pE-COME   ARRANGE-inf

           t-ee
           3s-RN/pat

           'We came to arrange it.'

158 THE NOUN PHRASE

    b.   *aax n-q-uul qo7-ya b'iincha'l t-ee

(5-50) a. <u>aa-qa</u> ∅-i7ex   k'aaya-n t-e   axi7n
          ∅-chi-xi
          DEM-pl past dep-3pA-dir SELL-ap 3s-RN/pat CORN

          '<u>They</u> sold the corn.'

4.2 <u>Classifiers</u>

There is a set of noun classifiers which are used when third person noun phrases are deleted from a sentence. They are suffixed to the verb, nonverbal predicate, or relational noun which cross-references the deleted noun phrase, and specify the noun more precisely. Many of the noun classifiers are related to common nouns. The complete set is:

Classifier		Common Noun	
jal	'nonhuman'	jiil	'wild animal'
nu7xh	'baby'	nu7xh	'baby'
xhlaaq'	'child'	xhlaaq'	'child'
b'ixh	'person of the same status, fondly'		
q'a	'young man'	q'aa	'young man'
txin	'young woman'	txiin	'young woman'
ma	'man'	matiij	'big'
xu7j	'woman'	xu7j	'woman'
swe7j	'old man'	swe7j	'old man'
xhyaa7	'old woman'	yaab'aj	'grandmother'
xnuq	'old man, respectfully'	xiinaq	'man'
xuj	'old woman, respectfully'	xu7j	'woman'

Examples of the classifiers with verbs, statives, and relational nouns following.

(5-51) a. verb, noun phrase

          ma ∅-tzaj t-tzyu-7n Mal Luuch
          rec 3sA-dir 3sE-GRAB-ds María Pedro

'María grabbed Pedro.'

    b. verb, noun phrase deleted

       ma ∅-tzaj t-tzyu-7n

       'She grabbed him.'

    c. verb, classifier

       ma ∅-tzaj t-tzyu-7n-<u>txin</u>

                          cl/young woman

       '<u>She</u> grabbed him.'

(5-52) a. stative

       aa-∅-tzan   n-maan-a   aj q'i-l   t-witz-xax
       DEM-3sA-well 1s-FATHER-1s rel GIVE-agt 3s-HEAD-encl

       'It is my father who plans.'

    b. classifier

       aa-∅-<u>swe7j</u> aj q'i-l t-witz-xax

       'It is <u>he</u> who plans.'

(5-53) a. locative

       at-∅   jun ch'it t-uj   tzee7
       LOC PRED-3sA ONE BIRD 3s-RN/in TREE

       'There is a bird in the tree.'

    b. classifier

       at-∅-<u>jal</u>   t-uj tzee7
            cl/nonhuman

       'There <u>it</u> is in the tree.'

(5-54) a. relational noun

       n-∅-7aq'naa-n   Mal   t-uuk'al Xwaan
       prog-3sA-WORK-ap María 3s-RN/com Juan

'María works with Juan.'

b. classifier

n-∅-7aq'naa-n Mal t-uuk'al-q'a
                                     -cl/young man

'María works with him.'

6. THE VERB PHRASE

I am using verb phrase to refer to the maximal verb word, or verb complex, rather than to refer to the predicate including some nominal constituent. The reason for this is that Mam verbs have a relatively complex structure which needs to be described before going on to discuss the syntax of the sentence. Because verbs can include auxiliaries (directionals) as well as inflection for person and aspect, the verb complex is more than a simple word, even if less than what is usually meant by verb phrase.

The verb phrase is either transitive or intransitive depending on whether it cross-references one or two arguments. The distinction is as clear as it is for verb roots, although processes of transitivization and detransitivization create verb phrases which do not match their roots in transitivity. See 7.1 for a discussion of transitivity at different levels, from the word to the phrase to the sentence.

The verb phrase can include aspect, person marking, directionals, mode suffixes, and the verb stem. Each of these is described below and then the structure of the verb phrase with different elements is reviewed.

1. ASPECT

There are four principal aspects and two dependent aspects which are used in subordinate clauses:

    ma   'recent past'
    o   'past'
    ok   'potential'
    n-   'progressive'

x-   'recent past dependent'

∅-   'past dependent'

If the action is complete, <u>ma</u> or <u>o</u> are used. <u>Ma</u> indicates that the action just occurred, while <u>o</u> indicates that it was completed any time before just now (more or less a day ago or more). <u>X</u>- corresponds exactly to <u>ma</u> in certain subordinate clauses, while <u>∅</u>- corresponds exactly to <u>o</u> in the same types of subordinate clauses (see 8.2). Examples:

(6-1) a. ma   chin jaw tz'aq-a

    rec 1sA dir SLIP-1s

    'I slipped (just now).'

b. o   chin jaw tz'aq-a

    past

    'I slipped (a while ago).'

c. t-uj   b'ee xhin   jaw tz'aq-a

                  x-chin

    3s-RN/in ROAD rec dep-1sA

    'In the road I slipped (just now).'

d. t-uj b'ee in   jaw tz'aq-a

              ∅-chin

         past dep-1sA

    'In the road I slipped (a while ago).'

(See 3.1 for aspect morphophonemics and 8.2 for circumstances which require subordination.)

The aspect <u>ok</u> is used optionally to indicate future action, whether potential or expected. It is the only aspect which is optional; the reason for the optionality is that the potential is also indicated by a mode suffix, so the aspect is redundant. If a verb is neither potential nor imperative (also indicated by a mode suffix) then one of the other aspects is obligatory. Example:

(6-2) a. chin jawa-l tz'aq-a
      1sA dir-pot SLIP-1s

   'I will slip.'

or b. ok   chin jawa-l tz'aq-a
      pot

   'I will slip.'

n- indicates that the action is in progress. This aspect itself indicates nothing about time and is used for progressive action in any time. If there is no other indicator of time a sentence with n- is interpreted as the present:

(6-3) n-poon   a7
      prog-ARRIVE WATER

   'The water is arriving.'

Adverbs can clarify the time:

(6-4) yaa   n-poon a7
      JUST NOW

   'The water was just arriving.'

(6-5) ojtxa n-poon a7
      BEFORE

   'The water was arriving before.'

An aspect in another part of the sentence also clarifies time, since n- takes its time reference from context:

(6-6) aa-tzan   ∅-∅-ok   n-b'i-7n-a   kuxi7
      DEM-well past dep-3sA-dir 1sE-HEAR-ds-1s EVERY LITTLE

      n-∅-jaaw   nimaal
      WHILE prog-3sA-GO UP DEM

'According to what I heard, every little while it was tearing.'

Because the aspect in the first clause above is $\emptyset$- 'past dependent', then the action in the second clause is also past, but is in process at that time.

Aspect markers are first in the verb phrase.

2. PERSON

2.1 Ergativity

I have shown in 3.1 that there are two different sets of person markers (Set A and Set B) which have different functions in the verb phrase. Set A is the ergative set and is used to indicate the agent of a transitive verb, while Set B is the absolutive set and is used to indicate the patient of a transitive verb and the subject of an intransitive verb. Set A functions as well to indicate the possessor of a noun (3.2), while Set B also functions to indicate the subject of a nonverbal predicate (3.3).

Although there are circumstances in subordinate clauses where this pattern is broken (8.1), the patient of a transitive verb and the subject of an intransitive verb are always cross-referenced on the verb by the same set of person markers. Thus while Mam has no morphological case marking on nouns, the morphological cross-referencing of verbal arguments on the verb is a typically ergative pattern. This is in contrast to an accusative system of grammatical relations, in which all "subjects" (transitive or intransitive) pattern together while the object of a transitive verb patterns differently. Ergativity in Mam functions at the syntactic as well as morphological level, as is shown in chapters 7 and 8. Briefly, agents (ergators) cannot be extracted for focus, question, negation, etc., but must be made absolutive before such processes can occur. Also, equivalent noun phrase deletion is only controlled by absolutives, never by ergatives. Last, if only one lexical noun phrase occurs in a sentence with a transitive verb, and the person markers are ambiguous as to referent (i.e. both third singular), it is interpreted as being cross-referenced absolutively; for an agent to be the only lexically represented direct noun phrase in this situation it must be cross-referenced by an absolutive marker on an intransitive (antipassive) verb.

Ergative prefixes on the verb are morphologically marked, while absolutives are unmarked. The evidence for this is that third person singular absolutive prefixes are ∅ (at least in some circumstances, see 3.1), while all other person prefixes have some phonological representation. This is entirely expected for ergative languages.

The ergative system preserves the clear distinction between transitive and intransitive verbs at the phrase level. Every verb is marked unambiguously as transitive or intransitive by whether it cross-references two arguments or one in the verb phrase. Absolutive markers follow the aspects and precede ergative markers, which precede the verb stem. If a verb is transitive and therefore has both an absolutive and an ergative marker, the two are usually, but not necessarily, separated by a directional.

2.2 <u>Emphatics</u>

Just as noun possessors could be contrastively emphasized by double possession, postposed ergative markers can be used on verbs to focus on one of the arguments. The form of the postposed marker is the ergative prefix plus the vowel <u>a</u>, which may be from the person enclitic. At any rate, there are only four possible emphatic person markers: -wa '1s', -ta '2s, 3s', -qa '1p', and -kya '2p, 3p'. Second and third person are distinguished in the singular and plural by whether there is a lexical noun phrase, where the emphatic is interpreted as cross-referencing third person, or no lexical noun phrase, where it is interpreted as cross-referencing second person. First person plural emphatics are always exclusive.

The emphatics used to focus on the subject of an intransitive verb match the absolutive prefixes in person and number:

   ma chin b'eet-wa   'I walked'
   ma Ø-b'eet-ta   'you walked'
   ma Ø-b'eet-ta xjaal   'the person walked'
   ma qo b'eet-qa   'we (excl) walked'
   ma chi b'eet-kya   'you-all walked'
   ma chi b'eet-kya xjaal 'the people walked'

If the agent is focused on in a transitive verb, the emphatics match the ergative marker in person and number. Here is an example with third person singular patient (aspect + A + dir + E + stem + ds + emph):

   ma Ø-tzaj n-tzyu-7n-wa   'I grabbed it'
   ma Ø-tzaj t-tzyu-7n-ta   'you grabbed it'
   ma Ø-tzaj t-tzyu-7n-ta xiinaq ch'it
                                  'the man grabbed the bird'

(Here it is necessary to have two lexical noun phrases to emphasize third person, because only one lexical noun phrase would be interpreted as referring to the patient. Thus ma Ø-tzaj t-tzyu-7n-ta xiinaq means 'You grabbed the man.')

   ma Ø-tzaj q-tzyu-7n-qa   'we (excl) grabbed it'
   ma Ø-tzaj ky-tzyu-7n-kya 'you-all grabbed it'
   ma Ø-tzaj ky-tzyu-7n-kya xiinaq ch'it
                                    'the men grabbed the bird'

To focus on the patient of a transitive verb, the emphatic agrees in person and number with the absolutive marker:

ma chin tzaj t-tzyu-7n-wa   'he grabbed me'
ma ∅-tzaj n-tzyu-7n-ta   'I grabbed you'
ma ∅-tzaj n-tzyu-7n-ta xiinaq
                            'I grabbed the man'
ma qo tzaj t-tzyu-7n-qa   'he grabbed us (excl)'
ma chi tzaj n-tzyu-7n-kya   'I grabbed you-all'
ma chi tzaj n-tzyu-7n-kya xiinaq
                            'I grabbed the men'

Now a single lexical noun phrase for third person is acceptable, since it is interpreted as the patient. There is no way to say 'you grabbed me' or 'you grabbed us'. With a first person patient emphatic and a nonfirst person ergative marker, the ergative marker always refers to third person.

3. DIRECTIONALS

3.1 Structure

Directionals are auxiliary elements in the verb phrase which indicate direction of movement and are derived from intransitive verbs of motion. The primary derivational process involved is that if there is a long vowel in the intransitive verb it is shortened in the directional. The simple directionals and the verbs from which they derive are:

Directional		Intransitive Verb	
xi	'away from'	xi7	'go'
tzaj	'toward'	tzaaj	'come'
ul	'there to here'	uul	'arrive here'
pon	'here to there'	poon	'arrive there'
kub'	'down'	kub'	'go down'
jaw	'up'	jaaw	'go up'

el	'out'	eel	'go out'
ok	'in'	ook	'go in'
kyaj	'remaining'	kyaj	'remain'
aj	'returning from here'	aaj	'return'
iky'	'passing'	iky'	'pass by'
b'aj	'complete'	b'aj	'finish'

<u>Xi</u> and <u>tzaj</u> frequently combine with other directionals, according to the semantics, to add the meaning 'away' or 'toward'. They are suffixed to the directional which they modify and have the reduced forms -<u>x</u> or -<u>tz</u> respectively. Eleven compound directionals are formed in this way:

ku7x	'down away'	(kub' + xi)
ku7tz	'down toward'	(kub' + tzaj)
jax	'up away'	(jaw + xi)
jatz	'up toward'	(jaw + tzaj)
ex	'out away'	(el + xi)
etz	'out toward'	(el + tzaj)
okx	'in away'	(ok + xi)
oktz	'in toward'	(ok + tzaj)
ajtz	'returning from there'	(aj + tzaj)
iky'x	'passing to the other side'	(iky' + xi)
iky'tz	'passing to this side'	(iky' + tzaj)

More rarely, other directionals combine with each other, almost always with phonological reduction. Examples:

i7pan	'passing there'	(iky' + pon)
japan	'up there'	(jaw + pon)
ajk	'returning down'	(aj + kub')
ku7xb'aj	'down there complete'	(kub' + xi + b'aj)

etzb'aj   'out here complete'
             (el + tzaj + b'aj)

Directionals follow absolutive markers, unless the verb is an intransitive verb of motion, in which event the directionals -x 'away' or -tz 'toward' can be suffixed to it, or unless the verb is an imperative, in which event the directional is final before the person enclitics. Directionals in final position have reduced forms:

xi → x	kub' → ka
tzaj → tz	ku7tz → katz
kyaj → kaj	ku7x → kax
jax → jx	etz → atz
jatz → jtz	ok → k
el → al	oktz → ktz
ex → ax	okx → kx

An example of a verb with each of the twelve simple and eleven common compound directionals follows. The verb stem is *ii-* 'take/bring':

ma ∅-txi w-ii-7n-a	'I took it'
ma ∅-tzaj w-ii-7n-a	'I brought it'
ma tz-ul w-ii-7n-a	'I brought it here'
ma ∅-pon w-ii-7n-a	'I took it there'
ma ∅-kub' w-ii-7n-a	'I lowered it from someone's back'
ma ∅-ku7-x w-ii-7n-a	'I took it down'
ma ∅-ku7-tz w-ii-7n-a	'I brought it down'
ma ∅-jaw w-ii-7n-a	'I lifted it on something'
ma ∅-ja-x w-ii-7n-a	'I took it up'
ma ∅-ja-tz w-ii-7n-a	'I brought it up'
ma tz'-el w-ii-7n-a	'I took it away from something'
ma tz'-e-x w-ii-7n-a	'I took it out'
ma tz'-e-tz w-ii-7n-a	'I brought it out'

170 THE VERB PHRASE

>   ma tz'-ok w-ii-7n-a   'I took it east'
>   ma tz'-ok-x w-ii-7n-a   'I took it inside'
>   ma tz'-ok-tz w-ii7n-a   'I brought it inside'
>   ma ∅-kyaj w-ii-7n-a   'I detained it'
>   ma tz'-aj w-ii-7n-a   'I took it on my return'
>   ma tz'-aj-tz w-ii-7n-a   'I brought it on my return'
>   ma tz-iky' w-ii-7n-a   'I passed by bringing it'
>   ma tz-iky'-x w-ii-7n-a   'I took it to the left'
>   ma tz-iky'-tz w-ii-7n-a   'I brought it from the left'
>   ma ∅-b'aj w-ii-7n-a   'I took, brought, or remained
>   with everything'

While directionals can be used with most verbs, almost all transitive verbs are always accompanied by directionals. They are not yet fully obligatory in that most (but not all) transitive verbs can be elicited without directionals with repeated questioning, but to all intents they are obligatory since Mam speakers do not like transitive verbs without directionals and will not use them. This is not a semantic matter, since the same transitive verbs in the syntactic passive with -eet usually do not take directionals. The only transitive verbs which I have found in texts or discourse without directionals are aj- 'want', ky'i7- 'not want', and il- 'see'.

3.2 Semantics

Not all transitive verbs take all the different directionals, and each transitive verb has a directional which is most closely associated with it. Furthermore, several of the directionals have secondary, nondirectional meanings associated with them. (England 1976b). The secondary meaning of the directionals are:

Primary		Secondary
xi	'away'	incipience
el	'out'	motion to the west
ok	'in'	motion to the east
aj	'return from here'	motion behind or to the back
ajtz	'return from there'	repeated action
kyaj	'leave here'	completive
iky'x	'pass to other side'	motion from right to left
iky'tz	'pass to this side'	motion from left to right
b'aj	'complete'	cessation of movement

An analysis of which directionals can accompany which verbs shows that there are three broad semantic categories of transitive verbs. One category consists of verbs which take all or almost all the directionals, and these are generally verbs referring to actions which involve movement but where the movement is rather unspecific so the directionals can be used to specify the particular movement involved. Examples are q'i- 'take/bring' or tx'aj- 'wash'. A second category is verbs which take very few directionals because the motion implied by the root is already so specific that only a few directionals complement it. Examples of this type are qeech- 'grind corn (nixtamal)' and saa- 'lay out clothing to dry'. The third category includes verbs which take a very few or only one directional because their meaning does not basically involve movement. Examples of this last type are q'iija- 'divine' and qaawa- 'scold'.

An analysis of which directional is most closely associated with each transitive verb fits the analysis of three verb categories. Xi and b'aj are the most general of the directionals, with the first used to indicate incipience and the second to indicate completion. They occur as the citation form directional (the directional most closely associated

172 THE VERB PHRASE

with the verb) in over a third of the transitive verbs. If the verb is from the category which does not intrinsically involve motion or from the category in which the motion is so general as to require further directional specification, then <u>xi</u> or <u>b'aj</u> is the usual citation form directional. Other verbs involve direction, but a more specific direction is included in the semantics of the verb stem itself. They take one of the other directionals in their citation forms, and the most common of these citation directionals are <u>kub'</u> 'down', <u>jaw</u> 'up', <u>el</u> 'out', and <u>ok</u> 'in'. These four directions also correspond to the four cardinal directions of the Mayans, both ancient and modern: down, up, west, and east.

Therefore an analysis of which citation form directional is associated with each verb and of whether verbs take a few or many directionals shows three semantic categories of verbs, as in the following chart:

	Citation Form:	
Co-occurrence With Directionals:	<u>xi, b'aj</u>	Other
Many	Class I general movement	
Few	Class III non-movement	Class II specific movement

4. MODE

If a verb is potential or imperative, it is suffixed for these two modes. The suffixes are different for transitive and intransitive verbs (3.1) and are:

	Potential:	Imperative:
Transitive:	-a7	-m (-n / __ directionals)
Intransitive:	-l	--

The mode suffixes follow the verb stem. If a transitive verb has a directional, the potential mode suffix is the <u>intransitive</u> form and it follows the directional stem. Therefore the transitive potential -<u>a7</u> is very rarely used. The aspect <u>ok</u> co-occurs optionally with the potential mode, and no aspect occurs with the imperative. Examples:

(6-7) Potential Intransitive

k-7ooq'a-<u>l</u>-a   t-i7j   t-waakaxh-a
2sA-CRY-pot-2s 3s-RN/thematic 2s-COW-2s

'You're going to cry about your cow.'

(6-8) Potential Transitive

ok ∅-t-b'i-<u>7</u>-ya   q'aan-b'il
pot 3sA-2sE-KNOW-pot-2s CURE-inst

'You will know the medicine.'

(6-9) Potential Transitive with Directional

kb'el   t-tx'ee7ma-n-a t-qan   kjo7n
k-kub'a-<u>l</u>
3sA-dir-pot 2sE-CUT-ds-2s 3s-FOOT CORN

'You will cut the cornstalks.'

(6-10) Imperative Intransitive

∅-txi7-ya b'eeta-l
2sA-GO-2s WALK-inf

'Go walk!'

(6-11) Imperative Transitive

    Ø-Ø-b'ii-m-a   aq'uuntl ky-uk'a   xjaal
    3sA-2s imp-KNOW-imp-2s   WORK   3p-RN/com PERSON

    'Ask about the work with the people!'

(6-12) Imperative Transitive with Directional

    Ø-Ø-tx'ee7ma-n-ka-ya   sii7   tzqiij
    3sA-2s imp-CUT-imp-dir-2s FIREWOOD DRY

    'Cut the dry wood!'

5. VERB STEM

The verb stem indicates the meaning of the verb. It is a verb root or a root of any class with appropriate derivational affixes. Each stem, whether derived or underived, is basically transitive or intransitive and takes inflection according to its class. Depending on what types of suffixes a verb takes, the stem formative vowel (4.1 #3) may be required. If a transitive verb includes a directional, then the suffix -7n (4.4 #59) is required.

6. STRUCTURE OF THE VERB PHRASE

The elements in the verb phrase change somewhat depending on whether the verb is transitive or intransitive, on whether it is imperative or not, and on whether there is a directional or not. The various structures follow:

Simple Transitive Verb:

   Aspect + Absolutive + Ergative + Stem + Mode + Enclitic

(6-13) ma   chi t-tzeeq'a-ya
        rec 3pA 2sE-HIT-2s

       'you hit them'

Transitive with Directional:
   Aspect + Absolutive + Directional + Mode + -x, -tz + Ergative + Stem + Enclitic

(6-14) a. ma   chi ku7-tz   t-tzyu-7n-a
           rec 3pA dir-dir   2sE-GRAB-ds-2s

   'you grabbed them'

   b. (ok) bk'elatz   t-tzyu-7n-a
             k-kub'-l-tz
       pot   3sA-dir-pot-dir   2sE-GRAB-ds-2s

   'you will grab them'

Transitive Imperative:
   Absolutive + Ergative + Stem + Mode + Directional + -x, -tz + Enclitic

(6-15) Ø-ky-yoo-m-a   maajan
       3sA-2pE-LOOK FOR-imp-2p   WORKER

   'Look for workers!'

(6-16) chi Ø-tzyuu-n-ka-tz-a
       3pA 2s imp-GRAB-imp-dir-dir-2s

   'Grab them!'

Simple Intransitive Verb:
   Aspect + Absolutive + Stem + Mode + -x, -tz + Enclitic
(Only intransitive verbs of motion can suffix -x or -tz; other intransitives take regular preposed directionals.)

(6-17) ma   chin b'eet-a
       rec 1sA   WALK-1s

   'I walked'

(6-18) ma   tz'-eex
            -eel-x
       rec 3sA-GO OUT-dir

'he went out'

<u>Intransitive with Directional</u>:

Aspect + Absolutive + Directional + Mode + -x, -tz + Stem + Enclitic

(6-19) ma   ∅-jaw   b'iit'j
        rec   3sA-dir   EXPLODE

'it exploded'

<u>Intransitive Imperative</u>:

Absolutive + Stem + Mode + Directional + -x, -tz + Enclitic

(6-20) chi mok'ee-∅-ka-x-a
        2pA CROUCH-imp-dir-dir-2p

'crouch down (you-all)'

7. SENTENCE FORMATION

Mam sentences are of two types: verbal and non-verbal. The predicate of a verbal sentence contains a transitive or intransitive verb while that of a non-verbal sentence contains a stative or a locative/existential predicate. This chapter describes the formation and typology of verbal sentences, including basic constituents, basic word order, and categories of voice, and then notes an instance of choice in oblique patient markers. The final topic discussed under verbal sentences is focus. Non-verbal sentences are then described, and this is followed by sections on negation, question formation, and coordination. These last three topics are considered again in chapter 8, as is focus, in that they also involve complex sentences.

1. VERBAL SENTENCES

1.1 Basic Constituents

1.1.1 The Verb. As in the previous chapters, I am using three terms for the arguments which stand in direct relation to the verb in simple sentences. The agent is the argument which is cross-referenced to a verb having two direct noun phrases (a transitive verb) by ergative markers. The patient is the argument which is cross-referenced to a transitive verb by absolutive markers. The subject is the argument which is cross-referenced to an intransitive verb (one which has only one direct noun phrase) by absolutive markers. I have deliberately chosen a morphological

definition of these arguments. One reason is that there is
theoretical disagreement as to how to classify them syntactically and I would like to describe the data from a neutral
position, at least on this issue. Although the terminology
mixes ₊syntactic and semantic terms, it clearly distinguishes
the three types of arguments, which helps clarify the discussion at various points. Where it is necessary to discuss
a semantic agent or patient I indicate the change in
convention.

   Verb roots in Mam are of two morphologically distinct
classes: transitive and intransitive (see chapter 3). Verb
phrases are also transitive or intransitive on the basis
of inflectional morphology (see chapter 6), and the distinction is equally important syntactically or semantically,
even though the classes of transitive and intransitive stems,
phrases, and sentences do not correspond exactly. There
are a few morphologically transitive stems which are used
only in their antipassive or passive forms (see chapter 4
and 7.1.3) so that the morphology of the verb phrase is
intransitive. Those which require the use of the antipassive
are semantically and syntactically intransitive as well
(other verbs, for which the antipassive is an <u>option</u>, to
be described later, are semantically transitive):

(7-1) milaay-x   qo   aanq'a-n qa-nti7 t-qan   q'iij
       NEG-always 1pA LIVE-ap   IF-NEG   3s-FOOT SUN

       q-iib'aj
       1p-RN/over

       'We can't live without sunlight over us.'

(7-2) ma-yax   ∅-jejeeya-n   xu7j   t-uj   nim-b'ee
       rec-intens   3sA-LAUGH-ap WOMAN 3s-RN/in BIG-ROAD

       'The woman laughed a lot in the road.'

In both example (7-1) and (7-2) the verb carries the antipassive suffix -n, showing that the stem is transitive but that it is marked intransitively with absolutive pronouns which cross-reference the subject. (The subject is presumably an original agent, since antipassives always cross-reference the agent rather than the patient of a verb, but the semantics of these verbs is sufficiently intransitive that it is not clear that it makes sense to speak of underlying agents and patients, so I will use subject for the actor who is marked on the verb, as I do for intransitive verbs.) In neither example can an object be expressed, so the surface syntax is also intransitive. Other transitive roots which require an antipassive are several roots that are derived from nouns, and semantically incorporate these nouns into the verb stem, for example:

(7-3)   ma   chin b'ooxha-n-a
         rec 1sA HUNT ARMADILLOS-ap-1s

         'I hunted armadillos.' (I armadillo-hunted.)

(7-4)   ma   chin chqiitz'a-n-a
         rec 1sA PLAY VIOLIN-ap-1s

         'I played the violin.' (I violin-played.)

-b'ooxha- 'hunt armadillos' is derived through the stem formative (4, #3) from b'ooxh 'armadillo' and -chqiitz'a- is similarly derived from chqiitz' 'violin'.

The few transitive verb stems which are used only in the passive are semantically transitive. By this I mean that the semantics imply an agent and a patient, even if the agent is not expressed in the surface form, and that an agent can be expressed in an oblique phrase, even though it is not required. The verb phrase morphology is of course intransitive, since only the original patient is

cross-referenced to the verb with absolutive markers.
Examples are:

(7-5) a. ma ∅-kan-eet   jun n-sentaabi-ya t-uj   tz'iis
            rec 3sA-FIND-pas ONE 1s-CENT-1s   3s-RN/in GARBAGE

   'I found my penny in the garbage.' (Lit: 'My penny was found in the garbage.')

   b. ma ∅-kan-eet jun n-sentaabi-ya w-u7n-a
                                        1s-RN/agt-1s

   'My penny was found by me.'

(7-6) a. ma-a7   ∅-juk'-eet   nimaal mariimp
            rec-emph 3sA-PLAY MARIMBA-pas dem   MARIMBA

   'The marimba started.' (Lit: 'The marimba was played.')

   b. ma-a7 ∅-juk'-eet nimaal mariimp w-u7n-a
                                        1s-RN/agt-1s

   'I played the marimba.' (Lit: 'The marimba was played by me.'

Neither of the verbs in the above sentences can be used in the transitive active, due apparently to a peculiarity of these roots. In the examples with the antipassive the semantics and verb phrase morphology coincide (intransitive) and are at variance with the stem class morphology (transitive), while in the examples with the passive the semantics and the verb stem morphology coincide (transitive) and are at variance with the verb phrase morphology (intransitive).

The other possibility, that the verb stem class and verb phrase morphology might coincide but be at variance with the semantics, also exists, with morphologically intransitive verb stems. Intransitive verbs of motion can

be used transitively in a causative sense without
changing the morphology but with transitive semantics:

(7-7) k-tzaaj-al   a7   w-u7n-a
       3sA-COME-pot   WATER   1s-RN/agt-1s

       'I will bring water.'   (Lit: 'Water will come by me.')

(7-8) t-wiixh o   ∅-kub'   t-ee   ich'
       3s-CAT   past 3sA-GO DOWN   3s-RN MOUSE

       'His cat killed mice.'   (Lit: 'His cat went down
       at mice.')

In (7-8) <u>twiixh</u> 'his cat' is focused in the pre-verb position
(7.1.5), but this is immaterial to the transitivity of the
sentence. (7-7) cross-references the semantic patient on
the verb while (7-8) cross-references the semantic agent.
In both sentences the stem and verb phrase are intransitive,
while the semantics is transitive.

The point of this discussion has been to show inconsistencies between the categories transitive and intransitive as defined on the basis of verb stem morphology (chapter 3), verb phrase morphology (chapter 6), and semantics. The preceding chapters show that the transitive/intransitive distinction is very clear at the morphological level; it is also important at the semantic level, although it is perhaps not as clear as (see the discussion of voice, 7.1.3), nor entirely consistent with, the morphological distinction.

Semantically transitive sentences in Mam have transitive verbs (with the exception noted above) which are cross-referenced to an agent and a patient (but see 7.1.3). Third person agents and patients can be specified in noun phrases:

(7-9) ma   chi kub' t-tx'ee7ma-n xiinaq tzee7
       <u>rec 3pA dir   3sE-CUT-ds   MAN   TREE</u>
            verb   agent patient

'The man cut the trees.'

Intransitive sentences have intransitive verbs (again with the exceptions noted above) which are cross-referenced to the subject, which can express either the semantic agent:

(7-10) ma   tz-uul   tx'yaan
        <u>rec 3sA-COME HERE DOG</u>
             verb   agent

'The dog just came here.'

or the semantic patient:

(7-11) ma   ∅-kyim   xiinaq
        <u>rec 3sA-DIE   MAN</u>
             verb   patient

'The man died.'

Here also third person arguments can be specified in noun phrases, as in (7-10) and (7-11). Since independent pronouns are only used in verbal sentences for emphasis (5.4.1), there is usually no lexical representation of first or second person agents or patients.

1.1.2 <u>Nominal Constituents</u>. In addition to verbs, the basic constituents of verbal sentences are adverbs (discussed in the next section) and various nominal constituents. These include the (semantic) agent, (semantic) patient, dative, instrument, benefactive, comitative, locative, causative, and thematic. Two other types of noun phrases which are not sentence constituents are reflexives and possessives. These are structurally like other nominal

SENTENCE FORMATION   183

constituents and are discussed below. Of the sentence
constituents, both a semantic agent and patient are required
in transitive sentences, while either a semantic agent or
patient is required in intransitive sentences. There is
a very limited set of transitive verbs which require an
indirect object (dative). These are the usual verbs such as
'give' or 'tell', and they are morphologically indistinguish-
able from other transitives. Other nominal constituents
occur where permitted or dictated by verb and sentence
semantics.

All nominal constituents except the agent and patient
are obligatorily indicated by relational noun phrases
introduced by characteristic relational nouns (3.2.10).
Under certain circumstances (see below) agents and patients
also appear in relational noun phrases. Again, first
and second persons are not represented lexically and are
only indicated by the possessive morphology on the
relational noun, while third person constituents are
indicated by the morphology of the relational noun and
by optional specification in a noun phrase which is the
object (or more precisely, the possessor) of the relational
noun.

Dative:

(7-12) a. ma-a7   ∅-tzaj   ky-q'o-7n   pwaq   q-ee
            rec-emph 3sA-dir   3pE-GIVE-ds   MONEY   1p-RN/dat

        'They gave us the money.'

        b. ma-a7 ∅-tzaj q-q'o-7n pwaq t-e   Marí
                         1pE   3s-RN/dat   María

        'We gave María the money.'

(7-12a) and b) use two different forms of the relational
noun. -ee, -iib'aj, and -uuk'al are the phrase final forms

of -e, -iib', and -uk' respectively. The relational
nouns which introduce the benefactive and dative constituents
are the same:

Benefactive:

(7-13)   ...b'ix juun-tl-jal   k-b'ant-eel
         AND ONE-other-cl/nonhuman 3sA-BE MADE-pot

         ky-e   aj   t-uj   Ch'yaq
         3p-RN/ben DEM 3s-RN/in Tuchiac

         '...and the other one will be made for those
         from Tuchiac.'

Instrument:

(7-14)   ma   chi kub' t-tx'ee7ma-n Kyel   tzee7 t-u7n
         rec 3pA dir   3sE-CUT-ds   Miguel STICK 3s-RN/inst

         maachit
         MACHETE

         'Miguel cut the sticks with a machete.'

(7-15)   ma   ∅-kub' w-aq'na-7n-a   t-uk'   asdoon
         rec 3sA-dir 1sE-WORK-ds-1s   3s-RN/inst   HOE

         'I worked (it) with a hoe.'

The instrument is indicated by two different relational
nouns, -u7n or -uuk'al. The use of -u7n, which is also the
relational noun for the causative and for the agent under
certain circumstances (see below) perhaps implies causation
more strongly than does the use of -uuk'al. The closest
analogy I can think of in English would be the difference
between:

'I broke the window by using a rock.' and

'I broke the window with a rock.'

Unlike English, Mam does not require the inclusion of a verb

form after -u7n, so the difference between the use of this
relational noun and -uuk'al is less marked than in the English
and the two vary relatively freely. The comitative also
uses the relational noun -uuk'al.

Comitative:

(7-16) o-o7   qo-xiima-n-a   t-i7j   t-uk'   Looxh
        past-emph 1pA-THINK-ap-1p   3s-RN/pat   3s-RN/com   Alonso

        Tmink   b'ix t-uk'   n-maan-a   b'ix t-uk'
        Domingo AND   3s-RN/com   1s-FATHER-1s   AND   3s-RN/com

        aja Cheep Toontz
        DEM José   Ordóñez

        'We have thought about it with Alonso Domingo, with
        my father, and with that José Ordóñez.'

Locative (two of many):

(7-17) at-∅   juun xjaal   n-∅-taan   t-uj
        LOC PRED-3sA   ONE   PERSON   prog-3sA-SLEEP   3s-RN/in

        juun t-tx'aaqan jaa   t-jaq'   chik'uul   t-e
        ONE   3s-OLD   HOUSE 3s-RN/under   MOUNTAIN   3s-RN/pos

        Chna7jal
        Huehuetenango

        'There was a person who slept in his old house under
        the mountain of Huehuetenango.'

Thematic:

(7-18) o   ∅-tzaalaj   xjaal   t-i7j   t-paa
        past 3sA-BE CONTENT   PERSON   3s-RN/thematic   3s-BAG

        'The person was content about his bag.'

Causative:

(7-19) b'i7x   jaka   Ø-lam-eet   aja t-xeew
        IMMEDIATELY AFFIRM   3sA-CLOSE-pas   DEM 3s-RESPIRATION

        a7   t-u7n   kyq'iiq'
        WATER   3s-RN/caus WIND

    'Immediately the movement of the water because of
    the wind can be closed off.'

The relational noun which introduces a causative is the same as one of the relational nouns which introduce an instrument and also the same as that which introduces an agent in an oblique phrase. There is actually no reason to separate causatives from agents in Mam--they are structurally identical at all levels.

The other two noun phrases which are similar in structure to the above sentence constituents are those that indicate possession and reflexivization. The possessive is indicated by the relational noun -ee, cross-referenced to the possessor:

(7-20) kwanto t-kan-eet   saant t-e   I7tzal...
        WHEN   3sE-FIND-pas   SAINT 3s-RN/pos Ixtahuacán

    'When they found the patron saint of Ixtahuacán...'

It is used pronominally if the object of possession is unspecified:

(7-21) b'ala jaka   Ø-xiika-n   w-ee-y7
        MAYBE AFFIRM   3sA-REACH-ap   1s-RN/pos-1s

    'Maybe mine can reach.'

Reflexives have a complicated structure which seems to be unique to Mam, among the Mayan languages. The relational noun -iib'aj indicates the reflexive, which directly follows the verb and carries the person enclitic for both, showing that the reflexive is incorporated into the verb. The

verb itself must have the antipassive suffix (see 7.1.3.2)
but cross-references the agent (who of course is equal to
the patient in a reflexive sentence) with <u>ergative</u> markers:

(7-22) a. ma kub' t-b'iyoo-n t-iib' xiinaq
        rec dir 3sE-KILL-ap 3s-RN/refl MAN

    'The man killed himself.'

Omitting the antipassive is ungrammatical:

    b. *ma kub' t-b'iyo-7n t-iib' xiinaq
                         -ds

as is using the absolutive markers to cross-reference the
agent:

    c. *ma kub' Ø-b'iyoo-n t-iib' xiinaq
                 3sA-

I have not indicated an absolutive marker before the directional in the a) sentence above (where the patient is normally marked; it would be Ø in this example to concord with the third person singular) because if the person of the agent/patient is changed to one that has a pronounced morpheme in the absolutive markers, nothing shows up:

    d. ma _kub' ky-b'iyoo-n ky-iib' xiinaq
             3pE-   3p-

    'The men killed themselves.'

    e. *ma <u>chi</u> kub' ky-b'iyoo-n ky-iib' xiinaq

Therefore the structure of the reflexive is that the reflexive noun phrase is incorporated into the verb, since enclitics follow the reflexive but not the verb:

(7-23) ma b'aj n-tx'ajoo-n w-iib'-<u>a</u>
       rec dir 1sE-WASH-ap 1s-RN/refl-1s

    'I washed myself.'

The verb is antipassive and certainly intransitive since only one argument is cross-referenced to it, but that argument is marked ergatively. Further, the argument occupies the position normally occupied by the agent of a transitive verb and not that occupied by the subject of an intransitive (i.e., before the directional). One would expect either that the verb is antipassive, it cross-references the argument absolutively and the person affix occurs before the directional, or that the verb is transitive, it cross-references the agent ergatively and the ergative affix occurs before the stem, but neither of these possibilities is grammatical. Instead the structure of a reflexive is a mixture of the two.

The agent and patient are also introduced by relational nouns under certain circumstances. With a simple intransitive or active sentence the agent and patient occur in direct noun phrases, as in examples (7-9), (7-10) and (7-11). Under the various circumstances in which verb phrase morphology indicates only one actor but the semantics indicates two actors, either the agent or the patient can appear in an oblique noun phrase (subject to certain restrictions which are discussed in the appropriate sections). These conditions include the passive and antipassive voices (see 7.1.3) and the type of situation mentioned above in which a morphologically intransitive verb is made causative through transitive semantics (examples 7-7, 7-8). The agent also appears in an oblique noun phrase when it is focused preverbally with an active transitive verb (see 7.1.3.2, 7.1.5). Patients also appear in oblique noun phrases after verbal nouns (see 7.1.4, 8.4). The passive and antipassive are discussed more thoroughly in section 7.1.3, so I will only give brief examples here.

SENTENCE FORMATION 189

Passive verbs cross-reference the patient so that the agent, if it can be expressed, appears in a relational noun phrase introduced by the relational noun -u7n.

(7-24) ma   chi b'iy-eet   kab' xjaal   w-u7n-a
        rec 3pA HIT-pas   TWO   PERSON 1s-RN/agt-1s

'Several[1] people were hit by me.'

Whenever an agent is expressed in an oblique phrase the relational noun which introduces that phrase is -u7n. Antipassive verbs cross-reference the agent, so that the patient, if expressed, appears in an oblique phrase introduced by either the relational noun -i7j or by -ee. The distribution of these two relational nouns for indicating the patient is discussed in 7.1.3 and 7.1.4.

(7-25) ma   Ø-tzyuu-n   Cheep ky-i7j   xiinaq
        rec 3sA-GRAB-ap   José   3p-RN/pat MAN

'José grabbed the men.'

An example of the use of an oblique noun phrase for the patient after an infinitive is:

(7-26) ...i7e7x   xjaal laq'oo-1 t-ee
        Ø-chi-e7x
        past dep-3pA-GO PERSON BUY-inf 3s-RN/pat

'...(when) some people went to buy it.'

1.1.3 Adverbs. There are several types of adverbs which are distinct with regard to their syntactic behavior. Most adverbs are morphologically "particles" in that they do not inflect and cannot be derived, but a small class of adverbs are derived from other words (e.g., words for time in the future and time in the past, see 4.7). Locative adverbs are last in the sentence. This is unlike locative relational noun phrases, which, while often last, can also precede other relational noun phrases. Locative adverbs can be fronted to a pre-verb position with no other changes in the sentence.

(7-27) a. k'ala-7tz-a   cheej maajlaj
          TIE UP-proc imp-2s HORSE OTHER SIDE

          'Go and tie up the horse there on the other side!'

      b. maajlaj k'ala-7tz-a cheej

(7-28) a. k-pool   iqatz maax
          k-poon-l
          3sA-ARRIVE THERE-pot CARGO UP TO THERE

          Xhniil
          Colotenango

          'The cargo will arrive there in Colotenango.'

      b. maax k-pool iqatz Xhniil

(7-29) ma Ø-txi   t-yek'a-n   Cheep u7j   t-e   tij-xjaal
       rec 3sA-dir 3sE-SHOW-ds José BOOK 3s-RN/dat old-MAN

       t-u7n   t-qan   q'aaq' machii7w
       3s-RN/inst   3s-FOOT   FIRE   THERE

       'José showed the man the book there by the firelight.'

In (7-28) the toponym that follows the locative adverb maax cannot be fronted, even though the locative is fronted.

Manner adverbs occur first in the sentence before the verb and do not move. Some require dependent person marking (8.1).

(7-30) a. cheeb'a b'iincha-n-kub'-t-a   q-mees
          SLOWLY MAKE-imp-dir-2s emph-2s   1p-TABLE

          'Make our table slowly!'

SENTENCE FORMATION 191

    b. *b'iinch-n-kub'-t-a q-mees cheeb'a

(7-31) a. qa-pa   chiix   t-ku7-tz   jb'aal
        IF-encl SUDDENLY 3sE-GO DOWN-dir RAIN

       'Maybe suddenly it will rain.'

     b. *t-ku7-tz jb'aal qa-pa chiix

(7-32) a. qit   t-xi   aaj   yoola-l   t-jaa   xu7j
        SOMETIMES 3sA-dir RETURN TALK-inf 3s-HOUSE WOMAN

       'Sometimes he went to talk in the woman's house.'

     b. *t-xi aaj yoola-l t-jaa xu7j qit

Time adverbs are unmarked in initial position in the sentence, and replace the usual aspect markers. A sentence with a future temporal adverb optionally includes the potential mode suffix.

(7-33) Past

     eew   tz-ul   aaj   nan   yaa7
     YESTERDAY 3sA-dir RETURN MA'AM GRANDMOTHER

     'Grandmother came yesterday.'

(7-34) Recent Past

     maaky'   Ø-jaw   we7
     A WHILE AGO 3sA-dir STAND

     'He got up a little while ago.'

(7-35) Future

     a. jnab'xa   Ø-b'aj   b'ant   t-ajlaa-l   yool
        NEXT YEAR 3sA-dir BE MADE 3s-COUNT-abs n WORD

        t-e   I7tzal
        3s-RN/pos Ixtahuacán

       'Next year the Ixtahuacán dictionary will be done.'

or b. jnab'xa k-b'aj-al² b'ant t-ajlaa-1 yool t-e
           3sA-dir-pot

       I7tzal

If the time adverbs occur at the end of the sentence they require dependent aspect markers in the past and near past and obligatory use of the potential mode suffix in the future.

(7-36) ∅-∅-ul   aaj   nan   yaa7   eew
        past dep-3sA-dir RETURN MA'AM GRANDMOTHER YESTERDAY

        'Grandmother came yesterday.'

(7-37) x-∅-jaw   we7   maaky'
        rec dep-3sA-dir STAND A WHILE AGO

        'He got up a while ago.'

(7-38) k-b'aj-al   b'ant   t-ajlaa-1   yool t-e
        3sA-dir-pot BE MADE 3s-COUNT-abs n WORD 3s-RN/pos

        I7tzal   jnab'xa
        Ixtahuacán NEXT YEAR

        'Next year the Ixtahuacán dictionary will be done.'

Otherwise, the use of the regular past and recent past aspects instead of dependent aspects with a temporal adverb at the end of the sentence is interpreted as a question.

(7-39) o   tz-ul   aaj nan yaa7 eew
        past 3sA-dir

        'Did grandmother come yesterday?'

(7-40) ma   ∅-jaw we7 maaky'
        rec

        'Did he get up a little while ago?'

The adverbs which refer to the present do not follow these rules, probably because there is no aspect marker for the present. Ja7la 'now' if at the end of the sentence is interpreted as present (without an aspect marker), and if at the beginning as future. Ch'ix 'right now' only occurs before the verb, which is marked by ergative rather than absolutive markers.

(7-41) a. tz-uul   taat   ja7la
       3sA-COME FATHER NOW

       'Father comes now.'

       b. ja7la tz-uul taat

       'Father will come now.'

(7-42) a. ch'ix   t-kyim q'iinan
       RIGHT NOW 3sE-DIE RICH PERSON

       'Right now the rich person dies.'

       b. *t-kyim q'iinan ch'ix

1.2 Basic Word Order and Typology

Mam basic word order is verb-agent-patient (VSO; i.e., verb-ergative-absolutive). Unlike some other Mayan languages, for instance Kekchí (Pinkerton, 1978) or Yucatec (Durbin and Ojeda, 1978), there is no difficulty determining basic word order. A simple active transitive sentence with noun phrases for agent and patient neither of which is expressed obliquely, focused, or topicalized always has that order, and in fact an overwhelming percentage of transitive sentences in texts follows verb-agent-patient order.

(7-43) ma Ø-kub' ky-tzyu-7n xiinaq cheej
       rec 3sA-dir 3pE-GRAB-ds MAN   HORSE
               V   AGT   PAT

       'The men grabbed the horse.'

(7-44) nn-∅-ok   ky-ki-7n   xjaal   jun wech
        prog-3sA-dir 3pE-SEE-ds PERSON ONE FOX
        V   AGT   PAT

'The people were seeing a fox.'

Other orders are not grammatical:
(7-45) a. *xiinaq ma ∅-kub' ky-tzyu-7n cheej

       b. *cheej ma ∅-kub' ky-tzyu-7n xiinaq

       c. *xiinaq cheej ma ∅-kub' ky-tzyu-7n

       d. *cheej xiinaq ma ∅-kub' ky-tzyu-7n

If only one lexical noun phrase which could be cross-referenced by either person marker on the verb appears on the surface, it is interpreted as the patient:

(7-46) ma ∅-kub' ky-tzyu-7n xiinaq

       'They grabbed the man.'
       not *'The men grabbed it.'

The person marker prefixes on the verb are in the opposite order: patient-agent-verb:

(7-47) ma   chi kub' n-b'iyo-7n-a
       rec 3pA dir   1sE-HIT-ds-1s
            PAT   AGT-V

'I hit them.'

Because independent pronouns are only used in a verbal sentence in emphatic constructions (see 5.4.1), sentences with a full nominal expansion of verb-agent-patient always involve third person nouns for both agent and patient. Agents and patients of first or second person are cross-referenced on the verb but have no lexical representation in the sentence, as is the situation with unspecified third person noun phrases.

Constituents indicated by oblique noun phrases have a characteristic order. All oblique noun phrases follow direct noun phrases. The dative follows the patient; other oblique noun phrases follow the dative in the preferred order of: locative + instrument + comitative + benefactive.

(7-48) ma ∅-txi   t-yek'a-n   Cheep u7j   t-e   ti7j-xjaal
       rec 3sA-dir 3sE-SHOW-ds José   BOOK 3s-RN/dat OLD-PERSON
               V   AGT   PAT   DAT

'José showed the book to the elder.'

(7-49) ma ∅-b'aj   t-aq'na-7n   Cheep t-jaq'   kjo7n
       rec 3sA-dir 3sE-WORK-ds José 3s-RN/under CORNFIELD
               V   AGT   LOC

t-uuk'   Xwaan t-e   xjaal
3s-RN/com Juan   3s-RN/ben PERSON
     COM   BEN

'José worked in the cornfield with Juan for the person.'

(7-50) ma ∅-b'aj   t-aq'na-7n   Cheep t-jaq'   kjo7n
       rec 3sA-dir 3sE-WORK-ds José 3s-RN/under CORNFIELD
               V   AGT   LOC

t-u7n   asdoon
3s-RN/inst HOE
     INST

'José worked in the cornfield with a hoe.'

Other typological characteristics of Mam conform by and large to a verb initial order. Although there are no prepositions as such, possessors follow possessed nouns (this applies to relational noun phrases as well as other possessive constructions).[3]

(7-51) nn-∅-ok-x   ky-q'o-7n   saant   t-uj   tal   jaa
       prog-3sA-dir-dir 3pE-GIVE-ds SAINT 3s-RN/in SMALL HOUSE

'They placed the patron saint in the little house.'

As an alternative to interrogative intonation contours, Mam has an enclitic -pa which is suffixed to the first word in a sentence and indicates yes/no questions.[4]

(7-52) at-∅-pa   aatz'an?
       LOC PRED-3sA-int SALT

'Is there salt?'

(7-53) ∅-uul-pa?
       3sA-ARRIVE-int

'Did he arrive?'

(7-54) noq-l-pa   n-∅-choora-n   a7   t-zi
       ONLY-doubt-int prog-3sA-FLOW-ap WATER 3s-RN/edge

t-jaa-ya?
2s-HOUSE-2s

'Is the water running at your house?'

Similarly, interrogative words are first in a sentence.[5]

(7-55) alkyee saj   tzyuu-n ky-e   kab' xiinaq?
              x-∅-tzaj
       WHO   rec dep-3sA-dir GRAB-ap 3p-RN/pat TWO MAN

'Who grabbed the men?'

(7-56) al-u7n   k-b'aj-al   t-jaacha-n-a   sii7?
       WHAT-RN/inst 3sA-dir-pot 2sE-SPLIT-ds-2s FIREWOOD

'What are you going to split the wood with?'

(7-57) tza7n ta7-∅-ya?
       HOW   LOC PRED-2sA-2s

'How are you?'

Mam has a set of verbal auxiliaries, the directionals (see 6.3), which precede the main verb (except imperatives) and to which are preposed the absolutive pronouns and are postposed the suffixes of mode.[6]

(7-58) k-tzaj-al   w-ii-7n-a
        3sA-dir-pot 1sE-TAKE/BRING-ds-1s

   'I will bring it.'

Mam adjectives follow the noun, <u>if</u> there is a demonstrative or numeral before the noun. If there is no other modifier before the noun, adjectives precede it. There is a small class of adjectives which do not follow this rule and can precede the noun even if other modifiers also precede it. These are <u>matiij</u> 'big', <u>nim</u> 'a lot', <u>nii</u> 'small', and <u>tal</u> 'small'.[7]

(7-59) a. kab' tx'yaan saq
           TWO DOG   WHITE

           'two white dogs'

        b. *kab' saq tx'yaan

        c. saq tx'yaan

           'the white dog'

(7-60) a. jun xiinaq matiij
           ONE MAN   BIG

           'a big man'

        b. jun matiij xiinaq

           'a big man'

        c. matiij xiinaq

           'the big man'

Thus Mam shows no contradiction to the Greenberg universal

hypotheses. It conforms to expectations about verb-initial languages.

1.3 Voice

I am using voice to mean the relationship between a transitive verb and its nominal dependents. A change in that relationship is a change in voice. There is some difficulty using traditional terms when discussing ergative languages because there is disagreement as to whether the agent of a transitive verb is its subject (traditional terminology), or whether it would be better to consider that for ergative languages the agent of a transitive verb is its object and the patient of a transitive verb, as well as the actor of an intransitive verb, is the subject. For this reason I have used agent and patient rather than subject and object. This leads to further difficulties with the terms passive and antipassive as applied to ergative languages.

Passive traditionally refers to a change in verb/argument relationships whereby the patient (transitive object) appears as the subject of an intransitive form of the verb and the original agent (transitive subject) appears in an oblique phrase. In Mam there are a number of verb forms in which this seems to happen; however, since this does not require a change in agreement between the verb and patient--the patient continues to be marked with absolutive pronouns--it may not be analogous to the passive in accusative languages. The verb does, however, change from a two-argument to a one-argument verb, which requires that the original agent be expressed obliquely. I will continue to use the term "passive" for these constructions, for lack of a better term.

The antipassive has been used for a change in verb/

argument relationships in ergative languages which has been claimed to be analogous to the passive in accusative languages (Silverstein, 1976: 140). The agent of a transitive verb appears as the subject of an intransitive form of the verb and the original patient appears in an oblique phrase. There is a new relationship established between the verb and the original agent, because person marking for the agent changes from ergative to absolutive. This is thought to be analogous to the passive in accusative languages because in both voices the "unique" case (that which marks only one type of argument, which is the accusative in accusative languages and the ergative in ergative languages) switches case while the "paired" case (the nominative in accusative languages or the absolutive in ergative languages) is expressed obliquely if at all. I will use the term "antipassive" for these constructions, in spite of the fact that the term may be misleading and that there is still no theoretical agreement on what precisely it means.

It still remains to justify considering the "passive" in ergative languages a voice. While the original patient continues to be marked absolutively and there is therefore no change in agreement induced by this noun phrase, the verb becomes intransitive and the original agent becomes oblique. These is a change in verb/dependent relations which I think warrants the use of the term "voice" in discussing it.

1.3.1 <u>Passives</u>. There are at least four and possibly five passive constructions in Mam. The four clear passives are marked morphologically by a passive suffix on the verb, and all involve a change in verb/argument relationships whereby the original agent of a transitive verb appears in an oblique phrase if at all. The original patient continues to be marked on the verb with absolutive pronouns. There is no restriction as to person of the patient on a passive verb, but several of the passives restrict the person of a possible oblique agent. Agents, if they appear, are expressed through a relational noun phrase introduced by the relational noun -u7n.

Before discussing the formation and functions of the different passives it is necessary to review certain characteristics of transitive verb stems. Transitive roots are monosyllabic and of the shape CVC. Stems are derived from other classes of roots either through derivational suffixes (such as -saa 'causative', or -b'aa 'positional to transitive'), through vowel lengthening (4.1.1 #5), or through the stem formative vowel (4.1 #3). Stems derived through suffixes will be called lexically derived stems, while stems which are transitive roots or are derived through vowel length or the stem formative will be called underived stems. The distinction is important in the formation of several of the passives.

The regular syntactic passive is formed with the suffix -eet (4.1.2 #28). Almost any underived or lexically derived stem with very few exceptions can be passivized through this suffix and its only function is to create an intransitive form in which the original agent is indicated obliquely. The few exceptions to passivization through this suffix are lexical. Underived stems with this passive permit an agent of any person, while most lexically derived stems with -eet do not permit an oblique agent. I have been unable to discover a rule which predicts which few lexically derived stems do not permit an oblique agent.

(7-61) a. transitive: underived

    ma ch-ok   t-b'iyo-7n Cheep kab' xjaal
    rec 3pA-dir 3sE-HIT-ds José TWO PERSON

    'José hit some people.'

b. passive

    ma chi b'iy-eet kab' xjaal t-u7n   Cheep
    rec 3pA HIT-pas TWO PERSON 3s-RN/agt José

    'Some people were hit by José.'

c. ma chi b'iy-eet kab' xjaal w-u7n-a
                                    1s-RN/agt-1s

    'Some people were hit by me.'

d. ma chi b'iy-eet kab' xjaal t-u7n-a
                                    2s-RN/agt-2s

    'Some people were hit by you.'

The verb-patient-oblique agent order is invariable in passive sentences. The agent or patient can be focused in pre-verb position, but the order after the verb is fixed. Other examples of this passive are:

(7-62) a. transitive: underived

    ma Ø-jaw   t-tx'ee7ma-n Cheep tzee7
    rec 3sA-dir 3sE-CUT-ds   José TREE

    'José cut the tree.'

b. passive

    ma Ø-tx'eem-at tzee7 t-u7n   Cheep
    rec 3sA-CUT-pas TREE 3s-RN/agt José

    'The tree was cut by José.'

(7-63) a. transitive: lexically derived

ma chi ku7-x t-noj-sa-7n Mal saaku
rec 3pA dir-dir 3sE-FILL-caus-ds María SACK

'María filled the sacks.'

b. passive

ma chi noj-s-eet saaku t-u7n Mal
rec 3pA FILL-caus-pas SACK 3s-RN/agt María

'The sacks were filled by María.'

(7-64) a. passive: lexically derived

ma ∅-kub' mutz-b'aa-t qe7n
rec 3sA-dir UPSIDE DOWN-P→t-pas TORTILLA HOLDER

'The tortilla holder was put down upside down.'

b. *ma ∅-kub' mutz-b'aa-t t-u7n Mal

(7-65) a. passive: lexically derived

ma tz'-ok a7-la-t kjo7n
rec 3sA-dir WATER-N→t-pas CORNFIELD

'The cornfield was irrigated.'

b. *ma tz'-ok a7-la-t kjo7n t-u7n Cheep

(7-66) a. passive:lexically derived

ma tz'-el tunk-pii-t t-txa7n
rec 3sA-dir TREE W/O POINT-caus-pas 3s-RN/at edge

tzee7
TREE

'The point of the tree was felled.'

b. *ma tz'-el tunk-pii-t t-txa7n tzee7 t-u7n Kyel

While the lexically derived stem formed by -saa in (7-63) above permits an agent in an oblique phrase, the other cited stems do not permit an agent in their passive forms.

A second passive is formed through the suffix -njtz (4.1.2 #30). It is semi-productive in that only certain underived stems take it. It has the lexical function of indicating that the agent has lost, or does not have, control of the action. A third person agent (only) can be expressed optionally in an oblique phrase.

(7-67) a. ma ∅-tzeeq'a-njtz Cheep t-u7n Kyel
          rec 3sA-HIT-pas José 3s-RN/agt Miguel

    'José was hit by Miguel.' (by accident)

  b. ma ∅-tzeeq'-at Cheep t-u7n Kyel
               -pas

    'José was hit by Miguel.' (on purpose)

  c. *ma ∅-tzeeq'a-njtz Cheep w-u7n-a
                                1s-RN/agt-1s

(7-68) a. ma chi b'ii-njtz   kab' ch'it t-u7n   Mal
          rec 3pA HEAR/KNOW-pas TWO BIRD 3s-RN/agt María

    'Some birds were heard by María.' (By chance she heard their song.)

  b. ma chi b'ii-t   kab' ch'it t-u7n Mal
           -pas

    'María knew there were some birds.' (ex: She wanted to buy birds, and heard that there were some.)

(7-67) and (7-68) compare the -njtz forms in the a) examples with the same sentences with -eet in the b) examples. In both sentences the action of the a) forms comes about by accident or chance while that of the b) forms implies that the agent has some purpose in performing the action.

Another use of the -njtz passive is in generic constructions of the form 'It is good/bad to do X.'. In these constructions the ergative rather than the absolutive markers are used on the verb (see chapter 8), and there can be no agent, since the statement is of a "general truth" type.

(7-69)   naach t-k'aa-njtz   a7
        BAD   3sE-DRINK-pas WATER

       'It is bad to drink water.', or 'Water is bad.'
       (Lit: 'It is bad that water is drunk.')

(7-70)   walaan t-k'aa-njtz a7
        GOOD

       'It is good to drink water.', or 'Water is good.'

(7-71)   miib'an t-waa7-njtz
        NEG   3sE-EAT-pas

       'It is not edible.' (Lit: 'It is not to be eaten.')

A third passive which has very similar functions to the -njtz passive is formed through the suffix -j (-1 with CVC roots) (4.1.2 #29). This passive is common with underived stems and functions lexically to indicate loss or lack of agent control, as does the -njtz suffix. Is is unclear whether the suffix exists with lexically derived stems-- there are several intransitive verbs which end in -j, but this is now frozen. It may have come from this passive. Different stems take one or another of the -njtz or -j suffixes, but there are some stems which take both with apparently no difference in meaning, and some stems which take neither. Passive verbs with -j can take an agent of any person in an oblique noun phrase, unlike -njtz which restricts agent to third person. Agents are not obligatory.

(7-72) a. ma ∅-kub'   tiil-j   axi7n t-u7n   Kyel
          rec 3sA-dir BROADCAST-pas CORN 3s-RN/agt Miguel

   'The corn was spilled all over by Miguel.'

   b. ma ∅-kub' tiil-at axi7n t-u7n Kyel
                     -pas

   'The corn was sown broadcast by Miguel.'

   c. ma ∅-kub' tiil-j axi7n w-u7n-a
                                1s-RN/agt-1s

   'The corn was spilled by me.'

(7-73) a. ma ∅-ku7-x   yuup-j   q'aaq'
          rec 3sA-dir-dir PUT OUT FIRE-pas FIRE

       t-u7n   Cheep
       3s-RN/agt José

   'The fire was put out by José.' (He wasn't watching what he was doing.')

   b. ma ∅-ku7-x yuup-at q'aaq' t-u7n Cheep
                      -pas

   'The fire was put out by José.' (on purpose)

(7-74) a. ma ∅-juus-j   chib'aj   t-u7n   Mal
          rec 3sA-BURN-pas MEAT/FOOD 3s-RN/agt María

   'The food was burned by María.' (by accident)

   b. ma ∅-juus-at chib'aj t-u7n Mal
                   -pas

   'The food was cooked well-done by María.' (on purpose, therefore not burned because no one burns food on purpose)

c. ma Ø-juusa-njtz chib'aj t-u7n Mal
          -pas

'The food was burned by María.' (by accident, same meaning as a) above)

(7-75) a. ma Ø-niim-j   Kyel   t-u7n   Mal
           rec 3sA-ACCEPT-pas Miguel 3s-RN/agt María

'Miguel was accepted by María.' (ex: He is asking something of her, and María says yes, but he wasn't sure ahead of time.)

b. ma niim-at Kyel t-u7n Mal
         -pas

'Miguel was accepted by María.' (ex: They had an arrangement ahead of time, he went to ask it of her, and she said yes.)

Again, the a) sentences in (7-72) through (7-75) show the use of the -j passive and compare it to the -at passive in the b) sentences. -juus- 'burn' is one of the verbs which can take either -j or -njtz to form a passive, so the a) and c) sentences in (7-74) have the same meaning. A further example of the -j passive follows (this time with its -l alternant):

(7-76) noqanx xhi ja-tz   b'oq-l
       JUST   3pA dir-dir UPROOT-pas

'It is just broken.' (Uprooting something without care causes it to break.)

A fourth passive is formed with the suffix -b'aj. This suffix is productive with underived and lexically derived stems and permits a third person agent in an oblique phrase. It requires the use of a directional and includes motion or process in its meaning: 'X happened because someone went to do it.'

(7-77) ma-a7   ch-ex   q'i-b'aj   eky'   t-u7n   Mal
        rec-emph   3pA-dir TAKE/BRING-pas   HEN   3s-RN/agt   María

'María went to bring the hens.' (María went to get them, and therefore they are brought.)

(7-78) k-x-el   tutz'-b'a-b'aj   xhoq'   t-txa7n
        3sA-dir-pot   SITTING-P→t-pas   WATER JAR 3s-RN/at edge

pe7n
PATIO

'The water jar will be placed in the patio.' (Because someone will go and do it.)

There are also suffixes which form an active transitive and an imperative which, like -b'aj, include the meaning of 'go and do X' and which require a directional, also like -b'aj. The three suffixes form a set in complementary distribution.

(7-79) a. -7kj: transitive

   chi x-el   ky-i-7kj-a   eky'
   3pA dir-pot 2pE-BRING/TAKE-proc-2p HEN

   'You all will go and bring the hens.'

b. -7tz: imperative

   chi ky-i-7tz-a   eky'
   3pA 2pE-BRING/TAKE-proc imp-2p HEN

   'You (all) go and bring the hens!'

c. -b'aj: passive

   chi x-el   q'i-b'aj   eky'
   3pA dir-pot BRING/TAKE-pas   HEN

   'The hens will be brought.' (When you go and do it.)

This is the only passive which requires the use of a
directional, but other passives may take directionals.
Whether they do or not depends on meaning, and directionals
are not nearly as frequently used with the other passives as
they are with active transitives, where they are almost
required.

A last possible instance of a passive is an agentless
construction in which the only difference between the
transitive and passive forms is that there is no agent
marking (ergative pronoun) on the verb, and the agent, if
expressed, must be in an oblique phrase. This can be
analyzed as a ∅ passive, as Aissen (1979) has done for
a somewhat different passive in Tzotzil. It is used when the
agent is unknown or when, if the agent is known, the statement is primarily about the patient (for instance, in answering the question 'What happened to the patient?'). Only
third person agents can be expressed in an oblique noun
phrase.

(7-80) a. ma   ch-ok   b'iyo-7n-∅ kab' xiinaq
           rec 3pA-dir HIT-ds-pas? TWO MAN

'The men were hit.' (who knows by whom)

b. ma ch-ok b'iyo-7n-∅ kab' xiinaq t-u7n   Cheep
                                  3s-RN-agt José

'The men were hit by José.'

c. *ma ch-ok b'iyo-7n-∅ kab' xiinaq w-u7n-a
                                  1s-RN/agt-1s

It is more common for the patient to be focused in pre-verb
position, since this type of sentence is used primarily
in patient focus (see 7.1.5).

```
   d.  kab' xiinaq xh-ok              b'iyo-7n-∅
                   x-chi-ok
                   rec dep-3pA-dir
```

'The men were hit.'

The reason why this is only possibly a passive is that there is contradictory evidence as to its status. On the one hand, the verb morphology is transitive; i.e., the stem suffix -7n is that required by transitive verbs with directionals. Intransitive verbs with directionals, including other passives, do not take that suffix. On the other hand, agents are expressed in oblique phrases, which is characteristic of passives, and the function the form serves--to remove agent (ergative) marking from the verb-- is the same as that of other passives. The form could therefore be analyzed as either a passive or an agentless transitive, and I do not have a good reason so far for preferring one or the other analysis. Table 3 reviews the major characteristics of the different passives.

1.3.2 The Antipassive. The Mayan antipassive has been well-discussed in the literature in recent years. In addition to a number of papers which describe the phenomenon is specific languages (e.g., Bricker, 1978 for Yucatec, Lengyel, 1978 for Ixil, Smith-Stark, 1976a for Pocomam, Pinkerton, 1978 for Kekchí), several papers are important in placing the antipassive in a general Mayan or theoretical context. Ayres, 1977 pointed out that the rather different constructions which have been called antipassive in Mayan languages may not all be best characterized as a "voice" in at least some of the languages. Norman and Campbell, 1978 discuss the reconstruction of proto-Mayan

Table 3. Passives

Passive suffix	Function	Stem class	Directional	Oblique Agent third person	Oblique Agent other person
-eet	syntactic	underived	optional	yes	yes
		lexically derived		usually no	usually no
-njtz	1) lexical -agt control	underived	optional	yes	no
	2) generic qualifiers	underived	?	no	no
-j	lexical -agt control	underived	optional	yes	yes
-b'aj	syntactic +process	all	obligatory	yes	no
-∅ (?)	syntactic	all	usually +dir suf	yes	no

antipassive rules, and Larsen and Norman , 1980 discuss the
antipassive in the general context of syntactic ergativity in
Mayan languages. Smith-Stark, 1978 reviewed what was known
about antipassives in Mayan languages at the time, outlined
the different functions of the "antipassive," proposed
terminology to discuss the phenomenon, and reconstructed
the *PM forms and functions. Craig, 1979 adds Jacaltec
data and compares Mayan languages to show how the agentive
construction has evolved into an antipassive voice. This
section shows how the antipassive works in Mam, and addresses
issues raised in this group of papers; specifically, what
are the functions of the Mam antipassive, are those functions
instances of voice, and where does Mam fit into the develop-
mental scheme proposed by Craig. Smith-Stark's terminology
is used.

The Mam antipassive is a voice category with several
different functions. Is is morphologically marked by the
addition of a suffix -n on a transitive verb, and the verb
then cross-references the agent with absolutive markers.[8]

(7-81)   n-chi   kamb'aa-n xjaal
         prog-3pA WIN-ap   PERSON

         'The people are winning.'

This structure is a change in voice because the relation
between a transitive verb and its agent is affected: the
ergative agent of a transitive verb becomes an absolutive
subject (still the agent) of an intransitive verb. Mam
always cross-references the original agent on a verb
marked by the -n suffix, never the original patient,
unlike for instance Ixil (Ayres, 1977). Patients, if
expressed, are relegated to an oblique phrase (see below
for exceptions) introduced by the relational noun -i7j or

the relational noun -ee (see 7.1.4 for further discussion of the difference between -i7j and -ee for indicating the patient).

(7-82) a. transitive

    ma Ø-tzaj t-tzyu-7n Cheep ch'it
    rec 3sA-dir 3sE-GRAB-ds José BIRD

    'José grabbed the bird.'

  b. antipassive

    ma Ø-tzyuu-n Cheep t-i7j   ch'it
    rec 3sA-GRAB-ap José 3s-RN/pat BIRD

    'José grabbed the bird.'

Pluralizing 'bird' shows that the original agent is the constituent cross-referenced on the verb, because otherwise one would expect the prefix chi to appear:

  c. ma Ø-tzyuu-n Cheep ky-i7j ch'it
                            3p-

    'José grabbed the birds.'

An exception to the rule that the patient is expressed in an oblique phrase is that it can be expressed directly if there is no confusion as to which noun phrase is the agent and which is the patient. By "no confusion" I mean that with specific verbs and specific actors there are certain actors who are expected to be the agents of the action and others who are expected to be the patients. For instance, in (7-82) it is expected that people grab birds, but not that birds grab people. Such judgments involve lexical hierarchies, to be sure, but these hierarchies are more subtle and complex than most that have so far been proposed, and may well involve some very specific cultural

information. The patient of (7-82b) can be expressed in
a direct noun phrase:
(7-83)   ma ∅-tzyuu-n Cheep ch'it

   'José grabbed the bird.'

The meaning is, however, somewhat different from that in
(7-82). (7-83) implies that the action was unintentional,
while (7-82) implies nothing about intention. If, however,
the patient of this sentence is 'man', for instance, rather
than 'bird', it must be put into an oblique phrase, because
between 'José' and 'man' there is no way of judging who
is the agent.
(7-84)   a.   ma ∅-tzyuu-n Cheep t-i7j xiinaq
                                         man

       'José grabbed the man.'

      b.   *ma ∅-tzyuu-n Cheep xiinaq

The other instance in which the patient is expressed
directly rather than obliquely is in the object incorporation
function of the antipassive, which is discussed below.
In this construction the patient is both obligatory and
expressed directly.

Functions which have been identified for the Mayan antipassive are three (Smith-Stark, 1978): 1) absolutive
function: occurs when a transitive verb has no mentioned or
implied patient; 2) agent promotion function: occurs with
information questions formed on the agent of a transitive
verb, with agent focus, and with relativization of the agent;
and 3) incorporative function: occurs when certain generic
direct objects (patients) are incorporated into the verb.
The Mam antipassive performs all of these functions plus
another which I will call the lexical function. Because they

are not morphologically distinct from one another (in terms of verb inflection or morphology) I subsume them all under the term antipassive voice, rather than using the terms absolutive, agentive, or incorporative voice.

Absolutive Function: (unknown or unmentioned patient)

(7-85)   ma   chin aq'naa-n-a
         rec 1sA WORK-ap-1s

         'I worked.'

(7-86)   toons n-chi   yoola-n xjaal
         THEN prog-3pA TALK-ap PERSON

         'Then the people were talking.'

   The absolutive use of the antipassive cannot include an expressed patient, in either a direct or an oblique noun phrase. Because the agentive antipassive can express a patient (both indirectly and directly, as noted above), and distinguishing between the functions is sometimes a matter of interpretation of the sentence, it could be argued that some examples of the absolutive antipassive include a patient. On closer inspection however, sentences such as (7-82), (7-83), and (7-84) involve agent promotion, in that they are used to answer a question about the agent, and are therefore not examples of the absolutive antipassive. Further, by definition the absolutive antipassive should preclude an expressed patient.

Agent Promotion Function: (interrogation, focus, relativization, and negation of agent)

   Interrogation (obligatory):

(7-87) a.   alkyee ∅-∅-tzyuu-n   ky-e   xiinaq?
             WHO   past dep-3sA-GRAB-ap 3p-RN/pat MAN

             'Who grabbed the men?'

    b. *alkyee Ø-Ø-kub'   t-tzyu-7n   ky-e xiinaq?
            past dep-3sA-dir 3sE-GRAB-ds

In addition to the use of the antipassive in question of
the agent, it is used to answer a question about the agent:

(7-88) ma-a7   Ø-k'aaya-n   Cheep t-i7j   t-cheej
        rec-emph 3sA-SELL-ap José   3s-RN/pat 3s-HORSE

        'José sold his horse.' (answers 'What did José do?')

Focus (optional, see below):

(7-89) Cheep Ø-Ø-tzyuu-n   ky-i7j   kab' xiinaq
        José   past dep-3sA-GRAB-ap   3s-RN/pat TWO MAN

        'José grabbed the men.'

The focused agent precedes the verb, and the dependent
aspect (see 8.2.1) is optional with fronted constituents.
The verb itself can be transitive with a fronted agent,
but the resulting sentence is interpreted as giving new
information about the agent rather than agent focus.
The degree of difference is small, to be sure, but Mam
speakers recognize that difference and say that (7-89) does
not mean the same thing as (7-90) below.

(7-90) Cheep o   chi tzaj t-tzyu-7n   kab' xiinaq
        José past 3pA dir 3sE-GRAB-ds TWO MAN

        'José grabbed the men.'

(7-90) is only possible because the agent and patient are of
different number. If they were both singular or plural
some additional disambiguating mechanism would be necessary
in order to clarify which person marker on the verb refers to
which noun phrase. A sentence with a transitive verb and
no fronting neither focuses on the agent nor gives new
information about it and is the baseline from which these
sentences are judged:

(7-91) o   chi tzaj t-tzyu-7n   Cheep kab' xiinaq
        past 3pA dir 3sE-GRAB-ds José TWO MAN

        'José grabbed the men.'

It is also possible to focus on the agent using a transitive verb, in which event the agent appears as a fronted oblique phrase:

(7-92) t-u7n   Cheep i   tzaj t-tzyu-7n
                        Ø-chi
        3s-RN/agt José past dep-3pA dir 3sE-GRAB-ds

        kab' xiinaq
        TWO MAN

        'José grabbed the men.'

The interpretation of this sentence is the same as that of (7-89).

Relativization (optional):

The antipassive is optionally used with a relativized agent, but has a different meaning from the use of an active transitive with a relativized agent. The action in the relative clause with the antipassive takes place before the action in the main clause, while the action in a relative clause with an active transitive takes place at the same time as that of the main clause.

(7-93) a.   antipassive

             ma-a7   w-il-a   tii-xiinaq saj
                                               x-Ø-tzaj
             rec-emph 1sE-SEE-1s BIG-MAN   rec dep-3sA-dir

             tzyuu-n ky-e   xjaal
             GRAB-ap 3s-RN/pat PERSON

             'I saw the gentleman who had grabbed the people.'
             (I saw him later on.)

b. transitive

    ma-a7   w-il-a   tii-xiinaq xhi
                                       x-chi
    rec-emph 1sE-SEE-1s BIG-MAN   rec dep-3pA

    tzaj t-tzyu-7n   xjaal
    dir   3sE-GRAB-ds PERSON

    'I saw the gentleman who was grabbing the
    people.' (I saw him at the time he was going it.)

(7-94) a. antipassive

    aj   xiinaq ∅-∅-ku7-x   awaa-n
    DEM MAN   past dep-3sA-dir-dir PLANT-ap

    (ky-e)   laanch ma ∅-tzaj t-q'o-7n   kab'
    3pE-RN/pat   ORANGE rec 3sA-dir 3sE-GIVE-ds TWO

    wi7   q-ee-ky'
    PLANT 1p-RN/dat-1p

    'The man who planted the orange trees gave us
    some plants.' (after he planted)

b. transitive

    aj   xiinaq i   ku7-x   t-awa-7n
                 ∅-chi
    DEM MAN   past dep-3pA dir-dir 3sE-PLANT-ds

    laanch ma ∅-tzaj t-q'o-7n   kab' wi7
    ORANGE rec 3sA-dir 3sE-GIVE-ds TWO PLANT

    q-ee-ky'
    1p-RN/dat-1p

    'The man who planted the orange trees gave us
    some plants.' (while he was planting)

Negation (optional):

I have added negation to Smith-Stark's examples of the agent promotion function. Since, however, the agent is fronted to a pre-verb position when it is negated, this is entirely expectable.

(7-95) a. miya7 Cheep saj   tzyuu-n ky-e
                      x-∅-tzaj
           NEG   José rec dep-3sA-dir GRAB-ap 3p-RN/pat
           kab' xiinaq
           TWO MAN

           'It wasn't José who grabbed the men.'

This is really another example of focus. Negation of an agent in a direct noun phrase must use the antipassive:

       b. *miya7 Cheep xhi   tzaj t-tzyu-7n   xiinaq
                      x-chi
                      rec dep-3pA dir   3sE-GRAB-ds

Negation of an agent in an already fronted oblique noun phrase uses the antipassive optionally:

       c. miya7 t-u7n   Cheep saj tzyuu-n ky-e xiinaq
                 3s-RN/agt

           'It wasn't José who grabbed the men.'

       d. miya7 t-u7n Cheep xhi tzaj t-tzyu-7n xiinaq

           'It wasn't José who grabbed the men.'

Incorporative Function: (object incorporation)

Object incorporation is similar to that described by Smith-Stark and Craig and requires the use of the antipassive with a limited set of non-specific (generic) objects which accompany certain verbs. The object is expressed in a direct noun phrase and the verb is cross-referenced with absolutive markers to the agent:

(7-96) n-∅-tx'aa-n   t-q'ool poon
        prog-3sA-CHEW-ap 3s-SAP COPAL

   'She was chewing copal sap.'

(7-97) ma   ∅-b'iincha-n qa-jaa
        rec 3sA-MAKE-ap pl-HOUSE

   'He constructed houses.'

<u>Lexical Function</u>:

A number of verbs are derived from nouns and semantically include those nouns as patients. Such patients are not usually expressed in either direct or oblique noun phrases and the verbs require the use of the antipassive suffix (see 7.1.1.1). If however there is some reason to mention the patient, it can occur in an oblique noun phrase. There is no evidence that sentences with such verbs bear any syntactic relation to transitive sentences. While this may not, therefore, be a change in voice, I am discussing it here because it involves a further use of the antipassive suffix. The following examples illustrate the verb <u>-ky'ajla-</u> 'father children (biologically)' which is derived from <u>ky'aajb'aj</u> 'male child (of a man)' and <u>-makaaxa-</u> 'look for a type of edible ant grub' from <u>makaax</u> 'ant grub'.

(7-98) kuuya   ti-∅-teen   at-∅   xiinaq
        WHO KNOWS WHAT-3sA-EXIST LOC PRED-3sA MAN

        miib'an ∅-ky'ajlaa-n
        NEG   3sA-FATHER CHILD-ap

   'Who knows why there are men who can't have children.'

(7-99) ma qo makaaxa-n   t-uj   t-tx'otx' Toono
        rec 1pA LOOK FOR GRUBS-ap 3s-RN/in 3s-LAND   Antonio

   'We looked for ant grubs on Antonio's land.'

With some of these verbs it is possible to express a
patient. For instance, with the verb -b'iitza- 'sing',
derived from b'iitz 'song', one could mention the name
of the song being sung:

(7-100) a. ma   chin b'iitza-n-a
            rec 1sA SING-ap-1s

            'I sang.'

        b. ma chin b'iitza-n-a manyaniitas

            'I sang "mañanitas".'

Sentences (7-3) and (7-4) are other examples of this use
of the antipassive. The verbs which fall into this class
are few and there are verbs derived from nouns which do
not necessarily incorporate the patients in this way.

To review, the Mam data include all of the functions
which Smith-Stark has identified for what has been called
the Mayan antipassive, plus a lexical function. All but
the lexical function are characterized by a change in
grammatical relations, or a change in voice. Table 4
summarizes the data.

The agent promotion function in Mayan languages is the
most diverse and it has been shown that it is not the same
as the antipassive voice in several of the languages
because in these languages it cross-references the original
patient with absolutive markers and therefore does not
involve the same change in grammatical relations (Ayres,
1977; Craig, 1979). That is, in some of the Mayan languages
there is an antipassive which cross-references the original
agent on the verb and there is also an agentive which
cross-references the original patient on the verb.
Historically there were two different suffixes which performed these functions, *-Vn and *-Vw (Smith-Stark, 1978).

Table 4. Antipassive Functions

	Absolutive Function	Agent Promotion Function	Incorporative Function	Lexical Function
suffix:	-n	-n	-n	-n
agent:	absolutive subject	absolutive subject	absolutive subject	absolutive subject
patient:	∅	oblique; direct if clear	direct -specific	oblique (rare)
use:	unknown patient	+Agt question +Agt focus +Agt relativization +Agt negation	object incorporation	lexical derivation

Craig (1979) hypothesizes that the proto-Mayan agentive
construction cross-referenced the patient rather than the
agent and that it evolved into an antipassive voice in some
languages through several steps: "One analogical step
consisted of the reanalysis of all one-argument verbs as
intransitive verbs; another was to re-interpret an absolutive
marker as cross-referencing the subject rather than the object when not accompanied by an ergative marker." Using
her criteria the Mam ergative construction has evolved all
the way to an intransitive antipassive, in that it has no
ergative marking, takes a suffix cognate with a proto-Mayan
antipassive suffix (*-Vn, Smith-Stark, 1978), and cross-references the agent with absolutive markers. Another
criterion she proposes for identifying intransitive verbs,
the presence of an intransitive phrase-final marker, is
not applicable in Mam because there are no phrase-final
verb markers in Mam.

1.4 The Distribution of Oblique Patient Markers

Patients appear in oblique noun phrases in two situations:
in antipassive constructions and after an infinitive
(see 8.4). There are two relational nouns which can
introduce oblique noun phrases expressing the patient. One
is -i7j and the other is -ee, which also introduces the
indirect object (dative). The relational noun -i7j is
always used with the antipassive if the agent follows the
verb.

(7-101) a. ma-a7   Ø-b'iyoo-n Cheep ky-i7j   kab' xiinaq
            rec-emph 3sA-HIT-ap José 3s-RN/pat TWO MAN

            'José hit the men.'

       b. *ma-a7 Ø-b'iyoo-n Cheep ky-e kab' xiinaq

If, however, the agent precedes the verb, the patient can
be introduced by either relational noun. If introduced by
-i7j, the implication is that the action was purposeful,
while if introduced by -ee, the implication is that the
action was accidental, uncompleted, or by surprise.

(7-102) a. Cheep ∅-b'iyoo-n ky-i7j kab' xiinaq

'José hit the men.' (I saw it and he was in
the fight the whole time and intended to hit
them.)

b. Cheep ∅-b'iyoo-n ky-e kab' xiinaq

'José hit the men.' (All of a sudden he came
on the scene and in helping those who were in
the fight hit someone.)

(7-103) a. aa   qiin-a xhin   kii-n-a   t-i7j
                         x-chin
         DEM PRO 1s-1s rec dep-1sA SEE-ap-1s 3s-RN/pat
         u7j
         BOOK

'I read the book.' (I saw it purposefully--
for reading.)

b. aa qiin-a chin kii-n-a t-e u7j

'I saw the book.' (I chanced to see it.)

(7-104) a. Kyel   x-∅-7awaa-n   t-i7j   kjo7n
         Miguel rec dep-3sA-PLANT-ap 3s-RN/pat CORNFIELD

'Miguel planted the cornfield.'

b. Kyel x-∅-7awaa-n t-e kjo7n

'Miguel planted the cornfield.' (It was either
not the time or not the place to do it.)

Because -ee is also used for the dative, it is possible to interpret the b) examples above as instances of patient demotion to indirect object. An analogy can be drawn with the English sentences such as 'I stabbed it.' vs. 'I stabbed at it.' where the use of 'at' implies incompleteness or lack of complete success.[9] In Mam the use of the dative relational noun for the patient likewise implies incompleteness or nonpurposefulness of action, but is only used that way when the agent is before the verb.

The other situation in which a dative relational noun is used to indicate the patient is after an infinitive, and here the use is obligatory.

(7-105) n-chi   ku7 teen xjaal   belaara-l t-e
         prog-3pA dir EXIST PERSON WATCH-inf 3s-RN/pat

         jun weech
         ONE FOX

         'The people began to watch the fox.'

The use of -i7j after an infinitive indicates the theme about which an action is performed, rather than the patient.

(7-106) n-ch-ok   teen t-aal   ooq'a-l
         prog-3pA-dir EXIST 3s-WOMAN'S CHILD CRY-inf

         t-i7j
         3s-RN/thematic

         'Her children began to cry about her.'

This use of -ee for a patient may likewise be an instance of demotion, but it does not carry any of the implications of incompleteness or surprise and is simply required by the infinitive.

1.5 Focus

This section discusses two phenomena: focus of nominal constituents in a sentence, and fronting of certain adverbial constituents which also seem to be instances of focus.

1.5.1 Nominal Focus. In general, focus, or contrastive emphasis, of nominals is accomplished through fronting the constituent to precede the verb. Other changes which may occur depend on the type of constituent focused. Focus of an agent or patient is more complex than focus of other constituents in that the former involves a change of voice as well as fronting, and agents or patients may appear in both direct or oblique noun phrases. Agent and patient focus are discussed first, then other nominals.

Agent Focus:

One way to focus agents of active transitive verbs is to front them to precede the verb in an oblique noun phrase, with no change in the verb.

(7-107) a. non-focus

        ma Ø-kub' ky-tzyu-7n xiinaq cheej
        rec 3sA-dir 3pE-GRAB-ds MAN   HORSE

        'The men grabbed the horse.'

   b. agent focus

        ky-u7n   xiinaq ma Ø-kub' ky-tzyu-7n cheej
        3p-RN/agt

        'The *men* grabbed the horse.'

This is not a voice change or a change in grammatical relations. The oblique noun phrase indicates focus and serves as a disambiguating mechanism for distinguishing agent and patient. If the agent does not precede the verb it cannot be expressed in an oblique phrase.

    c. *ma Ø-kub' ky-tzyu-7n cheej ky-u7n xiinaq

The sentence in c) is possible only if the agent is not marked on the verb, which then makes it into the Ø passive (or agentless transitive) (see 7.1.3.1).

    d. ma Ø-kub' tzyu-7n-Ø cheej ky-u7n xiinaq

        'The horse was grabbed by the men.'

Agents are also focused by preposing them to an antipassive verb in its agent promotion function.

(7-108) a. active, non-focus

        ma   chi tzaj t-q'o-7n   Mal   kab' xkoo7ya
        rec 3pA dir   3sE-GIVE-ds María TWO   TOMATO

        w-ee-ky'
        1s-RN/dat-1s

        'María gave me some tomatoes.'

  b. antipassive, focus

        Mal   saj   q'oo-n t-e   xkoo7ya
            x-Ø-tzaj
        María rec dep-3sA-dir GIVE-ap 3s-RN/pat TOMATO

        w-ee-ky'
        1s-RN/dat-1s

        '<u>María</u> gave me some tomatoes.'

A dependent aspect marker appears in (7-108b). The uses of the dependent aspects are discussed further in 8.2, but they are optional and preferred with fronted constituents.

    Finally, agents of passive verbs can be focused by preposing the entire relational noun phrase for the agent to the verb, with no other changes in the sentence.

(7-109) a. passive, non-focus

       ma chi tzy-eet cheej t-u7n xiinaq
       rec 3pA GRAB-pas HORSE 3s-RN/agt MAN

       'The horses were grabbed by the man.'

    b. passive, focus

       t-u7n xiinaq ma chi tzy-eet cheej

       'The horses were grabbed <u>by the man</u>.'

<u>Patient Focus</u>:

Patients of active transitive verbs are focused by being preposed to the verb. They are usually preceded by a demonstrative or other qualifier, which is necessary to distinguish focused patients from agents which have been fronted to precede a transitive verb in order to indicate new information about the agent (see examples 7-90, 8-35). The presence of a demonstrative also suggests that the preposed noun phrase for the patient is a stative predicate and the resulting construction is a complex sentence (see 7.2).

(7-110) a. non-focus

       ma Ø-kub' ky-tzyu-7n xiinaq cheej
       rec 3sA-dir 3pE-GRAB-ds MAN   HORSE

       'The men grabbed the horse.'

    b. patient focus

       aa cheej ma Ø-kub' ky-tzyu-7n xiinaq
       DEM

       'The men grabbed the <u>horse</u>.'

(7-111) a. non-focus

    ma ch-ok   t-b'iyo-7n Cheep kab' xiinaq
    rec 3pA-dir 3sE-HIT-ds José TWO MAN

    'José hit some men.'

b. patient focus with numeral qualifier

    kab' xiinaq xh-ok   t-b'iyo-7n Cheep
                x-chi-ok
                rec dep-3pA-dir

    'José hit <u>some men</u>.'

c. patient focus with negative qualifier

    miya7 xiinaq-qa xh-ok   t-b'iyo-7n Cheep
                    x-chi-ok
    NEG   -pl

    'It wasn't <u>men</u> that José hit.'

The dependent past aspect is used in (7-111b) and c), while the regular aspect is used in (7-110b). The use of dependent aspects in this context is not obligatory. In (7-111c) it is necessary to focus the patient because all negatives occur preverbally. The sentences in (7-111b) and c) distinguish between agent and patient by differential number marking of the absolutive and ergative pronouns on the verb and by clearly marking the patient as plural, through a number in (7-111b) and through the plural clitic in (7-111c). Thus the plural patient is matched by a plural absolutive marker. Also, the agent in (7-111c) is a proper noun and therefore singular, and is matched by a singular ergative marker. A sentence such as the following is uninterpretable because both noun phrases and both markers are singular.

         d. *xiinaq s-ok   t-b'iyo-7n Cheep
                 x-tz'-ok
             MAN   rec dep-3sA-dir 3sE-HIT-ds José

             *'The man hit José.' or 'José hit the man.'?

   Patient focus would add the demonstrative aa before xiinaq
and agent focus would most likely use the antipassive
construction. Sentences like (7-111d) above are possible
only if the actors and action are clear because they
permit just one interpretation.
(7-112) kjo7n   ma-a7   ∅-kub'   t-tooqa-n   tzee7
         CORNSTALK rec-emph 3sA-dir 3sE-BREAK-ds STICK

         'The stick broke the cornstalk.'

Sticks break cornstalks, but cornstalks do not under
normal circumstances break sticks. Note that the same
lack of ambiguity permits a patient to be expressed directly
in the antipassive construction (see 7.1.3.2 for an example).
   It is not possible to focus a patient with the antipassive
construction, since the construction serves basically for
agent focus.
(7-113) a. ma chi tzyuu-n xiinaq t-i7j   cheej
             rec 3pA GRAB-ap MAN   3s-RN/pat HORSE

             'The men grabbed the horse.'

         b. *t-i7j cheej ma chi tzyuu-n xiinaq

         c. *t-e cheej ma chi tzyuu-n xiinaq

         d. *t-i7j cheej xhi   tzyuu-n xiinaq
                    x-chi

         e. *t-e cheej xhi   tzyuu-n xiinaq
                    x-chi

The patient can be focused with the passive constructions by being preposed to the verb, either directly or with a preceding demonstrative. The demonstrative is not necessary since the agent is unambiguously marked in a relational noun phrase.

(7-114) a. ma chi tzy-eet cheej t-u7n   xiinaq
           rec 3pA GRAB-pas HORSE 3s-RN/agt MAN

   'The horses were grabbed by the man.'

b. aa-qa cheej ma chi tzy-eet t-u7n xiinaq
   DEM-pl

   'The horses were grabbed by the man.'

c. cheej ma chi tzy-eet t-u7n xiinaq

   'The horses were grabbed by the man.'

Other Nominal Constituents:

All other nominal constituents can be focused by being preposed to the verb with their preceding relational nouns. There are no other changes in the sentence except that dependent aspects can be used optionally (see below and 8.2).

(7-115) dative

   a. non-focus

      ma ∅-txi   t-q'o-7n   Cheep pwaq t-e
      rec 3sA-dir 3sE-GIVE-ds José MONEY 3s-RN/dat

      Mal
      María

      'José gave money to María.'

   b. focus

      t-e Mal ma ∅-txi t-q'o-7n Cheep pwaq

      'José gave money to María.'

(7-116) instrument

    a. non-focus

        ma   Ø-kub'   t-tx'ee7ma-n Kyel   tzee7
        rec 3sA-dir 3sE-CUT-ds Miguel TREE

        t-uk'   maachit
        3s-RN/inst MACHETE

        'Miguel cut the tree with a machete.'

    b. focus

        t-uk' maachit ma Ø-kub' t-tx'ee7ma-n Kyel tzee7

        'Miguel cut the tree with a <u>machete</u>.'

There is no instrumental suffix on verbs which are preceded by their instruments, as in some other Mayan languages, nor can the relational noun be omitted, nor is there an instrumental voice in which the instrument becomes the subject and the original agent is expressed in an oblique phrase (see Ayres, 1977 for an analysis of these phenomena in Ixil, another Mamean language).

    c. *maachit ma Ø-kub' t-tx'ee7ma-n Kyel tzee7

    d. *ma Ø-kub' t-tx'ee7ma-n maachit tzee7 t-u7n
                                                                3s-RN/agt

Many sentences with pre-verb focus optionally indicate aspects with the dependent recent past and past markers (<u>x</u>- and Ø respectively). The difference in meaning or context between a sentence with a dependent aspect marker after fronting and one with a regular aspect marker is minimal. Native speakers repeatedly interpret the sentences as "the same" in meaning.

(7-117) a. kab' xiinaq o   chi tzaj t-tzyu-7n Cheep
              TWO   MAN   past 3pA dir 3sE-GRAB-ds José

   'José grabbed the men.'

   b. kab' xiinaq i   tzaj t-tzyu-7n Cheep
              ∅-chi
              past dep-3pA

   'José grabbed the men.'

(7-117a) and b) were given as synonymous alternates, and further questioning did not reveal a difference between them. They both focus the patient in front of an active transitive verb. The distribution and use of dependent aspect markers is discussed in 8.2, but I would like to point out here that the use of these markers in focus sentences as well as the use of a demonstrative with patient focus suggests that the sentences may be complex. The focused part can be analyzed as a stative predicate and the rest as an embedded clause. (See 7.2 for a discussion of non-verbal predicates and 8.2 for more examples of dependent aspect markers.)

1.5.2 <u>Adverbial Focus</u>. There are three different qualifying constructions which appear pre-verbally and in that position are a kind of focus, or emphasis. The preceding discussion of nominal focus used the term "focus" for contrastive emphasis. With qualifiers contrast is not involved; instead these constructions serve to direct attention to the quality of an action, and in so doing emphasize that quality. I am using focus as a term to cover this kind of emphasis also because it, like nominal contrastive emphasis, is a pre-verb construction. Thus the mechanisms of qualifier focus have something in common with those of nominal contrastive emphasis, and the differences can be attributed to the basic distinction between nominals and qualifiers.

The qualifying constructions considered here are two adverbial constructions--affect words and affect verbs-- and one adjectival construction with an adverbial function-- positionals. Affect words and positionals obligatorily occur before the verb and are emphatic, while affect verbs optionally occur before the verb and in this position are emphatic.

Affect Words:

Affect words (3.7) belong to a special word class and describe the sound or movement characteristic of an action at its moment of inception. Most affect words are related to transitive or positional roots.[10] Various phonological devices, such as reduplication of the final consonant of the word, or paralinguistic vowel lengthening, are used to characterize certain types of actions. Affect words are always sentence initial and require either dependent person marking, in which ergative prefixes are cross-referenced to the subject of intransitive verbs (see 8.1), or dependent aspect marking (see 8.2).

(7-118) a. jotx   t-aaj-tz   meeb'a
            BOOM! 3sE-RETURN-dir   ORPHAN

   'Boom! the orphan returned.'

   b. jotx ∅-aaj-tz   meeb'a
           ∅-tz'-aaj-tz
           past dep-3sA-RETURN-dir

   'Boom! the orphan returned.'

These sentences are interpreted as "the same." I think that dependent aspect marking is used when the time frame of the action must be specified, while dependent person marking is

used when the time is apparent from context. If, for
instance, the action in this sentence had just happened,
dependent aspect marking would be used:

    c. jotx s-aaj-tz   meeb'a
        x-tz'-aaj-tz
        rec dep-3sA-RETURN-dir

  'Boom! the orphan just returned.'

(7-119) ch'uq t-eel   t-xaajb'a
       CLUNK! 3sE-GO OUT 3s-SHOE

  'Clunk! off went his shoe.'

    The motivation for calling the use of affect words an
instance of focus is that the use of affect verbs, discussed below, is analyzed as focus and by analogy affect
words, which have a syntactic distribution and usage similar
to affect verbs, can be analyzed as instances of focus
as well. The problem is that there is no contrast between
affect words as "focus" and affect words as non-focus,
since the syntax does not vary. Therefore direct evidence
for a focus function does not really exist. The semantics
of these constructions certainly involves emphasis, since
naming an action or noise of an action emphasizes the
action itself. In addition to being first in a sentence,
affect words are often further emphasized paralinguistically--
by extra loudness, extra vowel length, extra repetition of
the first consonant, or extra laryngealization of the
vowels.

<u>Affect Verbs</u>:

    Affect verbs, another type of adverbial, are derived
verbal forms (4.1.2 #25) which describe the characteristic
movement of an action in progress. Affect verbs are not
limited to sentence initial position. They are either

sentence initial and followed by an intransitive verb of
motion cross-referenced to the subject with ergative markers,
or they are regular intransitive verbs cross-referenced
with absolutive markers. If they are sentence initial and
followed by an intransitive verb of motion, then person marking appears on the intransitive verb rather than on the
affect verb (unless one considers that these forms are always
marked by the ∅ third person singular absolutive marker).
If an affect verb is sentence initial it focuses on the
quality of the action, while if it is used as an intransitive
verb it simply asserts that the action occurred, deriving
an intransitive verb of motion from a positional or other
root.

(7-120) mal-alaan   t-xi7   tzee7 ja7la
 SWELL-af vb 3sE-GO TREE NOW

 'Swelling, went the tree.' (i.e., 'The tree
 swelled up.')

(7-121) jow-owoon   t-iky'-tz
 PULL-af vb 3sE-PASS BY-dir

 'Pulling along it came by.' (i.e., 'It came by
 pulling itself along.')

(7-122) ma   chin tz'link-ikiin-a t-jaq'   kjo7n
 rec 1sA NAKED-af vb-1s 3s-RN/under CORNFIELD

 'I was walking naked in the cornfield.'

(7-123) ma   ch-ok-x   leq-eqeen   t-uj   t-q'ab'
 rec 3pA-dir-dir CROUCHED-af vb 3s-RN/in 3s-HAND
 xaq eew-al
 ROCK HIDE-inf

 'They went crouched down in the arroyo to hide.'

(7-120) and (7-121) direct attention to the kinetics of
an action, while (7-122) and (7-123) are descriptive of an
action without being emphatic. The semantics of the initial
affect verbs coupled with the ergative cross-referencing
provide evidence for the interpretation of affect words
as focus.

Positionals:

Positionals in their adjectival form precede the verb
and require dependent person marking with ergative rather
than absolutive markers (see 8.1).

(7-124) xjetx'-l   tex   t-txa7n   biiga
                          t-el-x
         UNEVEN-pos adj 3sE-GO OUT-dir 3s-RN/edge BEAM

         ky-witz   txqan-tl
         3p-RN/on BUNCH-other

         'Sticking out from the rest is a beam.'

(7-125) piky'-l   t-teen   xjaal   t-uj
         FACE UP LEGS OPEN-pos adj 3sE-EXIST PERSON 3s-RN/in

         b'ee
         ROAD

         'Lying face up in the road is a person.'

The function of the positional adjective is to focus on
the way an object is placed. Since the emphasis is on
the quality of the object in terms of its collocation or
position the positional adjective actually has an adverbial
function. This is a result of a salient characteristic
of positionals--that they conflate descriptive and verbal
semantics. Comparing a sentence with a positional adjective
and one with an underived adjective having the same root
shows the difference between the use of the positional

adjective for focus and that of the adjective for nonemphatic description.

(7-126) a. b'at'-1 t-kub'
LIGHT THINK THROWN DOWN-pos adj 3sE-GO DOWN

txqan k'uul t-miij b'ee
BUNCH BRUSH 3s-MIDDLE ROAD

'Lying in the middle of the road is a bunch of brush.'

b. b'at' txqan k'uul (aj) t-kub' t-miij b'ee
(adj) (rel)

'There is a bunch of brush (which is) in the middle of the road.'

(7-26a) focuses on the physical orientation ('thrown down') of a certain type of object ('light thing'), while the b) sentence describes the quality of the object (an unordered light bunch). Another difference is structural, since the b) sentence is a complex sentence in which the part after k'uul is a relative clause, optionally indicated by aj, embedded in the first clause (a stative predicate). What the positional adjective focuses on--the combination of characteristics of spatial orientation and physical state-- is a category which has its own unique root class, and is special to Mayan languages.

Because all of these examples of qualifier focus involve dependent aspect marking it is best to analyze them as complex sentences in which the focused element is a stative predicate and the rest of the sentence is an embedded clause. Other introductory dependent markers are absent from the embedded clause.

2. NON-VERBAL SENTENCES

Non-verbal sentences are sentences which instead of a verbal constituent contain a predicate of either the stative or existential/locative type (3.3). Stative predicates link the subject with some attribute, while existential/locative predicates link the subject with a place (locative), or assert the existence of the subject. The close connection between location and existence is reflected in the single set of predicates for both kinds of sentences.

The base of a stative predicate is a demonstrative, noun, or adjective, to which is suffixed person markers resembling the absolutive markers and the usual enclitics. The base then indicates the attribute while the suffixes indicate the subject.

(7-127) xu7j   qiin-a
         WOMAN 1sA-1s

         'I am a woman.'

(7-128) saq-∅
         WHITE-3sA

         'It is white.'

(7-129) sikynaj-∅-a
         TIRED-2sA-2s

         'You are tired.'

The base of an existential/locative predicate is -t- and signals its type. If used locatively, the predicate is accompanied by a locative phrase, while if existential there is no locative phrase. Person markers, again resembling the absolutive pronouns, and enclitics are suffixed to the base to indicate the subject. If the subject is a third person it is usually specified in a third person noun phrase or by the use of one of the noun classifiers (5.4.2) suffixed to the predicate.[11] A noun phrase specifying third person optionally follows the predicate.

(7-130) t-e7   T-i7j Raanch
         LOC PRED-3pA Turrancho

         'They are in Turrancho.'

(7-131) tzluu7 at-∅   jun aq'uuntl
         HERE   LOC PRED-3sA ONE WORK

         'Here is work.'

(7-132) t-o7   neqaa7
         LOC PRED-1pA NEAR

         'We are near.'

(7-133) t-iin-a
         LOC PRED-1sA-1s

         'I am.'

(7-134) at-∅   pwaq
         LOC PRED-3sA MONEY

         'There is money.'

Temporals and other adverbials excluding manner adverbs can also occur with non-verbal sentences, following the same rules already noted for verbal sentences (7.1.1.3).

(7-135) baqa   at-∅   am-b'il
         SCARCELY LOC PRED-3sA HAVE TIME-inst

         'There's scarcely time.'

(7-136) at-∅   jun aq'uuntl ojtxa
         LOC PRED-3sA ONE WORK   BEFORE

         'There was work before.'

(7-137) b'a-la   at-∅   qaq xjaal
         MAYBE-doubt LOC PRED-3sA SIX PERSON

'Maybe there are six people.'

Non-verbal predicates themselves are not inflected for tense/aspect, unlike verbs, so they do not indicate time and the addition of temporal adverbs is often necessary to place a non-verbal sentence in its temporal context. A non-verbal sentence with no temporal adverb and no contextual indication of time is interpreted as the present. Whether it is as a specific immediate present or an indefinite present depends on further context.

(7-138) a. indefinite

             at-∅   jun woo7
             LOC PRED-3sA ONE TOAD

             'There is a toad.'

         b. generic

             at-∅ woo7

             'There are toads.'

         c. specific

             tzluu7 at-∅ jun woo7
             HERE

             'Here is a toad.'

Adverbs clarify time other than the present:

         d. at-∅ jun woo7 ojtxa
                              BEFORE

             'There was a toad before.'

The time of a non-verbal sentence is also interpreted according to further context, including immediately adjacent clauses or the entire narrative context.

(7-139) at-∅   jun xjaal jun el   ∅-∅-xi7
        LOC PRED-3sA ONE PERSON ONE TIME past dep-3sA-GO

'There was a person who went.'

Here the time (past) of the predicate <u>at</u> is given by the past aspect marker on <u>xi7</u> in the second clause.

One characteristic of non-verbal predicates which is important to the interpretation of complex sentences is that third person stative predicates have zero markers for person, and they do not indicate pronominalization in any other way, as do the existential/locative predicates through the -<u>t</u>- base. Therefore any adjective, demonstrative, or noun phrase which is not in normal constituency (that is, a demonstrative or adjective which does not directly modify a noun, or a noun phrase which does not follow the verb directly as agent or patient or appear in a relational noun phrase) can be analyzed as the attribute of a stative predicate. The consequence that this has for the analysis of complex sentences is that any fronted nominal or adjectival constituent which does not appear in a relational noun phrase might be a non-verbal sentence with the rest of the sentence being an embedded clause. (See especially the discussion of focus, 7.1.5.) The lack of any truly independent pronouns (by this I mean a pronoun which indicates person and possibly even case, but does not indicate a relationship such as stative) further complicates the analysis. I should point out that while these facts may create problems of analysis, they do not create problems for speakers of the language.

(7-140) a. ma Ø-ku7-x   t-juusa-n   xu7j   chib'aj
            rec 3sA-dir-dir 3sE-BURN-ds WOMAN FOOD

'The woman burned the food.'

b. xu7j   x-Ø-juusa-n   t-e   chib'aj
    WOMAN rec dep-3sA-BURN-ap 3s-RN FOOD

'The <u>woman</u> burned the food.'

Sentence (7-140b) is the antipassive of the a) sentence and has fronted the agent for focus. If the fronted <u>xu7j</u> is analyzed as a stative predicate with Ø person marking, then the translation of the sentence is more accurately 'It was the woman who burned the food.'. Both translations are possible in Spanish as well, and native speakers give both for this type of sentence. The interpretation of <u>xu7j</u> as a stative predicate makes this sentence a complex sentence with <u>xjuusan te chib'aj</u> an embedded clause. The use of the dependent aspect marker adds weight to this analysis. One way to check what is happening is to change 'woman' to a first or second person.

c. aa qiin-a xhin   juusa-n-a t-e   chib'aj
                x-chin
        DEM 1sA-1s rec dep-1sA BURN-ap-1s 3s-RN FOOD

'<u>I</u> burned the food.' or 'It is I who burned the food.'

Here we definitely get a stative predicate, but then there really is no choice since there are no independent pronouns. Other evidence relative to the argument is that the negative of a fronted noun phrase uses the same negative particle which negates statives (7.3; 3.9.2). The analysis which I favor is that nominal constituents preposed to verbs without relational nouns are statives, and are therefore

non-verbal sentences followed by embedded clauses. The
alternate analysis, that nominal fronting is a simple
reordering of constituents which by position alone indicates
focus, is not however ruled out. The same reasoning
holds for positional adjectives--they are reduced noun
phrases appearing as statives when they are in pre-verbal
position, and are then followed by embedded clauses.

(7-141) jop-1   t-kub'   xjaal t-witz
         HOLLOW-EYED-pos adj 3sE-GO DOWN PERSON 3s-RN/on

         tx'otx' t-u7n   yaa-b'il
         GROUND   3s-RN/because   SICK-inst

         'Hollow-eyed the person is on the ground because
         of the illness.'

The difference here is that ergative markers instead of
absolutive markers cross-reference the subject of the
verb, which does not happen with focus of nominal
constituents. They, on the other hand, use dependent
aspect markers, at least optionally. Both types of
construction mark some sort of dependency (8.1; 8.2).

If this analysis is correct, then the focus constructions
which involve complex sentences, in which the focused element is part of a stative predicate and therefore an
independent clause, are agent focus with antipassive verbs,
patient focus with active transitives, and positional
focus. Other nominal focus constructions place the
focused constituent in relational noun phrases. Although
adverbial focus probably does not include a stative attribute,
it does trigger dependent marking and therefore may also
be part of a complex sentence.

3. NEGATION

Negation is accomplished through the use of negative particles which are first in the sentence and followed immediately by the phrase or clause being negated. This automatically focuses negated nominals. There are a number of different negative particles which are complementary in usage. Many of them are formed on the stem mii 'negative'.

3.1 Statives

Statives are negated by miyaa7 (nyaa7).

(7-142) a. xiinaq qiin-a
             MAN   1sA-1s

             'I am a man.'

         b. miyaa7 xiinaq qiin-a

             'I am not a man.'

(7-143) a. matiij-∅
             BIG-3sA

             'It's big.'

         b. miyaa7 matiij-∅

             'It's not big.'

3.2 Agent and Patient

These are negated by miyaa7 (nyaa7), the same particle which negates statives. They must be pre-verbal to be negated, and the verb is marked with dependent aspect markers. Agent negation requires either the antipassive or an oblique noun phrase, and can include both. A fronted negated patient requires no special marking but is probably a stative predicate.

(7-144) a. ma chi tzaj t-tzyu-7n Cheep kab' xiinaq
rec 3pA dir 3sE-GRAB-ds José TWO MAN

'José grabbed some men.'

b. miyaa7 Cheep saj   tzyuu-n ky-e
                  x-∅-tzaj
   NEG   José rec dep-3sA-dir GRAB-ap 3p-RN
   kab' xiinaq
   TWO MAN

'It wasn't José who grabbed some men.'

c. miyaa7 t-u7n   Cheep xhi   tzaj
                           x-chi
          3s-RN/agt   rec dep-3pA
   t-tzyu-7n kab' xiinaq

'It wasn't José who grabbed some men.'

d. miyaa7 t-u7n Cheep saj tzyuu-n ky-e kab' xiinaq

'It wasn't José who grabbed some men.'

e. *miyaa7 Cheep xhi tzaj t-tzyu-7n kab' xiinaq

f. miyaa7 xiinaq-qa xhi   tzaj t-tzyu-7n
                   x-chi
   NEG   MAN-pl   rec dep-3pA dir 3sE-GRAB-ds
   Cheep
   José

'It wasn't some men that José grabbed.'

3.3 Existential and Locative Predicates

These are negated by <u>mi7aal</u> if they refer to people.
<u>Mi7aal</u> takes the place of the existential/locative predicate
and is inflected like a stative.

(7-145) a. t-iin-a   tzluu7
             LOC PRED-1sA-1s HERE

             'I'm here.'

         b. mi7aal qiin-a tzluu7
             NEG   1sA-1s HERE

             'I'm not here.'

(7-146) a. at-∅-a   tzluu7
             LOC PRED-2sA-2s HERE

             'You're here.'

         b. mi7aal-∅-a tzluu7
             NEG-2sA-2s HERE

             'You're not here.'

Existential and locative predicates are negated by <u>miti7</u>
(<u>nti7</u>) if they refer to third person non-human noun phrases.

(7-147) a. at-∅   chib'aj
             LOC PRED-3sA MEAT

             'There is meat.'

         b. nti7 chib'aj
             NEG

             'There isn't meat.'

(7-148) a. at-∅   a7   t-zi
             LOC PRED-3sA WATER 3s-RN/at entrance

             q-jaa-y7
             1p-HOUSE-1p ex

             'There's water by our house.'

         b. nti7 a7 tzi q-jaa-y7
             NEG

             'There isn't water by our house.'

3.4 Verbs

Verbs are negated by mti7 (nti7) or by mii7n. Mii7n only negates imperative and potential verbs, and when negating the potential the aspect or mode suffixes are omitted.

(7-149) a. k-tzaaj-al   jb'aal ja71a
           3sA-COME-pot RAIN   TODAY

           'It will rain today.'

       b. mii7n ∅-tzaaj jb'aal ja71a
          NEG   3sA-COME

          'It won't rain today.'

(7-150) a. b'eet-a
           WALK-2s

           'Walk!'

       b. mii7n b'eet-a
          NEG

          'Don't walk!'

(7-151) a. ∅-tzyuu-m-a
           3sA-GRAB-imp-2s

           'Grab it!'

       b. mii7n ∅-tzyuu-m-a
          NEG

          'Don't grab it!'

Nti7 is used with the nonpotential and non-imperative.

(7-152) a. o   tz'-e-tz   n-laq'o-7n-a
           past 3sA-dir-dir 1sE-BUY-ds-1s

           'I bought it.'

b. nti7 o tz'-e-tz n-laq'o-7n-a
   NEG

   'I didn't buy it.'

(7-153) a. ma chin b'eet-a
   rec 1sA WALK-1s

   'I walked.'

b. nti7 ma chin b'eet-a
   NEG

   'I didn't walk.'

3.5 Negative Words and Constructions

There are a number of special forms, some of them suppletive, for certain negatives:

juu7n	'each one'	mijuun	'no one, nothing'
ja7ka	'it's possible'	milaay (nlaay)	'it's not possible'
kukx	'still'	na7x	'still not'
joo7	'yes'	mii7n	'no'
-aj-	'want'	-ky'i7-	'not want'

Many particles also combine with mii to form negatives:

iky'	'like this'	miky'	'not like this'
qa	'if'	qamii	'if not'

4. QUESTION FORMATION

4.1 Yes/No Questions

Yes/no questions are formed by the interrogative enclitic pa (8.6), by intonation pattern, or by placing a time adverb last in the sentence with the regular past or recent past aspects (7.1.1.3). The interrogative enclitic follows the first word in a sentence.

(7-154) a. at-∅   aatz'an

             LOC PRED-3sA SALT

         'There is salt.'

      b. at-∅-pa aatz'an
              -int

         'Is there salt?'

Yes/no intonation consists of rising rather than falling intonation on the last word of the sentence.

(7-155) a. at aatz'an

         'There is salt.'

      b. at aatz'an

         'Is there salt?'

If a time adverb is last in the sentence it normally requires dependent aspect markers in the past and recent past. If independent markers are used instead, a question is formed.

(7-156) a. i   aq'naa-n-a eew
             ∅-chi
             past dep-2pA WORK-ap-1p YESTERDAY

         'You-all worked yesterday.'

      b. o   chi aq'naa-n-a eew
             past 2pA-

         'Did you-all work yesterday?'

4.2 Information Questions

Information questions are formed according to several strategies which include direct agent question, direct patient question, question of constituents expressed in relational noun phrases, and interrogative word question of constituents other than nominals.

Agent Question:

The direct question of agents is accomplished by using an interrogative word for the agent (<u>alkyee</u> for people, <u>tqal</u> for things) and the antipassive. Dependent aspects mark the verb in the past and recent past.

(7-157) a. ma-a7   chi tzaj t-tzyu-7n   Cheep kab' xiinaq
          rec-emph 3pA dir 3sE-GRAB-ds José TWO MAN

       'José grabbed the men.'

   b. alkyee saj   tzyuu-n ky-e kab' xiinaq
      x-∅-tzaj
      WHO   rec dep-3sA-dir GRAB-ap 3p-RN TWO MAN

       'Who grabbed the men?'

(7-158) a. o   tz'-ok t-juusa-n   xu7j txa-tz'iis
          past 3sA-dir 3sE-BURN-ds WOMAN dregs-DIRT

       'The woman burned the garbage.'

   b. alkyee ∅-∅-ok   juusa-n t-e   txa-tz'iis
      WHO   past dep-3sA-dir BURN-ap 3s-RN dregs-DIRT

       'Who burned the garbage?'

Patient Question:

Patients are questioned directly by using the question word (<u>alkyee</u> for people, <u>tqal</u> for things) before the verb, which remains an active transitive but does use the dependent aspect markers.

(7-159) a. ma-a7   chi tzaj t-tzyu-7n   Cheep kab' xiinaq
          rec-emph 3pA dir 3sE-GRAB-ds José TWO MAN

       'José grabbed the men.'

```
         b.  alkyee-qa xhi           tzaj t-tzyu-7n    Cheep
                      x-chi
             WHO-pl   rec dep-3pA dir 3sE-GRAB-ds José

             'Whom did José grab?'

(7-160)  a.  ma  Ø-tzaj   t-q'o-7n-a    pwaq  q-ee-ky'
             rec 3sA-dir  2sE-GIVE-ds-2s MONEY 1p-RN/dat-1p

             'You gave us money.'

         b.  tqal saj              t-q'o-7n-a      q-ee-ky'
                  x-Ø-tzaj
             WHAT rec dep-3sA-dir  2sE-GIVE-ds-2s  1p-RN/dat-1p

             'What did you give us?'
```

The use of the antipassive for agent question, with the patient in an oblique phrase, disambiguates agent from patient question. (7-159b) is not interpretable as *'Who grabbed José?', for instance, because active transitives are only used for patient question.

Relational Noun Phrase Question:

Question of all nominals except direct agents and patients is obligatorily expressed in relational noun phrases. Agents and patients can also be questioned in relational noun phrases in certain contexts. The question word al is preposed to the unpossessed relational noun (this is the only situation in which relational nouns are not possessed), the question phrase is first in the sentence, and the dependent aspects are used. The question phrases are therefore:

```
     al u7n        agent
     al u7n        causative
     al u7n     }
     al uuk'al  }  instrument
```

        al uuk'al   comitative
        al i7j   patient
        al i7j   thematic
        al ee   dative
        al ee   benefactive
        al ee   possessive

(7-161) agent

    a.   o   Ø-jaw   patq'u-7n-Ø   xaq   t-u7n
         past 3sA-dir TURN OVER-ds-pas? ROCK 3s-RN/agt

         Kyel
         Miguel

         'The rock was turned over by Miguel.'

    b.   al u7n   Ø-Ø-jaw   patq'u-7n-Ø
         INT RN/agt past dep-3sA-dir TURN OVER-ds-pas?

         xaq
         ROCK

         'By whom was the rock turned over?'

(7-162) instrument

    a.   ma   Ø-kub'   t-tx'ee7ma-n Kyel   tzee7
         rec 3sA-dir 3sE-CUT-ds   Miguel TREE

         t-u7n   maachit
         3s-RN/inst MACHETE

         'Miguel cut the tree with a machete.'

    b.   al u7n   x-Ø-kub'   t-tx'ee7ma-n
         INT RN/inst rec dep-3sA-dir 3sE-CUT-ds

         Kyel   tzee7
         Miguel TREE

         'With what did Miguel cut the tree?'

(7-163) dative

    a. o   ∅-txi   q'o-7n-∅   pwaq   t-e   Mal
       past 3sA-dir GIVE-ds-pas? MONEY 3s-RN/dat María

    'The money was given to María.'

    b. al   ee   ∅-∅-xi   q'o-7n-∅   pwaq
       INT RN/dat past dep-3sA-dir GIVE-ds-pas? MONEY

    'To whom was the money given?'

The phrase final forms of the relational nouns are used, because the sentence after the question phrase is an embedded clause, signalled by the dependent aspect markers.

<u>Interrogative Words</u>:

All other interrogative words occur sentence initially, followed by verbs marked with dependent aspect markers.

(7-164) tii-tzan x-∅-b'aj   t-tzeeq'a-n-a nii-tal
        WHY-then rec dep-3sA-dir 2sE-HIT-ds-2s small-SMALL

        t-iitz'an-a
        2s-YOUNGER BROTHER-2s

        'Why did you hit your little brother?'

(7-165) jte7   ne71 x-∅-b'aj   t-ajla-7n
        HOW MANY SHEEP rec dep-3sA-dir 3sE-COUNT-ds

        'How many sheep did he count?'

(7-166) jatuma setz   q'i-7n-∅   u7j
        x-tz'-el-tz
        WHERE rec dep-3sA-dir-dir BRING/TAKE-ds-pas? BOOK

        'Where did the book come from?'

4.3 <u>Indirect Questions</u>

Indirect questions are formed exactly like direct questions, with the exception that they are separate embedded clauses

in complex sentences. That fact, however, requires no
additional changes in the structure of the question.

(7-167) k-x-el   n-ma-7n-a   t-ee-ya   al u7n
         3sA-dir-pot   1sE-SAY-ds-1s   2s-RN/dat-2s   INT RN/agt

         ∅-∅-b'aj   b'iincha-n-∅   jaa
         past dep-3sA-dir   MAKE-ds-pas?   HOUSE

         'I'll tell you by whom the house was built.'

(7-168) miti7 b'a7n w-u7n-a   jatuma setz
                                               x-tz'-el-tz
         NEG   GOOD   1s-RN/agt-1s   WHERE   rec dep-3sA-dir-dir

         q'i-7n-∅   u7j
         BRING/TAKE-ds-pas?   BOOK

         'I don't know where the book came from.'

5. COORDINATION

Two or more simple sentences can be conjoined by any one of
the enclitics ka 'but' or tzan 'then, well', or by a conjunctive particle such as b'ix 'and', ii 'and', pera 'but',
entoons 'then', pwees 'then, well', yajtzan 'and then',
ax 'also', or sineke 'but rather, on the other hand'. Note
that the particles ii, pera, entoons, pwees, and sineke are
borrowed from Spanish. The enclitic ka is mutually exclusive
with the particle pera, but the enclitic tzan co-occurs
freely with any of the conjunctive particles, especially
the Spanish-derived entoons which has approximately the
same meaning.

Conjunctive particles occur at the beginning of the
sentence or clause which they are conjoining while conjunctive
enclitics occur affixed to the first word or phrase in the
sentence or clause they are conjoining. This is usually an

adverb, phonologically independent aspect marker, directional, conjunctive particle, or demonstrative. Tzan also appears very commonly on the quotative verb -chi-. Examples of conjoined sentences are:

(7-169)   entoons-tzan-la n-b'aj   nimaal t-k'aloo-n
          THEN-then-doubt prog-dir DEM   3sE-TIE-ap

          t-iib'-jal   b'ix n-∅-xi7
          3s-RN/refl-cl/nonhuman AND   prog-3sA-dir

          jak'u-7n-∅-jal   entoons b'i7x-la
          PULL-ds-pas?-cl/nonhuman   THEN   ALL AT ONCE-doubt

          ∅-tooq-jal
             -j-jal
          3sA-BREAK-pas-cl/nonhuman

          'Then maybe it started to be tied up all by itself,
          and it was pulled, and then all at once it broke.'

(7-170)   b'a7n chi-chi-tzan xjaal pera aax-ax-ta   pwaq
          GOOD 3pA-SAY-then PERSON BUT SAME-clt-emph   MONEY

          '"That's fine," said the people then, "but what's
          important is the money."'

(7-171)   pera tii   tz'-ok-x   q-se-7n   komo ax
          BUT WHAT 3sA-dir-dir 1pE-DO-ds LIKE ALSO

          mangeera-x naach
          HOSE-also   BAD

          'But what are we going to do, because the hose is
          no good.'

Section 8.6 includes further discussion and examples of the conjunctive enclitics.

NOTES

1. Just as the number _juun_ 'one' functions as the indefinite article, the number _kab'_ 'two' functions as an indefinite plural.
2. Remember that _k-_ is the 3sA marker in the potential.
3. Typological characteristics follow Greenberg (1963). Greenberg Universal #3: "Languages with dominant VSO order are almost always prepositional." and #2: "In languages with prepositions, the genitive almost always follows the governing noun, while in languages with postpositions it almost always precedes."
4. Greenberg Universal #9: "With well more than chance frequencies, when question particles or affixes are specified in position by reference to the sentence as a whole, if initial, such elements are found in prepositional languages, and, if final, in postpositional."
5. Greenberg Universal #12: "If a language has dominant order VSO in declarative sentences, it always puts interrogative words or phrases first in interrogative word questions; if it has dominant order SOV in declarative sentences, there is never such an invariant rule."
6. Greenberg Universal #16: "In languages with dominant order VSO, an inflected auxiliary always precedes the main verb. In languages with dominant SOV, an inflected auxiliary always follows the main verb."
7. Greenberg Universal #17: "With overwhelmingly more than chance frequency, languages with dominant order VSO have the adjective after the noun." Greenberg Universal #19: "When the general rule is that the descriptive adjective follows, there may be a minority of adjectives which usually precede, but when the general rule is that descriptive adjectives precede, there are no exceptions."

8. I have stated unequivocally that the antipassive constructions outlined here cross-reference the agent on the verb. This is relatively easy to determine in Mam by manipulating third person nouns for number, since the absolutive markers are different for third person singular and plural. The examples given in the discussion were mostly chosen with agents and patients of different number to facilitate showing how the cross-reference works. Furthermore, I am unaware of any constraints on person for either the agent or patient in the absolutive function of the antipassive, so these constituents can be manipulated for different persons to check cross-referencing.
9. I am indebted to Judith Aissen, who pointed out the analogy to me.
10. The relationship is often a matter of lengthening a root vowel, or the affect word might have a short vowel while the transitive verb has a long vowel. In the latter instance the affect word, with a CVC shape, looks like a root, while the transitive verb, with CVVC, looks like a derived form. I doubt, however, that transitives are derived from affect words. In these examples both might be derived from transitive or positional CVC roots, which may no longer exist in their underived forms.
11. Any further specification of a third person stative pronoun is part of the attribute itself, rather than a separate noun phrase. Noun classifiers can be suffixed to the attribute, for example:

(7-128')   saq-jal-∅
            WHITE-nonhuman-3sA

            'It is white.'

8. COMPLEX SENTENCES

This chapter addresses several issues in the formation of complex sentences. First, two morpho-syntactic strategies which are used in different types of dependent clauses are discussed: the replacement of absolutive with ergative person markers (dependent person marking) and the use of dependent aspects. Some of the data has been presented in the previous chapter, and is here drawn together to develop a more comprehensive statement on the differences between dependent person marking and dependent aspect marking. Secondly, several specific kinds of complex sentences, including relative clauses and complement clauses, are described. Finally, an index of syntactic enclitics, many of which function in complex sentences, is given.

1. DEPENDENT PERSON MARKING[1]

Before describing the contexts in which this type of dependent marking occurs, it is necessary to outline the mechanics of the phenomenon in Mam and discuss its relationship to the general category of ergativity. It has been proposed that ergative languages are characterized by having split ergativity (Silverstein, 1976): under certain conditions grammatical relations are marked by nominative/ accusative rather than ergative principles. Larsen and Norman (1980) discuss this phenomenon in Mayan languages and state that the factors which precipitate split verb agreement are the category of person (only in Mochó), particular tenses or aspects, subordinate clauses, and certain types of focused constituents immediately preceding the verb. They go on to say that (p.353):

In all such cases, split ergativity results from the use of the ergative rather than the absolutive person markers to cross reference intransitive subjects. If transitive verbs in the same environment maintain their normal agreement pattern, then this gives rise to an accusative configuration, all subjects being marked with Set A [ergative markers], all objects with Set B [absolutive markers].

In the context of focused adverbials and certain subordinate clauses (specified below) Mam marks the subjects of intransitive verbs with ergative pronouns.

(8-1) n-chi   ooq' t-poon   ky-txuu7
       prog-3pA CRY   3sE-ARRIVE 3p-MOTHER

'They were crying when their mother arrived.'

In this sentence the second clause indicates the subject with ergative prefixes because of the temporal dependence. So far the Mam system looks like a classic instance of split ergativity triggered by dependent clauses and focused abverbials.

Transitive verbs in the same contexts, however, cross-reference their <u>patients</u> (objects) with ergative markers (as well as their agents) and so do not "maintain their normal agreement pattern."

(8-2) ok   t-ku7-x   ky-awa-7n   xjaal kjo7n
       WHEN 3sE-dir-dir 3pE-PLANT-ds   PERSON CORNFIELD

       b'i7x   n-∅-xi7   cheenaq' t-i7j
       ALL AT ONCE   prog-3sA-GO BEAN   3s-RN/pat

'When the people plant the cornfield at the same time the beans go in.'

The dependent particle <u>ok</u> 'when (potential)' requires ergative rather than absolutive markers, and in (8-2) this

applies to the marking on the patient of a transitive verb.
While most transitive verbs are accompanied by directionals,
the same pattern holds if a directional is absent:

(8-3) ok qo tzaalaj-al   ok <u>t-q</u>-il   u7j t-e
       pot 1pA BE HAPPY-pot WHEN 3sE-1pE-SEE BOOK 2s-RN/pos

yool   t-e   I7tzal
WORD 3s-RN/pos Ixtahuacán

'We will be happy when we see the Ixtahuacán
dictionary.'

Verb agreement in independent and dependent clauses, while
different, always marks the subject of an intransitive verb
and the patient of a transitive verb with the same set of
prefixes.

	Agent TV	Patient TV	Subject IV
Independent Clauses:	ergative	absolutive	absolutive
Dependent Clauses:	ergative	ergative	ergative

Thus there is no circumstance in which there is a
nominative/accusative pattern in which all "subjects" are
distinguished from all "objects". What happens in dependent
clauses is that the same markers are used for both the agent
and patient of a transitive verb, but also for the subject
of an intransitive verb.

Another factor which must be considered is marking
(Dixon, 1979). Accusative languages typically mark the
accusative while ergative languages typically mark the
ergative. Evidence such as zero person affixes for third
person singular absolutives in Mam and other Mayan languages
suggests that it is indeed the absolutive which is unmarked
and the ergative which is marked in Mayan. Under "split"
conditions where subjects of intransitives and agents of
transitives are both marked ergatively, what results is an

Agent-Subject/Patient (Object) configuration, like accusative languages, but the marking is reversed. Dixon suggests the term "extended ergative" for languages of this type, and cites Jacaltec as an example (1979: 97fn.).

Mam however does not have this configuration under split conditions, but rather marks all arguments ergatively. This may be what Dixon refers to as a "partly ergative" configuration (1979: 134), but I suggest that it be called "spreading ergativity" in Mam. First, something of the history of the Mam system can be reconstructed.

Ergative case marking is characteristic of the Mayan family, and while no one working on *PM syntax has made the explicit statement that *PM was ergative (e.g., Smith-Stark, 1976, begs the question), it has been used to establish a framework for other syntactic reconstruction (Campbell and Norman, 1978) and Kaufman feels that there is no doubt that *PM had ergative syntax (personal communication). Ergativity is well established for Classical Yucatec (Smailus, 1979), even though modern Yucatec is more accusative (Bricker, 1981). Ergativity certainly existed in seventeenth century Mam (Reynoso, 1644).

It is apparently true that most Mayan languages also have nominative/accusative (or extended ergative) marking in at least some contexts (Larsen and Norman, 1980) and that one of them--Yucatec--is more nominative/accusative than ergative (Bricker, 1981. This is, however, definitely innovative.). Whether Mam had split case marking previously is not clear. Reynoso, in his verb conjugations, shows the use of ergative instead of absolutive markers on intransitive verbs in dependent contexts,[2] but does not give paradigms for the same situations with transitive verbs. This might be because transitive verbs maintain their normal agreement patterns and therefore he did not find the paradigm noteworthy. He does mark the intransitive paradigm "other", suggesting that he found it puzzling. On the other hand, he might not have encountered the transitive examples for a number of reasons, so it is difficult to assess his lack of data on this point. Ixil, another Mamean language, does today have split ergativity (Ayres, 1977) in which intransitive subjects are marked ergatively after focused adverbials and transitive verbs maintain normal agreement. Ixil data, then, suggest that the Mamean subgroup had split ergativity, and the Reynoso data on earlier Mam is inconclusive.

Aguacatec has a system somewhere between the Ixil and Mam systems. In time adverbial clauses in the indefinite past, after focused time adverbs, and in purpose clauses intransitive verbs cross-reference their subjects ergatively. Transitive verbs without directionals or with following directionals maintain their normal agreement patterns (agent marked ergatively and patient absolutively), but transitive verbs which take a preceding directional mark both agent and patient ergatively (Tom Larsen, personal communication). The three Mamean languages I have information about therefore look like this:

Normal Configuration:

	Agent TV	Patient TV	Subject IV
Ixil	ergative	absolutive	absolutive
Aguacatec	ergative	absolutive	absolutive
Mam	ergative	absolutive	absolutive

Dependent Clauses:

	Agent TV	Patient TV	Subject IV
Ixil	ergative	absolutive	ergative
Aguacatec: none or			
following dir.:	ergative	absolutive	ergative
preceding dir.:	ergative	ergative	ergative
Mam:	ergative	ergative	ergative

Aguacatec then provides a model of how the Mam system developed historically.[3] We can assume that the earlier Mam system was like Ixil and a number of other Mayan languages and was a split or extended ergative system in which intransitive subjects were marked ergatively under certain conditions but transitives maintained normal agreement. Then, transitive verbs with preceding directionals marked both the agent and patient ergatively. Mam today has only preceding directionals, suggesting that it lost any following ones. Finally, even transitive verbs without directionals marked both the agent and patient ergatively, presumably through extending the marking pattern.

What were the steps that led to the reanalysis of transitive verbs in Mam? Two facts are important. First, all directionals which precede the verb in Aguacatec, and all directionals in Mam, are derived from intransitive verbs of motion and carry the person prefixes which cross-reference the patient. Second, Larsen analyzes the main verb in such complex verb phrases as an active verbal noun. It is possible that the Mam main verb is also a nominalized form, since a transitive verb with a directional always carries the participle suffix -_7n_. I propose that the following steps were involved in the emergence of the present Mam system:

1) The main verb in a transitive verb phrase with a directional cross-referenced the semantic agent with ergative (possessive) markers.

2) The absolutive markers on the directional were re-analyzed as cross-referencing subjects (see also Craig, 1979 and my discussion of the passive, 7.1.3.2).

3) Under split conditions, all subjects of intransitive verbs, including those of directionals, were marked ergatively.

4) The person marker on a directional was blocked from cross-referencing the semantic agent, since that was already cross-referenced by the ergative marker on the main verb, so it was interpreted as referring to the remaining argument, which is the semantic patient.

5) The pattern of double ergative marking under split conditions spread to transitive verbs without directionals. This implies that the person markers on directionals have been reanalyzed (or back-analyzed) as patients, while the form of the main verb in a transitive plus directional construction is perhaps not as "nominalized" as it was.

The historical development of the system does not affect the synchronic analysis. Under no circumstances does Mam have accusative marking. It always maintains the same marking for intransitive subjects and transitive patients. In certain dependent clauses transitive agents as well are marked the same (ergatively), but the strict order of affixes on verbs avoids ambiguity.

Dependent person marking occurs in a number of different contexts which have in common the absence of any overt aspect marking.[4] These contexts include one type of embedded clause, purpose or result clauses, clauses which follow focused adverbials, and clauses which follow a few other specific adverbials. In addition, certain verbs in relative clauses require dependent person marking, but only in a rather restricted semantic context. Most relatives require dependent aspects.

1.1 <u>Embedded Clauses</u>

One type of embedded clause which requires dependent person marking if it is aspectless is the temporally subordinate clause. A number of particles introduce such clauses: <u>aj</u> 'when, nonpotential', <u>ok</u> 'when, potential', <u>ela</u> 'when', and <u>kwanto</u> 'when' (the last is borrowed from Spanish[5]). <u>Aj</u> and <u>ok</u> are in strict complementary distribution with regard to aspect/time, and the specific time of an <u>aj</u> clause is inferred from context; i.e., from the aspect of the independent clause. Examples of aspectless subordinate clauses with the different particles are:

(8-4) o   Ø-tzaalaj   xjaal t-i7j   t-paa
       past 3sA-BE HAPPY PERSON 3s-RN/thematic 3s-BAG

       <u>aj</u> <u>t</u>-kan-eet   priim-x
       WHEN 3sE-FIND-pas EARLY-encl

       'The person was happy about his bag when it was found early.'

(8-5) at-Ø   txab'an siich'   <u>ok</u> q-ook-a
       LOC PRO-3sA BIT   CIGARETTE WHEN 1pE-ENTER-1p

       juu7n priim
       EACH EARLY

       'There are bits of cigarette there when we go by in the morning.'

(8-6) <u>ela</u> <u>t</u>-b'aj meq't n-Ø-xi7   t-waa7-n   xjaal
       WHEN 3sE-dir HEAT prog-3sA-dir 3sE-EAT-ds PERSON

       'When she finished heating them, the person ate them.'

(8-7) <u>kwanto</u> <u>t</u>-kan-eet   saant t-e   I7tzal
       WHEN   3sE-FIND-pas SAINT 3s-RN/pos Ixtahuacán

       'When the patron saint of Ixtahuacán was found...'

The use of dependent person marking in a complex sentence also implies temporal subordination even without an introductory 'when' particle, as in:

(8-8) n-chi   ooq' t-poon   ky-txuu7
       prog-3pA CRY 3sE-ARRIVE 3p-MOTHER

   'They were crying when their mother arrived.'

Ok and ela require that the clause they introduce be aspectless and marked with the dependent person markers. Aj can be followed by the aspect marker n- 'progressive' and the regular person markers in a statement of the general truth sort:

(8-9) aj   nti7 n-qo-kaamb'a-n   t-i7j   schab'il
       WHEN NEG   prog-1pA-WIN-ap   3s-RN/pat GAME

       n-qo-jaw   b'iisa-n
       prog-1pA-dir BE SAD-ap

   'When we don't win the game we become sad.'

Otherwise aj requires dependent person marking in an aspectless clause. Kwanto often occurs with dependent aspect marking rather than dependent person marking. Perhaps kwanto, as a Spanish borrowing, does not sufficiently imply or indicate time or aspect, so that the clause which is subordinate is additionally marked for aspect, at least some of the time. Because it is subordinate the dependent rather than independent aspects are used. An example is:

(8-10) kwanto sookl   tzluu7 x-∅-ku7
              x-tz'-ook-ul
       WHEN   rec dep-3sA-ENTER-dir HERE   rec dep-3sA-dir

       ky-iyiji-7n
       3pE-CARE FOR-ds

   'When he arrived here they took care of him.'

The 'when' clause of a complex sentence which is dependent on a clause with a perfect takes dependent aspect

marking, if it is not introduced by a 'when' particle which
implies time. This is because the time frame of a perfective is set by the dependent clause so aspect marking
either through the introductory particle or the 'when' particle is necessary.

(8-11) a. oo-taq   Ø-b'aj   waa7-n ok   t-tzaj
           past-perf 3sA-dir   EAT-ds WHEN/pot 3sE-dir

           q'o-7n-Ø   t-k'aa7
           GIVE-ds-pas?   3s-DRINK

           'He will have eaten when they give (him)
           his drink.'

      b.   oo-taq Ø-b'aj waa7-n Ø-Ø-xi   q'o-7n-Ø
                                 past dep-3sA-dir

           t-k'aa7

           'He had eaten when they gave (him) his drink.'

The a) sentence above uses dependent person marking after
the particle ok, but the b) sentence uses dependent aspect
marking to specify past time. See 8.2.1 for further examples.

1.2 Purpose and Result Clauses

Clauses which indicate the resultant motive or purpose of
an action expressed in another clause are subordinated by
the particle ii 'so that, it is necessary that' or by the
relational noun tu7n (always possessed by the third person
singular in this usage, in agreement with the entire clause
which follows) with the special meaning 'in order that, so
that'. Such subordinate clauses are aspectless and require
dependent person marking. Several examples illustrate
this type of clause:

268 COMPLEX SENTENCES

(8-12) <u>ii</u>   t-jaa-tz   miij mangeera
        IT IS NECESSARY THAT 3sE-RAISE-dir HALF HOSE

  <u>ii</u>   t-xi7 ky-jaa-qa-j
  SO THAT 3sE-GO 3p-HOUSE-pl-dem

  'It is necessary that half the hose be lifted, so
  that it will go to their house.'

(8-13) yaa n-∅-ku7-tzan   q-xii7ma-n-a   t-i7j
        NOW prog-3sA-dir-well 1pE-THINK-ds-1p 3s-RN/thematic

  <u>t-u7n</u>   t-ee-tz   oonb'il
  SO THAT 3sE-GO OUT-dir HELP

  'We were thinking about it so that help would arrive.'

(8-14) tii-tzan   tqal mooda k-b'ant-eel q-u7n   <u>t-u7n</u>
        WHAT-well WHAT WAY   3sA-DO-pot 1p-RN/agt SO THAT

  t-jaq-eet   xaq
  3sE-OPEN-pas ROCK

  'What are we going to do in order to open the rock?'

(8-15) n-∅-kub'   t-q'aaq' xjaal <u>t-u7n</u>
        prog-3sA-GO DOWN 3s-FIRE PERSON SO THAT

  t-meq't   t-waa7
  3sE-BE HEATED 3s-TORTILLA

  'The person was making a fire so that he could heat
  his tortillas.'

In this type of clause the resultant action expressed in the 'so that' clause is temporally dependent on the independent clause; it occurs or has the potential for occurring <u>after</u> the action in the independent clause. The other type of "motive" clause--that introduced by 'because'--does not have the same temporal dependence on the independent clause.

The Mam word for 'because' is tu7nj (again based on the relational noun -u7n) and clauses introduced by tu7nj require no special dependency marking.

1.3 Focused Adverbials

Section 7.1.5.2 described three types of focused adverbials in Mam: affect words, affect verbs, and positional adjectives. All have in common that in their pre-verb focused position they are followed by aspectless clauses marked with the dependent person prefixes (optionally for affect words). It was shown that affect words are obligatorily focused but that affect verbs in a focused position contrast with their non-emphatic occurrence in a regular intransitive verb phrase marked with aspect and with absolutive person prefixes. Positional adjectives as instances of adverbial focus contrast with non-emphatic adjectives formed on the same root, where these exist.

(8-16) txa7q'   t-eel   tanaq squk' t-uj   t-k'u7j
        CRUNCH! 3sE-GO OUT DEM   LOUSE 3s-RN/in 3s-STOMACH

        'Crunch! went the louse in its stomach (when it died).'

(8-17) pal-alaan   t-iky'   nimaal ich'
        LYING DOWN-af vb 3sE-PASS BY DEM   RAT

        'Floating, the big rat went by.'

(8-18) chik'-l   t-kub'   waa7j
        UNCOVERED, FACE UP-pos adj 3sE-GO DOWN TORTILLA

        t-uj   qe7n
        3s-RN/in TORTILLA HOLDER

        'Uncovered, the tortillas are in the holder.'

(8-16) shows an affect word in its obligatorily focused position, (8-17) shows an affect verb focused before an intransitive verb of motion, while (8-18) shows a positional adjective focused before an intransitive verb of motion. Positional adjectives also appear with great frequency in verb-less sentences, in which they are the head of a stative predicate, for instance:

(8-19) pew-1   muuqan   t-wi7   mees
        DISC, LYING THERE-pos adj TORTILLA 3s-RN/on TABLE

'The tortilla is tossed down on the table.'

The use of positional adjectives in such a stative construction does not involve explicit motion, as does the use of positional adjectives in sentences such as (8-18) above, so that the qualifier nature of the positional adjective in (8-19) is more adjectival, while it is more adverbial in (8-18).

Because of the obligatory use of dependent person markers after two types of focused adverbials, their optional use after affect words, and the occurrence of such marking in several other types of embedded or dependent clauses, it is reasonable to analyze these examples as complex sentences with an embedded clause introduced by the verb which carries dependent person marking. Focused positionals have been analyzed (7.2) as independent non-verbal sentences; other focused adverbials likewise constitute independent clauses, although they are perhaps not statives.

1.4 Other Adverbials

There are several manner adverbs which also require dependent person marking in aspectless clauses, although most manner adverbs do not (3.9.7 and 7.1.1.3). Those that do are b'aaka 'little by little', na7x 'still not', and qit 'at times'. Why these adverbs require dependent person marking is not obvious; they do not seem to have any feature, syntactic or semantic, which is not shared by at least some other adverbs. Examples are:

(8-20) noq <u>qit</u>   t-jaa-tz   nimaal a7
        ONLY AT TIMES 3sE-GO UP-dir DEM   WATER

        'Only sometimes did the water come out.'

(8-21) b'ix baqa   <u>qit</u>   q-ojlaa-n
        AND HARDLY AT TIMES 1pE-REST-ap

        'And at times we hardly rested.'

(8-22) <u>b'aaka</u>-tzan   t-we7   juun t-ajlaal
        LITTLE BY LITTLE-well 3sE-STAND ONE 3s-SUM

        q-u7n-a
        1p-RN/agt-1p

        'Little by little we raised the amount.'

(8-23) <u>b'aaka</u>   t-ja-pan   t-e   wiinqan laaj
        LITTLE BY LITTLE 3sE-GO UP-dir 3s-RN TWENTY TEN

        'Little by little it rose to thirty.'

(8-24)[6] <u>na7x</u>-tzan   t-e-x   q-laq'o-7n k'uxb'il-a
        STILL NOT-well 3sE-dir-dir 1pE-BUY-ds TOOL-1p

        noq-tzan
        ONLY-well

        'We still haven't bought the tool.'

(8-25) <u>na7x</u>   t-poon   a7
        STILL NOT 3sE-ARRIVE WATER

        'The water has still not arrived.'

1.5 Focused Generic Qualifiers

As was pointed out in 7.1.3.1, a generic qualifying statement of the form 'It is good/bad to do X.' consists of a focused qualifier (an adjective or negative) followed by a verb which is marked dependently with ergative rather than absolutive person markers and which is also a passive formed by the -njtz passive suffix (4.1.2 #30). Agents cannot be expressed in an oblique phrase. Examples of this use of dependent person marking are:

(8-26) nach t-k'aa-njtz   a7
       BAD 3sE-DRINK-pas WATER

       'It's bad to drink water.'

(8-27) walaan t-k'aa-njtz a7
       GOOD

       'It's good to drink water.'

(8-28) mii-b'an t-waa7-njtz
       NEG-GOOD 3sE-EAT-pas

       'It is inedible.' ('It is not good to be eaten.')

1.6 Relative Clauses

Dependent person marking appears occasionally in relative clauses, even though these, as will be shown in 8.2, usually have dependent aspect marking. In such clauses dependent person marking often appears on intransitive verbs of motion, but whether the verb is a verb of motion or not, the use of dependent person marking implies lack of movement; that is, it describes a state rather than an action. A comparison of a sentence with dependent person marking and the same sentence with dependent aspect marking shows the semantic change:

(8-29) a. aj txkup t-ook-x   t-uj   jaa
           DEM ANIMAL 3sE-ENTER-dir 3s-RN/in HOUSE

           ich'-jal
           MOUSE-cl/nonhuman

           'The animal that is in the house is a mouse.'

     b. aj txkup s-ook-x   t-uj jaa ich'-jal
             x-tz'-ook-x
             rec dep-3sA-ENTER-dir

           'The animal that went in the house is a mouse.'

In (8-29a) the dependent person marking implies a locative state, and says nothing about movement. (8-29b), on the other hand, describes the action which took place. The use of dependent person marking in relative clauses is reserved for locative or other static statements about the noun to which the relative clause refers. It may refer to the state which results from the completion of the action specified by the verb. Other examples are:

(8-30) jun serkyaan t-ook-x   luu7
        ONE SERPENT 3sE-ENTER-dir HERE

        'a serpent that is in here'

(8-31) Cheep Toontz t-jaa-x   t-iib'aj   q-jaa-y7
        José Ordóñez 3sE-GO UP-dir 3s-RN/above 1p-HOUSE-1p ex

        'José Ordóñez who is above our house...'

(8-32) masaat ky-kii-n-x   xhliiky-j
        DEER   3pE-SEE-ap-clt   STANDING

        'deer which they saw standing...'

The examples in (8-29a), (8-30), and (8-31) all have intransitive verbs of motion in the relative clause, but these

verbs are used locatively instead of being used to refer to
motion. Another way to interpret this is that the action
is completed and therefore the clause refers to the state
as a result of the movement involved. (8-32) does not
have an intransitive verb of motion in the relative clause,
but the word xhliikyj is a derived form from a positional
root xhliky- 'standing, referring to young plants or
children'. Positionals typically imply absence of
movement.

   This use of dependent person markers for states or
completed movement within relative clauses is very much
like their use in embedded clauses which follow positionals.
Furthermore, although the action in a clause following the
other focused adverbials (affect words and affect verbs)
is usually in process and not complete, the affect word
or verb itself describes the static kinetics of an action.
Therefore several of the characteristic (and obligatory)
uses of dependent person markers involve situations of
stasis.

1.7 Summary

Dependent person marking is the use of ergative pronouns
on verbs where absolutive pronouns normally occur. This
may reflect an earlier stage in the history of the language,
in which split ergativity resulted in an accusative
agreement pattern under certain circumstances, but since
objects of transitive verbs as well as subjects of intransitive verbs are marked ergatively in certain specific
situations (see examples (8-2), (8-3), and (8-24)), the
pattern which emerges is no longer an instance of nominative/
accusative marking.

   The situations which trigger dependent person marking

are temporally dependent clauses, purpose and result
clauses, focused adverbials, several specific adverbs,
focused generic qualifiers, and completed action in
relative clauses. Furthermore, dependent person marking
may show up with no obvious triggering mechanism; for
instance, first in a sentence.

(8-33) t-ja-tz   q-saa7-n   nimaal t-uj   chem-b'il
        3sE-dir-dir   1pE-CLEAN-ds   DEM   3s-RN/in   GATHER-inst

    t-ee-jal
    3s-RN-cl/nonhuman

    'We clean the big water tank.'

In sentences such as this the context of the whole
discourse must be taken into account, and what is invariably happening is that the use of the ergative markers
indicates some temporal dependency. Sentence (8-33)
appears in a conversation about installing a piped water
system, as part of an explanation of the steps involved in
the process. Although translation did not use an introductory 'when', the steps were clearly ordered so that
this particular statement was dependent on previous context.

2. DEPENDENT ASPECT MARKING

The dependent aspect markers x- 'recent past' and ∅- 'past'
function in several other types of subordinate clauses
(see 3.1 to review the morphophonemic characteristics of
these aspects). The principal use of dependent aspects is
in clauses which follow fronted nominals. A second use of
dependent aspect marking is with focused temporals and
in clauses that are dependent on a clause containing a
perfective. Another occurrence of dependent aspect marking
is obligatorily after the particle mes. Finally, there

are several examples of dependent aspect marking which are
still unclear but which seem to involve temporal dependency
on a perfective or some sort of fronting.

2.1 Fronted Nominals

Fronted nominals are any noun phrases which occur preverbally. These are usually instances of question, negation,
relativization, or focus of the noun phrase, with the
exception that fronting of the agent with a transitive active
verb is interpreted as new information about the agent rather
than agent focus (see 7.1.3.2). The fronting of a noun
phrase is usually, but not obligatorily, followed by
dependent aspect marking in the near past and past, and
no special marking in the progressive and potential. The
preferred form is invariably that with dependent aspect
marking, but further questioning almost always can elicit
the non-dependent aspects with no difference in meaning.
Why dependent aspect marking should be optional in this
context is puzzling, unless it has to do with the asymmetri-
cal nature of the system--the potential and progressive
have no correlate to the dependent past and recent past so
in at least some aspects regular affixes are used (see
examples (8-52) and (8-53)), and this is extended to aspects
which do have the dependent option. In other words, this
is an asymmetry in the morphological system which may be
somewhat unstable and sensitive to change, stylistics,
and sociological variation. The reason for having dependent aspects in only the past and recent past may have
to do with the fact that these aspects refer to completed
action while the others refer to incomplete action.

   Fronting of noun phrases occurs with contrastive
emphasis (focus), but also with question or negation of the

noun phrase, since the negative or question word is fronted. The final category which is a type of fronting is relativization, in that the noun phrase to which the relative refers always precedes the relative clause. Because these processes are similar in that they involve dependent aspect marking, and also similar in that the noun phrase or a reduced form of the noun phrase is preposed to the verb, they are here analyzed as one process, fronting, which triggers the dependent aspects. All of the processes, if they involve the agent, are what Smith-Stark calls agent promotion (1978; see also 7.1.3.2), but almost any fronted nominal is followed by dependent aspect marking, even if it is a relational noun phrase and therefore oblique. Apparently the only examples of fronting which are not at least optionally followed by the dependent aspects are those in which an agent is fronted in an oblique phrase and the verb is passive. The examples which follow illustrate the various types of fronted nominals. First are examples of fronting for focus or for new information about the agent.

(8-34) a. transitive active

   ma   ∅-ku7-x   ky-juusa-n   qa-xu7j   chib'aj
   rec   3sA-dir-dir   3pE-BURN-ap   pl-WOMAN   FOOD

   'The women burned the food.'

 b. agent focus with antipassive

   qa-xu7j   xhi   ku7-x   juusa-n   t-e   chib'aj
        x-chi
   pl-WOMAN   rec   dep-3pA   dir-dir   BURN-ap   3s-RN   FOOD

   '<u>The women</u> burned the food.'

The dependent aspect in (8-34b) is preferred, but optional:

278 COMPLEX SENTENCES

  c. qa-xu7j ma chi ku7-x juusa-n t-e chib'aj

   'The women burned the food.'

 If an agent is fronted to precede an active transitive for focus it is placed within an oblique phrase; if it is not in an oblique phrase the sentence gives new information about the agent and de-emphasizes the patient, rather than focusing on the agent. Either option, however, can facultatively use dependent aspects:

(8-35) a. active transitive

   o chi tzaj t-tzyu-7n Cheep kab' xiinaq
   past 3pA dir 3sE-GRAB-ds José TWO MAN

   'José grabbed some men.'

  b. new information about agent

   Cheep i   tzaj t-tzyu-7n kab' xiinaq
     Ø-chi
     past dep-3pA

   'José grabbed some men.'

  c. new information about agent, same as b)

   Cheep o chi tzaj t-tzyu-7n kab' xiinaq

   'José grabbed some men.'

  d. focus

   t-u7n Cheep i   tzaj t-tzyu-7n
        Ø-chi
   3s-RN/agt past dep-3pA

   kab' xiinaq

   'José grabbed some men.'

e. focus, same as d)

   t-u7n Cheep o chi tzaj t-tzyu-7n kab' xiinaq

   '<u>José</u> grabbed some men.'

The same sentence with patient focus is:

(8-36) a. kab' xiinaq i tzaj t-tzyu-7n Cheep

   'José grabbed the <u>men</u>.'

Or:

b. kab' xiinaq o chi tzaj t-tzyu-7n Cheep

   'José grabbed the <u>men</u>.'

An indirect object always appears in an oblique phrase, which can be fronted for focus.

(8-37) a. nonfocus

   ma ∅-tzaj t-q'o-7n Mal xkoo7ya w-ee-ky'
   rec 3sA-dir 3sE-GIVE-ds María TOMATO 1s-RN/dat-1s

   'María gave me a tomato.'

b. dative focus

   w-ee-ky' saj   t-q'o-7n Mal xkoo7ya
               x-∅-tzaj
               rec dep-3sA-dir

   'María gave <u>me</u> a tomato.'

Other nominals are similarly fronted for focus in relational noun phrases.

(8-38) t-uk'   maachit xi   tx'eem-at
                        ∅-∅-txi
   3s-RN/inst MACHETE past dep-3sA-dir CUT-pas

   tzee7 t-u7n   Kyel
   TREE 3s-RN/agt Miguel

   'The tree was cut by Miguel <u>with a machete</u>.'

(8-39) a. nonfocus

    ma   chin jaw tz'aq-a t-uj   b'ee
rec 1sA dir SLIP-1s 3s-RN/in ROAD

'I slipped in the road.'

b. locative focus

    t-uj b'ee xhin   jaw tz'aq-a
        x-chin
        rec dep-1sA

'I slipped in <u>the road</u>.'

The following are examples of dependent aspects with question of a nominal. Only examples with dependent aspects are given, because while optional, they are preferred.

(8-40) agent, antipassive

    alkyee saj   tzyuu-n ky-e kab' xiinaq
        x-∅-tzaj
    WHO   rec dep-3sA-dir GRAB-ap 3p-RN TWO MAN

'Who grabbed the men?'

(8-41) agent, in relational noun phrase with ∅ passive/indefinite agent

    al u7n   ∅-∅-jaw   patq'u-7n   xaq
    INT RN/agt past dep-3sA-dir TURN OVER-ds ROCK

'Who lifted the rock?'

(8-42) patient, animate

    alkyee-qa xhi   tzaj t-tzyu-7n   Cheep
           x-chi
    WHO-pl   rec dep-3pA dir 3sE-GRAB-ds José

'Whom-all did José grab?'

(8-43) patient, inanimate

tqal x-∅-kub'   t-tx'ee7ma-n Kyel
WHAT rec dep-3sA-dir 3sE-CUT-ds   Miguel

'What did Miguel cut?'

(8-44) dative

al ee   xi   t-q'o-7n   Mal   pwaq
          ∅-∅-txi
INT RN/dat past dep-3sA-dir 3sE-GIVE-ds María MONEY

'To whom did María give the money?'

Note that in (8-44) the relational noun is in its phrase final form.

(8-45) instrument

al u7n   x-∅-kub'   t-tx'ee7ma-n Kyel   tzee7
INT RN/inst rec dep-3sA-dir 3sE-CUT-ds   Miguel TREE

'With what did Miguel cut the tree?'

Negatives of noun phrases are similar:

(8-46) agent, antipassive

miya7 Cheep saj   tzyuu-n ky-e kab' xiinaq
            x-∅-tzaj
NEG   José rec dep-3sA-dir GRAB-ds 3p-RN TWO MAN

'It wasn't José who grabbed the men.'

(8-47) patient

miya7 xiinaq-qa xhi   tzaj t-tzyu-7n   Cheep
                x-chi
NEG   MAN-pl   rec dep-3pA dir 3sE-GRAB-ds José

'It wasn't the men that José grabbed.'

282 COMPLEX SENTENCES

Finally, all relatives are followed by the dependent aspects unless the verb implies a state rather than an action (see 8.1.5), in which event the verb is marked with dependent person markers. Examples of relative clauses follow. See 8.3 for more detail about relative clause formation.

(8-48) relative of main clause agent, = agent in relative clause

<u>aj xiinaq</u> [Ø-Ø-ku7-x   awaa-n   ky-e
DEM MAN   past dep-3sA-dir-dir PLANT-ap 3s-RN/pat

laanch] Ø-tzaj   t-q'o-7n   kab' wi7   q-ee-ky'
ORANGE 3sA-dir 3sE-GIVE-ds TWO PLANT 1p-RN/dat-1p ex

'The man who planted the oranges gave us some plants.'

(8-49) relative of main clause patient, = agent in relative clause

o   chi tzaj n-tzyu-7n-a   <u>aqaj   xiinaq</u>
past 3pA dir 1sE-GRAB-ds-1s DEM pl MAN

[e7x   ilq'aa-n t-e   maansan]
 Ø-chi-xi7
 past dep-3pA-dir ROB-ap   3s-RN/pat APPLE

'I grabbed the men who robbed the apples.'

(8-50) relative of main clause dative, = agent in relative clause

ma   Ø-txi7 n-q'o-7n-a   pwaq t-e   <u>aj xjaal</u>
rec 3sA-dir 1sE-GIVE-ds-1s MONEY 3s-RN/dat DEM PERSON

[x-Ø-7oona-n   w-i7j-a   ]
 rec dep-3sA-HELP-ap 1s-RN/pat-1s

'I gave money to the person who helped me.'

(8-51) relative of main clause agent, = patient in relative
clause

ma ∅-txi7   t-ilq'a-7n xiinaq kab' mansaan
rec 3sA-dir 3sE-ROB-ds MAN   TWO APPLE

$$\begin{bmatrix} aj & saj & & n\text{-}tzyu\text{-}7n\text{-}a \\ & x\text{-}\emptyset\text{-}tzaj & & \\ DEM & rec & dep\text{-}3sA\text{-}dir & 1sE\text{-}GRAB\text{-}ds\text{-}1s \end{bmatrix}$$

'The man whom I grabbed robbed apples.'

(8-52) relative of main clause agent, = dative in relative
clause

ma ∅-oona-n   xjaal   w-i7j-a $\begin{bmatrix} (aj) \\ DEM \end{bmatrix}$
rec 3sA-HELP-ap   PERSON 1s-RN/pat-1s

$$\begin{bmatrix} \emptyset\text{-}\emptyset\text{-}xi7 & & n\text{-}q'o\text{-}7n\text{-}a & pwaq & t\text{-}ee \\ past & dep\text{-}3sA\text{-}dir & 1sE\text{-}GIVE\text{-}ds\text{-}1s & MONEY & 3s\text{-}RN/dat \end{bmatrix}$$

'The person to whom I gave the money helped me.'

(8-53) relative of main clause patient, = patient in relative
clause

ma ch-ok   t-b'iyo-7n Cheep qa-xiinaq $\begin{bmatrix} xhi \\ x\text{-}chi \\ rec\ dep\text{-}3pA \end{bmatrix}$
rec 3pA-dir 3sE-HIT-ds José pl-MAN

$$\begin{bmatrix} tzaj & n\text{-}tzyu\text{-}7n\text{-}a \\ dir & 1sE\text{-}GRAB\text{-}ds\text{-}1s \end{bmatrix}$$

'José hit the men whom I grabbed.'

Several characteristics of sentences with fronted nominals support the analysis that these are all types of complex sentences. Relatives clearly are, since the relative clause is an entire sentence embedded in the main clause. The other types of sentences with fronted nominals considered here are like sentences with relative clauses in that they are all followed by the dependent aspects. In addition, any relational noun which is final in a fronted noun phrase is in its phrase final form (if there is one). Example (8-44) shows this, as does the following example:

(8-54) al   uuk'al k-aq'naa-l-a   nchi7j
                   k-aq'naa-n-l-a
       INT RN/com 2sA-WORK-ap-pot-2s TOMORROW

'With whom will you work tomorrow?'

The fronted nominals which function to focus the noun phrase might be called cleft, but I am reluctant to do so because I think the term is confusing and evokes the English syntactic structure, which is not appropriate to the description of Mayan languages. Rather, all types of fronting which have been discussed here consist of a predicate--the fronted noun phrase--and an embedded clause.

The following examples show that if the embedded clause is not in the past or recent past, the normal aspect markers appear with no other changes.

(8-55) al   u7n   k-b'aj-al   t-jaacha-n-a   j-sii7
       INT RN/inst 3sA-dir-pot 2sE-SPLIT-ds-2s dem-FIREWOOD

       luu7
       HERE

'With what will you split this firewood?'

(8-56) miya7 Cheep n-∅-tzaj   tzyuu-n ky-e kab' xiinaq
       NEG   José prog-3sA-dir GRAB-ap 3p-RN TWO MAN

'It's not José who is grabbing the men.'

2.2 Temporals

Two time related contexts in which the dependent aspects

appear are with focused temporals and in clauses which depend
on a clause containing a perfective. The distribution of
temporal adverbs is given in 7.1.1.3; briefly, they occur
first in the sentence when unmarked and replace aspect markers.
They can occur last also, but then they trigger dependent
aspect marking:

(8-57) a. o   chin jaw tz'aq-a
          past 1sA dir SLIP-1s

          'I slipped.'

    b. eew   chin jaw tz'aq-a
          YESTERDAY

          'I slipped yesterday.'

    c. in   jaw tz'aq-a eew
          ∅-chin
          past dep-1sA

          'I slipped <u>yesterday</u>.'

    d. *eew o chin jaw tz'aq-a

    e. *o chin jaw tz'aq-a eew

The a) sentence has a regular aspect marker and no temporal
adverb, b) uses an adverb to specify time instead of the
aspect marker, c) gives more emphasis to time by placing
the time adverb last in the sentence, d) is ungrammatical
because the adverb and aspect marker do no co-occur, and
e) is also ungrammatical because the adverb last requires
a dependent aspect marker. There is one more possibility,
however, which is to prepose the time adverb to the verb
<u>and</u> mark the verb with dependent aspects:

    f. eew in jaw tz'aq-a

          'I slipped <u>yesterday</u>.'

Sentence f) is much like c) in that both give emphasis to the time, while b) can be used to answer the question 'when?'.

Temporal adverbs, then, are emphatic if they are last in the sentence and in that position require dependent aspect marking, and can be emphatic when they are first in the sentence if dependent aspects are used. They do not co-occur with the regular past or recent past aspects because they either replace them or require dependent aspects.

In 8.1.1 it was shown that temporally subordinate clauses take dependent person marking. If, however, a clause is subordinate to one that includes a -taq perfective then it takes dependent aspect marking if time/aspect is not indicated by the 'when' particle. While perfectives imply temporal dependency, many sentences in normal discourse do not explicitly state it, so not all -taq clauses are accompanied by a clause marked with dependent aspect. If there is a 'when' clause, however, it is either marked with dependent aspects or with a specific (with regard to time) 'when' particle.

(8-58) ajaj   x-∅-poon   maa-taq   n-chin   waa7-n-a
        DEM   rec dep-3sA-ARRIVE rec-perf prog-1sA   EAT-ap-1s

        'When he arrived there, I was eating.'

The maa or oo aspects which combine with -taq can be in addition to other aspects and do not really indicate time.

(8-59) maa-taq   n-chim   b'eet-a   sok   n-kii-n
                                                        x-tz'-ok
        rec-perf prog-1sA   WALK-1s   rec dep-3sE-dir 1sE-SEE-ds

        w-iib'-a   t-uk'   jun xjaal
        1s-RN/refl-1s   3s-RN/com   ONE PERSON

        'I was walking when I met a person.'

In other than the past or near past, verbs in the 'when' clause of a perfective occur in a clause introduced by the particle <u>ok</u> 'when, potential', and are marked with dependent person markers. This is different from other contexts which trigger dependent aspect marking, and which use <u>unmarked</u> aspects <u>and</u> persons for progressive or potential.

(8-60) aj   ok   t-poon   maa-taq   n-chin   waa7-n-a
        DEM   pot   3sE-ARRIVE   rec-perf   prog-1sA   EAT-ap-1s

'When he arrives, I will be eating.'[7]

(8-60) is the same sentence as (8-58), in the potential.

2.3 The Manner Adverb <u>mes</u>

The particle <u>mes</u> requires dependent aspect marking. <u>Mes</u> indicates that an action took place unintentionally or by surprise, and always occurs first in a sentence, followed by dependent aspects.

(8-61) a. ma   ∅-tzeeq'-at   Cheep   t-u7n   Kyel
           rec   3sA-HIT-pas   José   3s-RN/agt   Miguel

   'José was hit by Miguel (on purpose).'

       b. mes   x-∅-tzeeq'-at   Cheep t-u7n Kyel
           rec   dep-3sA-HIT-pas

   'José was hit by Miguel (by accident).'

(8-62) mes   in   kab'a-n-a   t-u7n   t-laaj   q'e7n
        ∅-chin
        past dep-1sA   HURT-ap-1s   3s-RN/caus 3s-FAULT   BOOZE

   'I hurt myself because of the booze.' (The implication is that it was an accidental side effect of drinking.)

288 COMPLEX SENTENCES

2.4 Other Contexts

There are a number of examples which include dependent aspects and which do not clearly fall under the conditioning factors already discussed. I suspect that most of these on further investigation would be found to be examples of focus fronting or of temporal dependence on an implied perfect. Several of these examples are given here without further comment.

(8-63) kwanto sookl   tzluu7 x-∅-ku7
                x-tz'-ook-l
        WHEN   rec dep-3sA-ENTER-again HERE   rec dep-3sA-dir

        ky-iyiji-7n
        3pE-CARE FOR-ds

        'When he arrived here they took care of him.'

(8-64) pwees saj   w-ii-7n-a
                x-∅-tzaj
        WELL rec dep-3sA-dir 1sE-BRING/TAKE-1s

        'Well, I brought it.'

(8-65) iky-tzan   x-∅-b'aj   t-ma-7n-a   kee...
        LIKE THAT-well rec dep-3sA-dir 2sE-SAY-ds-2s THAT

        'Well, that's what you were saying, that...'

2.5 Summary

Dependent aspect marking occurs in sentences that are embedded after focused noun phrases, in sentences that have focused temporals, and with verbs that follow the particle mes. It also occurs in clauses that are temporally dependent on -taq perfective clauses. Dependent aspect marking is in general complementary to dependent person marking, occurring in different types of subordinate clauses. The one context in which the two types of dependent marking are complementary according to aspect is with -taq clauses, where the past and recent past are marked with dependent aspects while other aspects require dependent person marking. Other than this the potential and progressive are not specially marked in contexts where the past and recent past are marked with dependent aspects. Dependent aspect marking, while preferred in all the contexts outlined above, is in fact optional with fronted noun phrases. The most satisfactory explanation at the moment seems to be that since the potential and progressive in this context are not marked specially, Mam speakers will also produce and accept sentences in the past and recent past without special marking. This is, however, definitely an area where native speaker judgments of grammaticality are not entirely consistent.

A comparison of the occurrence of dependent person marking and dependent aspect marking follows:

	Dependent Persons	Dependent Aspects
Time	1. -taq perfectives in potential (with ok particle)	1. -taq perfectives in nonpotential
	2. temporally dependent clauses	
	3. purpose and result clauses	
Focus	1. generic qualifiers	1. temporals
	2. adverbials (-time)	2. adverbials (+time)
		3. nominals
Other	1. relative clauses complete action	1. relative clauses incomplete action
	2. some manner adverbs	2. mes (manner adverb)

A rough rule which approximately covers the difference between the use of dependent persons and dependent aspects in subordinate clauses is that if the clause must indicate time, then dependent aspects are used, while if time is indicated in the main clause and the time of the subordinate clause depends on the time in the main clause or can be inferred from it, or there is no time implied in the subordinate clause, dependent persons are used.

The frequency of dependent marking of one type or the other underlines the rigidity of the basic V-ERG-ABS word order in Mam. Almost all alterations of this word order create dependent (complex) structures.

3. RELATIVE CLAUSES

In general, relative clauses are formed by embedding a clause after the noun phrase in the main clause which it modifies. Except in the limited context of static or completed action (8.1.5) the embedded relative is marked by the use of dependent aspects in the past and recent past and is not specially marked in other aspects. The noun phrase on which the relative is formed is usually marked with the demonstrative aj. The mechanism of relative clause formation is:

1) The relative clause is placed after the noun phrase it modifies, as close as possible to it (see below).

2) The noun phrase in the relative clause which is equivalent to the noun phrase it modifies is moved in front of the verb. If the noun phrase in the relative is a relational noun phrase, the relational noun is not moved. If the relativized noun phrase functions as the agent in the relative clause, the verb in the relative clause can be made antipassive, but only if the action in the relative clause takes place before the action in the main clause.

3) The verb in the relative clause is marked with a dependent aspect in the past or near past (unless the verb is static, in which event dependent person markers are used without aspects).

4) The equivalent noun phrase in the relative clause is replaced by the demonstrative aj.

5) Under certain circumstances aj can be deleted. If aj immediately follows its referent noun they are metathesized, so that aj precedes the noun which is modified by the relative clause. There are actually several words which can be substituted for aj. Jun is the indefinite demonstrative (article), and plurals can be indicated by the demonstrative aqaj or a number.

Relative clauses almost always follow the nouns they modify:

(8-66) a. ma-a7   ∅-w-il-a   tii-xiinaq
          rec-emph 3sA-1sE-SEE-1s   intens-MAN

   'I saw the man.'

b. ma ∅-tzaj ky-tzyu-7n tii-xiinaq
   rec 3sA-dir 3pE-GRAB-ds

   'They grabbed the man.'

c. ma-a7 ∅-w-il-a tii-xiinaq ⎡saj   ⎤
                                ⎢x-∅-tzaj   ⎥
                                ⎣rec dep-3sA-dir⎦

   ky-tzyu-7n]

   'I saw the man whom they grabbed.'

According to the steps outlined above, the production of sentence (8-66c), which contains b) as a relative clause embedded in a), proceeds as follows:

1) Relative Clause Placement
   *ma-a7 Ø-w-il-a tii-xiinaq ma Ø-tzaj ky-tzyu-7n tii-xiinaq
   'I saw the man, they grabbed the man.'

2) Equivalent Noun Phrase Movement
   *ma-a7 Ø-w-il-a tii-xiinaq tii-xiinaq ma Ø-tzaj ky-tzyu-7n
   'I saw the man, the man they grabbed.'

3) Dependent Aspect
   *ma-a7 Ø-w-il-a tii-xiinaq tii-xiinaq saj ky-tzyu-7n
   'I saw the man, the man they grabbed.'

4) Aj
   *ma-a7 Ø-w-il-a tii-xiinaq aj saj ky-tzyu-7n
   'I saw the man whom they grabbed.'

5) Aj Deletion
   ma-a7 Ø-w-il-a tii-xiinaq ___ saj ky-tzyu-7n
   'I saw the man they grabbed.'

Another example is:

(8-67) a. lo-7n   xiinaq w-u7n-a
            SEE-part MAN   1s-RN/agt-1s

            'I know the man.' (Lit: 'The man is seen by me.')

        b. o   tz'-ok   t-b'iyo-7n xiinaq Luuch
            past 3sA-dir 3sE-HIT-ds MAN   Pedro

            'The man hit Pedro.'

        c. lo-7n xiinaq w-u7n-a ⎡(aj) Ø-Ø-ok   ⎤
                                 ⎣ DEM past dep-3sA-dir ⎦

            b'iyoo-n t-e   Luuch ⎤
            HIT-ap   3s-RN/pat Pedro ⎦

            'I know the man who hit Pedro.'

(8-67c) is derived through:
1) Relative Clause Placement
   *lo-7n xiinaq w-u7n-a <u>o tz'-ok t-b'iyo-7n xiinaq</u> Luuch
   'I know the man, the man hit Pedro.'
2) Equivalent Noun Phrase Movement
   *lo-7n xiinaq w-u7n-a <u>xiinaq</u> o tz'-ok t-b'iyo-7n Luuch
   'I know the man, the man hit Pedro.'
2a) Antipassivization
   *lo-7n xiinaq w-u7n-a xiinaq o tz'-ok <u>b'iyoo-n t-e Luuch</u>
   'I know the man, the man hit Pedro.'
3) Dependent Aspect
   *lo-7n xiinaq w-u7n-a xiinaq Ø-Ø-ok b'iyoo-n t-e Luuch
   I know the man, the man hit Pedro.'
4) <u>Aj</u>
   lo-7n xiinaq w-u7n-a <u>aj</u> Ø-Ø-ok b'iyoo-n t-e Luuch
   'I know the man who hit Pedro.'
5) <u>Aj</u> Deletion (optional)
   lo-7n xiinaq w-u7n-a ___ Ø-Ø-ok b'iyoo-n t-e Luuch
   'I know the man who hit Pedro.'

A relative clause can follow some constituent which intervenes between it and the noun it modifies if the intervening phrase is relatively short and if there is no confusion as to referent.

(8-68) ma Ø-xi7 <u>xu7j</u> t-jaa   ⎡x-Ø-w-il-a   ⎤
       rec 3sA-GO WOMAN 3s-HOUSE ⎣rec dep-3sA-1sE-SEE-1s⎦

   'The woman I saw went home.'

(8-69) ma Ø-oona-n   <u>xjaal</u> w-i7j-a   ⎡aj ⎤
       rec 3sA-HELP-ap   PERSON 1s-RN/pat-1s ⎣DEM⎦

       Ø-Ø-xi7   n-q'o-7n-a   pwaq t-ee   ⎤
       past dep-3sA-dir 1sE-GIVE-ds-1s   MONEY 3s-RN/dat   ⎦

   'The person to whom I gave the money helped me.'

In (8-68) the relative clause xwila modifies xu7j over the
intervening tjaa, while in (8-69) the relative clause
aj xi7 nq'o7na pwaq tee modifies xjaal over the intervening
wi7ja. Note that in this sentence the relational noun
tee remains in its position following the verb although the
rest of the relational noun phrase has been moved forward
and replaced by aj. The sentences from which (8-69) is
derived are:

(8-70) a. ma   Ø-oona-n   xjaal   w-i7j-a
            rec   3sA-HELP-ap   PERSON 1s-RN/pat-1s

            'The person helped me.'

        b. o   Ø-xi7   n-q'o-7n-a   pwaq   t-e   xjaal
            past 3sA-dir   1sE-GIVE-ds-1s   MONEY 3s-RN/pat   PERSON

            'I gave the money to the person.'

To go back for a moment to a discussion of (8-66c), there
is no ambiguity as to whether tii-xiinaq functions as the
agent or patient of the relative clause, because it is
identified as singular by the patient marker on the first
verb, and therefore is also the patient (singular) of the
second verb, and not the (plural) agent. If both of the noun
phrases cross-referenced to the verb in the relative clause
are of the same person and number, disambiguating
mechanisms, such as using the antipassive with the patient
in an oblique phrase, are available. For instance,
'I saw the man (singular) who grabbed him (singular).' uses
the antipassive:

(8-71) ma-a7   Ø-w-il-a   tii-xiinaq ⎡saj   ⎤
                                                       ⎢x-Ø-tzaj   ⎥
        rec-emph.   3sA-1sE-SEE-1s   dem-MAN   ⎣rec dep-3sA-dir⎦

        tzyuu-n   t-i7j   ⎤
        GRAB-ap   3s-RN/pat   ⎦

Reversing the agent and patient would involve a sentence
like (8-66c) with a singular marker on the second verb:

(8-72) ma-a7 Ø-w-il-a tii-xiinaq [saj t-tzyu-7n]
                                     [3sE-   ]

       'I saw the man he grabbed.'

Another example is:

(8-73) aj   xu7j   [x-Ø-kii-n   t-e   Cheep]
        DEM WOMAN   [rec dep-3sA-SEE-ap   3s-RN   José]

       ma   Ø-xi7   t-jaa
       rec   3sA-GO 3s-HOUSE

       'The woman who saw José went home.'

In (8-73) the antipassive with the patient in an oblique
phrase clarifies that José is the patient in the relative
clause, so the sentence cannot be interpreted as *'The woman
José saw went home.'.

(8-73) also is an example of a relative which modifies
a focused (pre-verb) noun phrase. Two characteristics
of this type of sentence are important. First, the fronted
noun phrase is obligatorily preceded by aj; and second,
the main verb does not take dependent aspects, in spite
of being preceded by a focused constituent, which optionally
but preferentially triggers dependent aspect marking in
other contexts (7.1.5). This helps distinguish the relative
clause, marked by dependent aspects, from the main clause,
not marked by dependent aspects. Another example is:

(8-74) a. nonfocused noun phrase, optional aj

ma Ø-tzaj t-q'o-7n   (aj) xiinaq
rec 3sA-dir 3sE-GIVE-ds DEM MAN

$\begin{bmatrix} \text{Ø-Ø-ku7-x} & \text{awaa-n} & \text{ky-e} & \text{laanch} \\ \text{past dep-3sA-dir-dir} & \text{PLANT-ap} & \text{3s-RN} & \text{ORANGE} \end{bmatrix}$

kab' wi7   q-ee-ky'
TWO PLANT 1p-RN/dat-1p ex

'The man who planted orange trees gave us some plants.'

b. focused noun phrase, obligatory aj

aj xiinaq [Ø-Ø-ku7-x awaa-n ky-e laanch]

ma Ø-tzaj t-q'o-7n kab' wi7 q-ee-ky'

'The man who planted orange trees gave us some plants.'

Aj can be optionally deleted except when the relativized noun phrase precedes the verb. (There are some further constraints on this rule which I do not fully understand.) If the relative clause appears after some constituent which intervenes between it and the noun it modifies, then aj simply replaces the fronted noun phrase in the relative clause, as in (8-69), but does not precede the noun being modified. Thus, (8-75) is an ungrammatical variant of (8-69).

(8-75) *ma Ø-oona-n aj xjaal w-i7j-a Ø-Ø-xi7 n-q'o-7n-a pwaq t-ee

When aj introduces a relative on an unfocused noun phrase it can be deleted, as in (8-68). If the relative directly follows its referent, however, then aj metathesizes with the referent noun phrase, as in (8-74). The following pair of sentences is another example of aj with a relative clause following a nonfocused and then a focused noun phrase. In (8-76) the variant aqaj is the plural demonstrative.

(8-76) a. nonfocused, optional aqaj

   o chi tzaj n-tzyu-7n-a (aqaj) xiinaq
   past 3pA dir 1sE-GRAB-ds-1s DEM MAN

$$\begin{bmatrix} \text{e7x} & \text{ilq'aa-n t-e} & \text{mansaan} \\ \text{Ø-chi-xi7} & & \\ \text{past dep-3pA-dir} & \text{ROB-ap} & \text{3s-RN APPLE} \end{bmatrix}$$

   'I grabbed the men who robbed apples.'

b. focused, obligatory aqaj

   aqaj xiinaq [e7x ilq'aa-n t-e mansaan]

   o chi tzaj n-tzyu-7n-a

   'I grabbed the <u>men</u> who robbed apples.'

In (8-76a) aqaj can be deleted, but the resulting sentence is not as good, probably because aqaj gives additional information about number and is therefore not deleted as readily as aj might be. (8-74a) was judged equally acceptable with or without aj.

As was noted in 8.1.5, dependent person marking is used on the verb in a relative clause instead of dependent aspect marking for non-aspectual states; i.e., static or completed action. Contrast is provided by the pair:

(8-77) a. dependent aspect

   aj txkup $\begin{bmatrix} \text{s-ook-x} & & \text{t-uj} \\ \text{x-tz'-ook-x} & & \\ \text{rec dep-3sA-ENTER-dir} & \text{3s-RN/in} \end{bmatrix}$
     DEM ANIMAL

$$\begin{matrix} \text{jaa} \\ \text{HOUSE} \end{matrix} \Big] \begin{matrix} \text{ich'-jal} \\ \text{MOUSE-cl} \end{matrix}$$

'The animal that <u>went</u> in the house is a mouse.'

b. dependent person

$$\text{aj txkup} \begin{bmatrix} \text{t-ook-x t-uj jaa} \\ \text{3sE-} \end{bmatrix} \text{ich'-jal}$$

'The animal that <u>is</u> in the house is a mouse.'

A final point to be noted in a discussion of relative clause formation is that the use of the antipassive in a relative clause formed on the agent implies that the action takes place before the action in the main clause, while the use of an active transitive in a relative clause formed on the agent implies that the action takes place at the same time as that in the main clause. See examples (7-93) and (7-94) in section 7.1.3.2.

4. COMPLEMENT CLAUSES

4.1 Infinitival Clauses

Dependent clauses which function as complements of intransitive verbs of motion or the intransitive verb -teen- 'be in a place, exist' use an infinitive form of the verb. The infinitive is formed by suffixing -<u>l</u> (4.3 #58) to the verb stem after the stem formative. It is a true infinitive in that it is not marked for person, aspect, or direction.

(8-78) a. o   chi e7x xjaal
           past 3pA GO PERSON

          'The people went.'

       b. o   tz'-ex   ky-laq'o-7n xjaal
           past 3sA-dir 3pE-BUY-ds   PERSON

           'The people bought it.'

       c. o   chi e7x xjaal   ⎡laq'oo-1 t-ee   ⎤
           past 3pA GO   PERSON ⎣BUY-inf   3s-RN/pat⎦

           'The people went to buy it.'

In (8-78c) the complement clause <u>laq'ool tee</u> uses the infinitive of the verb and is derived from (8-78b), which is the full independent form of the clause. Person and aspect marking is absent from the dependent clause, the agent noun phrase which is equivalent to the subject in the independent clause is deleted, and directionals are absent. Patients occur in oblique noun phrases always introduced by the relational noun -<u>ee</u>. Other examples are:

(8-79) a. ma   chin-x   aaj-a
           rec 1sA-dir   RETURN-1s

           'I went.'

       b. ma   chin b'eet-a
           rec 1sA   WALK-1s

           'I walked.'

       c. ma   chin-x   aaj-a   ⎡b'eeta-1⎤
           rec 1sA-dir   RETURN-1s   ⎣WALK-inf⎦

           'I went to walk.'

(8-80) chi tzaaj-∅-a   ⎡b'ii-1   tzluu7⎤
       2pA COME-imp-2p   ⎣HEAR-inf HERE ⎦

       'Come here to hear!'

The verb -<u>teen</u>- 'be in a place' is used in the independent clause of this type of construction to indicate that

an action has begun. A directional usually accompanies
-teen-; which directional is determined by the verb in the
dependent clause.

(8-81) n-chi   ku7 teen xjaal   ⌈belaara-1 t-e   ⌉
        prog-3pA   dir BE   PERSON ⌊WATCH-inf 3s-RN/pat⌋

        jun weech⌉
        ONE FOX ⌋

'The people began to watch the fox.'

(8-82) n-ch-ok   teen t-aal   ⌈ooq'a-1 ⌉
        prog-3pA-dir   BE   3s-CHILD OF WOMAN ⌊CRY-inf ⌋

        t-17j   ⌉
        3s-RN/thematic ⌋

'Her offspring started to cry about her.'

The infinitive is also used in clauses which are complements of certain causative verbs. In this type of complement the agent is also deleted, but it is equivalent to the patient in the independent clause, since the verb of the independent clause is transitive.

(8-83) ma   tz'-ok   n-q'o-7n-a   ⌈tx'eema-1 sii7   ⌉
        rec 2sA-dir   1sE-GIVE-ds-1s/2s ⌊CUT-inf   FIREWOOD⌋

'I made you cut wood.'

(8-84) ma   tz'-ok   t-lajo-7n   Kyel   ⌈tx'eema-1 sii7⌉
        rec 3sA-dir   3sE-OBLIGATE-ds   Miguel ⌊CUT-inf   WOOD⌋

'Miguel obliged him to cut wood.'

Patients in the complement clause are usually expressed in oblique phrases introduced by -ee; in (8-83) and (8-84) the relational noun was omitted because it is clear that 'wood' is an expected patient of the verb 'cut'.

There is one further use of the infinitive. It can

occur in a complement clause following a stative. The agent
of the verb in the complement clause which is equivalent to
the (absolutive) subject of the stative is deleted. Patients
can be expressed obliquely or directly.

(8-85) mejoor qiina [txako-1   yaa7y-j   ]
        BETTER 1sA   [CALL-inf GRANDMOTHER-abs n]

   'I'll call grandmother.'

(8-86) aa-wt   ch'iin   q-qo7   [leeq'a-1 t-witz]
        DEM-cont A LITTLE   1p emph-1pA   [LICK-inf 3s-RN/on]

   jj-tzee7]
   dem-TREE]

   'If only we could lick a little on the surface
   of the tree.'

<u>Qiina</u> in (8-85) and <u>q-qo7</u> in (8-86) are the heads of
stative predicates.

While the first type of infinitive clause described
above has traditionally been called "subject-controlled"
equivalent noun phrase deletion, and the second type has
been known as "object-controlled" equivalent noun phrase
deletion, this terminology obscures a critical fact about
Mam structure. What is important is that it is the
<u>absolutive</u> constituent in the main clause which controls
equivalent noun phrase deletion in both of these types of
infinitival complements as well as in the third type where
the main clause contains a stative. Thus all of the
different absolutive constituents can control such noun
phrase deletion. As far as I know an ergative constituent
<u>never</u> controls equivalent noun phrase deletion, and con-
sequently the complement of a transitive verb whose agent
is the same as the agent or subject in the complement

does not include an infinitive.[8] This provides additional evidence that ergativity in Mam is syntactic as well as morphological and has consequences at a deep level.

4.2 Other Complements

Much remains to be said about complex sentences, and at some later date more details will undoubtedly become available. One question to be investigated is what types of complements are associated with specific verbs. For instance, the complements of the verbs -aj- (-ajb'el-) 'want' and -ky'i7- 'not want' take aspectless finite verbs if the subject of both clauses is the same. Therefore person is marked on both the independent 'want' verb and the dependent verb, but neither dependent person marking nor dependent aspect marking appears in the dependent clause.

(8-87) Ø-w-ajb'el-a   chin aq'naa-n-a
        3sA-1sE-WANT-1s   1sA WORK-ap-1s

        'I want to work.'

(8-88) Ø-t-ky'i7   Ø-waa7-n
        3sA-3sE-NOT WANT   3sA-EAT-ap

        'He does not want to eat.'

If, however, the subject of the two clauses is different, the dependent clause is introduced by tu7n (see 8.2.1) and its verb takes dependent marking.

(8-89) Ø-w-ajb'el-a   t-u7n t-aq'naa-n
        3sA-1sE-WANT-1s   3s-RN 3sE-WORK-ap

        'I want him to work.'

Numerous questions remain about this type of construction, including what happens with various aspects in the main clause and whether there are other verbs which take similar complements.

There are a number of sentences which instead of having the structure 'independent verb-complement clause with dependent verb' have the structure 'stative-complement'. For example, 'I know X.' is usually rendered by b'a7n 'it is good' or lo7n wu7na 'seen by me' followed by a complement:

(8-90) b'a7n chin aq'naa-n-a
        GOOD   1sA   WORK-ap-1s

        'I know how to work.' or 'I work well.'

(8-91) lo-7n   w-u7n-a   tii   tqal   n-∅-b'ant
        SEE-part   1s-RN/agt-1s   WHAT   WHAT   prog-3sA-DONE
        w-u7n-a
        1s-RN/agt-1s

        'I know what to do.'

Which adjectival or qualifier constructions take complements, and the exact structure of such complements, remains to be analyzed. Directionals also express some ideas which in other languages might require complex sentence structures, especially aspectual ideas such as beginning or finishing an action.

(8-92) ma   chin b'aj aq'naa-n-a
        rec   1sA   dir   WORK-ap-1s

        'I finished working.'

Verbs with directionals could in fact be analyzed as complex sentences in which the main verb (semantically) is a complement of an intransitive verb for the direction--or aspect--of the movement involved.

The use of tu7n in clauses which express a resultant motive or reason has been discussed in 8.1.2. Tu7n is also used in certain types of 'that' clauses, such as (8-87) above, or the following:

(8-93) ma   Ø-kyaj   ky-ma-7n   ky-pokb'aal t-u7n ky-xi7
        rec 3sA-dir   3pE-SAY-ds   3p-NOTICE   3s-RN 3pE-dir

        aq'naa-l
        aq'naa-n-l
        WORK-ap-pot

'They said that they were going to work.'

In addition, the particle <u>kee</u> 'that' has been borrowed from Spanish and introduces many 'that' clauses.

(8-94) ma   Ø-txi   n-na-7n-a   kee   miti7 Ø-xi
        rec 3sA-dir 1sE-THINK-ds-1s   THAT NEG   3sA-dir

        aaj   b'ii-l   t-uj   tnam
        RETURN   LISTEN-inf   3s-RN/in   TOWN

'I imagine that he didn't go to listen in town.'

The differences between clauses introduced by <u>tu7n</u> and <u>kee</u> need to be specified. <u>Kee</u> does not require dependent person marking, as does <u>tu7n</u>, and its distribution is narrower in that it does not appear in motive or reason clauses, but it does overlap with <u>tu7n</u> in other 'that' complements.

This section has very briefly pointed out several remaining problems in the analysis of complex sentences. Others can be found with little difficulty. The work done so far lays the foundation for answering these questions.

5. SYNTACTIC CLITICS

Mam has a number of clitics which have not so far been mentioned. Most of these have a syntactic function, but all the clitics will be reviewed here, whether their function is strictly syntactic or not. Several of them have been discussed elsewhere and are not reviewed in

detail here, but only mentioned. If, however, a clitic
has not been described previously, the following information
is given:
1. clitic, gloss
2. related words or affixes, if any
3. functions, examples

Clitics are defined as such and not as affixes because they
are either a phonologically dependent form of some independent word or because they are not tied to a certain class
of stem, but rather are added to different words, including
particles, depending on syntactic structure. I have roughly
divided the different clitics into the following classes:
noun phrase, person, verb phrase, affirmative, adverbial,
sentential, and conjunctive.

5.1 Noun Phrase

There are three clitics which apply to the noun phrase,
two of which have been described previously. The clitic
qa (pre- or postclitic) optionally pluralizes nouns (5.1.3).
The noun classifiers are used pronominally to specify
third person noun phrases (5.4.2). One other clitic
needs to be discussed:
1) 1. -jo 'demonstrative'
   2. Related to aj 'this, that' and joo7 'yes, that's it'.
   3. This is a demonstrative enclitic which is either
      added to a noun, or if the noun has been deleted,
      is added to the constituent which cross-references
      the deleted noun (the verb, nonverbal predicate,
      or relational noun). Examples:
      aa-tzan-jo 'this is it'
      myaa7-jo 'that's not it'
      q'ii-n-tz-a-jo 'bring that'

t-uj xooch-jo 'in that well'
    It can also occur on particles:
iky-jo 'like that'

5.2 Person

All of the person clitics have been discussed. First, the normal person distinctions need enclitics to express a full set (3.1, 3.2, 3.3, 3.4). Second, ergative prefixes are used for contrastive emphasis on nouns (both preposed and postposed, 5.4.1) and on verbs (postposed only, 6.2.2).

5.3 Verb Phrase

Three enclitics are used along with aspects to indicate perfectives, conditionals, and contrary to fact statements.

2) 1. -taq 'perfective'
   2. No related forms.
   3. Indicates that an action is complete with respect to another action. -taq marks the independent clause in a sentence with a perfective, and is suffixed to either separable aspects or particles. The other clause in the sentence is marked with dependent aspects if it is in the past, and with dependent person marking if it is in the nonpast. Examples:

(8-95) oo-taq ∅-b'aj waa7-n ∅-∅-xi
       past-perf 3sA-dir EAT-ap past dep-3sA-dir

       q'o-7n-∅   t-k'aa7
       GIVE-ds-pas? 3s-DRINK

       'He had eaten when they gave the drink.'

(8-96) oo-taq ∅-b'aj waa7-n ok   t-tzaj q'o-7n-∅ t-k'aa7
                              WHEN 3sE-dir

       'He will have eaten when they give the drink.'

(8-97) kyja7-<u>taq</u>   t-ojlaa-n   ∅-∅-xi
       LIKE THIS-perf 3sE-REST-ap past dep-3sA-dir

   q'amo-7n-∅   juun-tl   aq'uuntl t-ee
   GIVE-ds-pas? ONE-other WORK   3s-RN/dat

   'He was going to rest when they gave him more work.'

(8-98) ch'iin-<u>taq</u>   ∅-txi7 sajtz   iila-n
                                  x-tz'-aj-tz
       A LITTLE-perf 3sA-GO rec dep-3sA-dir-dir SCOLD-ap

   w-i7j-a
   1s-RN/pat-1s

   'He had walked a little way when they scolded me.'

3) 1. -wt 'conditional'
   2. No related independent forms, the <u>t</u> may well come from -<u>taq</u> (2).
   3. This indicates a conditional clause or a potentially realizable situation. Example:

(8-99) aj aa-<u>wt</u>   ∅-tzaj t-ma-7n-a   aj t-neej-al
       DEM DEM-cond 3sA-dir 2sE-SAY-ds-2s DEM 3s-FIRST-ord num

   'You could say the first part.'

   See the next enclitic for examples in a conditional clause.

4) 1. -w(a)la 'contrary to fact'
   2. The -<u>la</u> might be the enclitic -<u>la</u>, which indicates doubt.
   3. This marks the 'then' clause in a conditional sentence or is used alone to indicate contrary to fact. Examples:

(8-100)   ma-a7-tzan   ∅-poon   yiin   qo-chi-wla-jo
          rec-emph-well 3sA-ARRIVE SOMEWHAT 1pA-SAY-cont-dem

          maax   q-xool-a
          UP TO 1p-RN/between-1p ex

          'Let's say that it arrived among us.'

(8-101)   oo-taq-wala   chin b'aj waa7-n-a   xhuul
                                                x-chi-uul
          past-perf-cont 1sA dir EAT-ap-1s rec dep-3pA-ARRIVE

          noqa-wt   ∅-tzaj   ky-ma-7n   oor
          ONLY-cond 3sA-dir   3pE-SAY-ds   HOUR

          'I would have finished eating when they arrived
          if only they had told me the time.'

(8-102)   ma-wla   chin waa7-n-a   noqa-wt   ∅-tzaj
          rec-cont   1sA EAT-ap-1s ONLY-cond   3sA-dir

          ky-ma-7n   oor
          3pE-SAY-ds   HOUR

          'I would have eaten if they had told me the time.'

(8-103)   ma-wla   ∅-aq'naa-n-a   nti7-wt   t-kub'
          rec-cont   2sA-WORK-ap-2s   NEG-cond   3sE-dir

          t-tooqa-n   t-q'ab'-a
          2sE-BREAK-ds   2s-HAND-2s

          'You would have worked if you hadn't broken your
          hand.'

5.4 Affirmation

Two enclitics are affirmative. They emphasive (contrastively?) the part of the sentence they are attached to.
5) 1. -na 'affirmative'

2. No related forms.
3. An emphatic which is added to some part of a predicate. Examples:

(8-104) baaya ma-a7-<u>na</u>   tz'-ee-tz   oox naq'atii
         OK   rec-emph-affirm 3sA-GO OUT-dir 3   DEM

         byeet t-ee   syeent
         BILL   3s-RN/pos 100

         'Well, now, three bills of a hundred <u>did</u> come.'

(8-105) iil-x-<u>na</u>-∅
         NECESSARY-encl-affirm-3sA

         '<u>Yes</u>, it's always necessary.'

(8-106) at-<u>na</u>-∅
         LOC PRED-affirm-3sA

         '<u>Yes</u>, there is.'

(8-107) ma   ∅-kub'-na   tutz'-ee7
         rec 3sA-dir-affirm   SITTING-P→i

         '<u>Yes</u>, he sat down.'

6) 1. -V7 'emphatic'
   2. No related forms.
   3. This is an emphatic which usually is found on separable aspects but also occurs on other types of words. It lengthens the vowel and adds glottal stop to the word being emphasized. Examples:

(8-108) ma-<u>a7</u>   ∅-poon   t-zi   ky-jaa
         rec-emph   3sA-ARRIVE 3s-RN/at entrance   3p-HOUSE

         '<u>Now</u> it arrived at their house.'

(8-109) o-<u>o7</u>-tzan   ∅-txi7   maquu-t-jal
         past-emph-well   3sA-dir   BURY-pas-cl/nonhuman

```
            t-jaq'      tx'otx'
            3s-RN/under GROUND

            'Well, it was buried in the ground.'

(8-110)   baqa       ch'ii7n-∅
          SCARCELY A LITTLE-3sA

          'It's scarcely a little.'

(8-111)   b'ala jaa7ka   'Maybe yes'
```

5.5 **Adverbial Clitics**

7) 1. -tl 'other'
   2. No related form.
   3. This goes on almost any type of word and indicates 'another' or 'again'. Examples:

```
(8-112)   n-∅-xi7      t-k'a-n-tl           txuub'aj txqan-tl
          prog-3sA-dir 3sE-DRINK-ds-again MOTHER   A LOT-other

          a7
          WATER

          'The mother was again drinking some more water.'

(8-113)   n-q-ee-x-tzan-tl-a              q'amaa-1
          prog-1pE-GO OUT-dir-well-again-1p ex SAY-inf

          t-e       ky-e        q-uuk'al-a
          3s-RN/pat 3p-RN/dat 1p-RN/com-1p ex

          'And we went out again to tell the others.'

(8-114)   o7k-tzan   n-∅-tzaaj      t-chii  ky-i7j    xjaal
          ONLY-WELL prog-3sA-COME 3s-FEAR 3p-RN/pat PERSON

          t-i7jaj          ch'iin-tl
          3s-RN/thematic A LITTLE-other

          'The people are afraid only because of another bit.'
```

8) 1. -x 'adverbial'
   2. Related to aax 'the same'.
   3. This enclitic has four functions, or there are four homophonous clitics: a) It means 'the same' and occurs with relational nouns and the particle iky 'like this':

(8-115) ky-u7n-x-la   xjaal
        3p-RN/agt-encl-doubt PERSON

        'by the same people'

(8-116) axax iky-x   aja t-naach-al   at-∅
        ALSO LIKE THIS-clt DEM 3s-BAD-abs n LOC PRED-3sA

        ky-uukal-ma
        3p-RN/com-cl/man

        'Also it's the same inconvenience with the men.'

   b) It means 'only' and occurs with numbers and the particles noq and o7k 'only'.

(8-117) nim-pa-tzan   jun syeent-x nee7
        MUCH-even-well ONE 100-only SMALL

        'Well, it's not much, only a hundred.'

(8-118) noq-x   ky-ee-ka   xu7j
        ONLY-only 3p-RN/dat-3p emph WOMAN

        'only for the women'

   c) It means 'still' and occurs with the locative predicate and its negative, or with the particle kuk- (kukx 'still').

(8-119) at-x-∅   oox   taanka
        LOC PRED-still-3sA THREE TANK

        'There are still three tanks.'

(8-120) nti7-x   Ø-kub'   t-uj   ky-witz nemaas-tl
         NEG-still 3sA-GO DOWN 3s-RN/in 3p-HEAD THE REST-other

         xjaal
         PERSON

         'The rest of the people still did not accept it.'

   d) It means 'always' and occurs with negatives, several particles and verbs.

(8-21)   pera tz-uul-x   t-u7n juun t-b'aan-al
         BUT 3sA-ARRIVE-always 3s-RN ONE 3s-GOOD-abs n

         'But it always comes in good condition.'

(8-122) jo-maj-x   kyaqiil q'iij
         ONE-TIME-always   EVERY   DAY

         'always every day'

9) 1. -la 'doubt'
   2. No related forms
   3. This is probably the same as the -la in -w(a)la. It indicates doubt. Examples:

(8-123) abeer   maaxa-la
         WHO KNOWS UP TO-doubt

         'Who knows until when.'

(8-124) per oo-t-la   tz'-ook   t-yaab'-jal
         BUT past-perf-doubt 3sA-GO IN 3s-ILLNESS-cl/nonhuman

         t-neej-al
         3s-FIRST-ord n

         'But maybe it was damaged from the beginning.'

10) 1. -pa 'even'
    2. No related forms.
    3. Examples:

(8-125) miky'l-pa ∅-txi7 t-xeewal ich' w-u7n-a
         NEG-even   3sA-GO 3s-ODOR MOUSE 1s-RN/aĝt-1s

         t-uj   xooch-jo
         3s-RN/in   WELL-dem

         'I didn't even perceive the odor of the mouse in that well.'

(8-126) aal-pa-tzan   qa t-ky'i7-ya   mii-wt-tzan
         DEM-even-well   IF 2sE-NOT WANT-2s NEG-cond-well

         sa   t-ii-7n-a
         x-∅-tzaj
         rec dep-3sA-dir 2sE-BRING/TAKE-ds-2s

         'Well, if you don't even want it you shouldn't have brought it.'

5.6 Sentence Clitics

The first of the sentence clitics is also -pa. This is either a clitic with two very different meanings, or more likely is two different clitics.

11) 1. -pa 'interrogative'
     2. No related forms.
     3. Indicates yes/no questions. Changes in intonation can indicate this type of question as well.
        Examples:

(8-127) b'a7n-pa-la   jun aq'uuntl
         GOOD-int-doubt ONE WORK

         'Will the work be good?'

(8-128) ∅-uul-pa
         3sA-ARRIVE-int

         'Did he arrive?'

12) 1. -chaq 'distributive'
    2. -chaq 'distributive suffix' is related.
    3. This clitic occurs on interrogatives. Examples:

(8-129) jaa-chaq-tzan-tuma   kb'el   qee7   juun
                                      k-kub'-1

WHERE-dist-well-WHERE 3sA-dir-pot BE BUILT ONE

'Where will each be built?'

(8-130) aax   qo7-ya   tii-chaq   tqal aq'uuntl
        THE SAME 1pA-1p ex WHAT-dist WHAT WORK

        t-aj   tii-chaq   tqal paalt
        3sE-WANT   WHAT-dist WHAT ERROR

'We're the ones who do whatever work he wants and commit whatever error.'

13) 1. -ch 'quotative'
    2. This is related to the quotative verb chi-.
    3. The full verb form is usually used to indicate quotes, but it can be shortened to -ch and postposed to the last word in a quote, if the person being quoted is third person singular.

(8-131) at-∅   jun xaq-ch
        LOC PRED-3sA ONE ROCK-quote

'"There's a rock," he says.'

(8-132) b'a7n-ch
        GOOD-quote

'"It's good," she says.'

5.7 Conjunction

There are two conjunctive enclitics. One is a paragrapher, the other means 'but'.

14) 1. -ka 'but'
    2. No related forms.
    3. This is a sentence level conjunction meaning
       'but'. The Spanish word pero has also been
       borrowed, but the two never co-occur. Examples:

(8-133) ma   chiin-x-a   aq'naa-l b'ala mii-ka   chin uul-a
        rec 1sA-GO-1s WORK-inf MAYBE NEG-but 1sA ARRIVE-1s

        'I'm going to work, but maybe I won't come here.'

(8-134) Ø-b'alq'ajee7   qa-nimaal t-uj   sesyoon
        3sA-WAVER   pl-DEM   3s-RN/in MEETING

        n-Ø-kub'-ka-tzan   t-uj   q-witz-ma
        prog-3sA-GO DOWN-but-well 3s-RN/in 1p-HEAD-cl/man

        'They wavered in the meeting, but at last they
        accepted it.'

15) 1. -tzan 'well, then'
    2. No related forms.
    3. This is the paragrapher. It means 'well' or 'then'
       and indicates that what the speaker says has
       something to do with what he said before. Examples
       abound throughout. Here is one more:

(8-135) n-Ø-tzaaj-tzan   n-qo-ku7-tzan   teen-a
        prog-3sA-COME-well prog-1pA-GO DOWN-well BE-1p ex

        yoola-l   t-uuk'al-ma
        TALK-inf 3s-RN/com-cl/man

        'And then we started, well, to talk with him.'

5.8 Order

As far as has been determined, enclitics combine according to the following order:

V7	taq	wa	pa	la	tzan	jo	tl	Emphatic Person	Person
		wt							
		ka							
		na							

NOTES

1. Much of the data and analysis presented in this section is also included in an article in IJAL (England, in press).
2. Reynoso gives the following paradigm under 'otro' (other) for the verb <u>vli</u> 'venir' (come) (1644: 35):

    v-uli   cuando yo vine   (when I came)
    t-uli-a   cuando tu veniste   (when you came)
    t-uli-hu   cuando aquel vino   (when he came)
    ε-uli-o   cuando nosotros venimos (when we came)
    ε-uli-e   cuando vosotros venistes (when you-all came)
    ε-uli-hu   cuando aquellos vinieron (when they came)

The prefixes here are clearly ergative, although the verb is intransitive, and are triggered by aspectless subordination, translated as 'when'. The ε in Reynoso's orthography is used for <u>k</u>, <u>k'</u>, <u>q</u>, <u>q'</u> indiscriminately, at least in this reprint. In the first person plural it can be interpreted as <u>q</u>, while in the second and third plural it is <u>k</u>. The second and third person forms are εi (<u>ky</u>) in other environments, showing that <u>ky</u> was not at that time a separate phoneme, for example:

    v-xi-<u>εi</u>-aεon-e 'vosotros distes' (you-all gave) (p.45)

Compare the prefixes above to those he gives for his next 'otro' category, which is the recent past with <u>ma</u> (p. 35):

    ma-chim-vli   ya yo vine   (I came now)
    ma-tz-uli-a   etc.   etc.
    ma-tz-uli-hu
    ma-ɛo-vli-o
    ma-che-vli-e
    ma-che-vli-hu

These are the absolutive prefixes. The $\underline{\varepsilon}$ of the first person plural is $\underline{q}$. Transitive verbs mark patients absolutively and agents ergatively, as in:

    ma-tz-el-ɛ-iɛim-o
    rec-3sA-dir-1pE-TAKE/BRING -1p ex

    'ya nosotros quitamos' (now we took it away, p. 41)

    ma-ɛubi-vu-aɛon
    rec-3sA.dir-1sE-PUT

    'ya yo lo puse' (I put it now, p. 49)

3. This is not the only place in which Aguacatec has a structure intermediate between the synchronic Mam structure and some earlier Mamean system; see England, 1976a, for a similar development in the person markers.

4. These clauses are called aspectless embedded clauses by Craig. The verbs in such clauses in Jacaltec require split case marking (Craig, 1977: 236ff.), which may by implication have been the situation in Mam at one time.

5. It is perhaps an interesting fact that Mayan languages seem to have borrowed "function" words from Spanish with relative ease, even when words with the same function existed in the Mayan language. Some of these loans are undoubtedly quite old; others are more recent. Further examples in Mam are <u>per</u> 'but' (from <u>pero</u>) which varies with the Mam enclitic -<u>ka</u>, <u>ii</u> 'and' (from <u>y</u>) which varies with <u>b'ix</u>, <u>entoons</u> 'then' (from <u>entonces</u>)

which has much the same function as the Mam enclitic -*tzan*, and *kee* 'that' (from *que*) which introduces embedded clauses.

6. This is a transitive verb in which the patient is marked with ergative pronouns (as well as the agent), as in example (8-2) and (8-3). Such examples are not unusual, and although they usually have a directional intervening between the two clauses, it is not required.

7. The tense marking here is in the opposite clause from the English: the potential is marked in the 'when' clause and the progressive in the perfect clause. The literal translation would be 'when he will arrive, I am eating.'.

8. This is unlike, for instance, Jacaltec, where verbs of desire take infinitival complements and equivalent noun phrase deletion applies to a subject which is the same as the ergative constituent (agent) of the main clause (Craig, 1977: 314).

APPENDIX I
VOWEL DISHARMONIC SUFFIXES

1. -pV

    -pii

    /i__   wiq'pii-   'uproot'
    /a__   tzaqpii-   'jump'
    /o__   b'onkpii-   'knock over a fat person'
            jolpii-   'change character'
            joq'pii-   'break off shoots; pull up plants entirely'
            q'ojpii-   'break off shoots, branches'
            t'ojpii-   'push someone stooped over'
            tzoqpii-   'free'
            tz'oypii-   'disinflate'
    /u__   chuypii-   'throw down branches'
            ch'uypii-   'destroy a construction'
            q'uqpii-   'transplant'
            tunkpii-   'fell'
            tunpii-   'lower something which is hanging in the air'
            tuch'pii-   'work land badly'
            yutzpii-   'frighten'

    -puu

    /i__   chitpuu-   'untie something leaving it open'
            jilpuu-   'cause to slip; slip in to something'
            jiqpuu-   'pull up, roots and all'
            kyitxpuu-   'push someone unkempt'
            lik'puu-   'stretch out thin material'
            lit'puu-   'stretch net, bag, etc'
            qitpuu-   'loosen'

APPENDIX I

/e__	wiq'puu-	'take out something buried'
	cheypuu-	'untie'
	chrenkypuu-	'knock over a fat person'
	ch'expuu-	'change'
	jenkypuu-	'knock over a fat person'
	jetz'puu-	'limp'
	lenkypuu-	'knock over a fat person'
	qejpuu-	'push someone seated'
	seky'puu-	'frighten'
	selpuu-	'throw something round and flat'
	tx'ekypuu-	'plant something long'
/a__	chak'puu-	'knock down persons or branches'
	jaspuu-	'cut with one chop'
	ky'aqpuu-	'perforate; insult'
	nach'puu-	'pick at your food'
	naxhpuu-	'slap the mouth and nose'
	txak'puu-	'push someone standing'
	txalpuu-	'put to one side'
/u__	tz'upuu-	'inject'

2. -q'V

-q'ii

/u__	mulq'ii-	'sink'

-q'uu

/i__	b'ilq'uu-	'swallow'
	pichq'uu-	'turn upside down'
	tzib'q'uu-	'spill'
	tzipq'uu-	'put something in something'
/e__	petxq'uu-	'carry by the tip'
/a__	b'alq'uu-	'roll down'
	patq'uu-	'turn something flat over, or earth'

3. -chV

-chaa
/o__   b'owchaa-   'cause to fall'
       k'owchaa-   'knock on door'
       poq'chaa-   'break dishes, fruits, or eggs with
                    the hand'
/u__   xmukchaa-   'joke, gossip about'
       ub'chaa-   'kiss'

-chii
/u__   ch'upchii-   'wash head'

-chuu
/i__   b'iq'chuu-   'swallow something whole'
/a__   k'apchuu-   'split firewood; remove key'
       q'amchuu-   'break branches'
       t'ab'chuu-   'snap at something in the air
                    (e.g. dogs)'

4. -tz'V
   -tz'aa
   /o__   koxtz'aa-   'limp'

   -tz'ii
   /a__   b'altz'ii-   'roll up string'
   /o__   qoptz'ii-   'illuminate, light instantly'

   -tz'uu
   /e__   meltz'uu-   'turn over; close eyes; exchange'
          weqtz'uu-   'throw away, lose'
   /a__   japtz'uu-   'shut door'
          maqtz'uu-   'return to someone'
          paqtz'uu-   'fold'
          tamtz'uu-   'cut something solid'
   /u__   putz'uu-   'squash'

5. -tzii

| | /a__ | ab'tzii- | 'charge with; anticipate' |
| | /u__ | ub'tzii- | 'cure pots' |

6. -tx'ii

| | /u__ | kumtx'ii- | 'make something return' |

7. -lV

-lee

	/i__	iky'lee-	'insult; pasture'
		itz'lee-	'stay up late'
	/o__	q'ojlee-	'fight'

-lii

| | /a__ | echaqlii- | 'check' |
| | | xpaplii- | 'criticize; blaspheme' |

-luu

| | /e__ | xmejluu- | 'plead' |

8. -k'uu

| | /a__ | jask'uu- | 'say softly' |
| | | taqk'uu- | 'cut at intervals' |

9. -b'V

-b'aa

	/e__	lepb'aa-	'leave a child with someone for a trip'
	/a__	k'alb'aa-	'start a job'
		lajb'aa-	'retire, go away'
		laq'b'aa-	'move away'
	/u__	xkuchb'aa-	'measure with cord'

-b'ee

	/a__	ajb'ee-	'want'
		sasb'ee-	'test'
		xalb'ee-	'step over'
	/ó__	oqb'ee-	'abandon'

VOWEL DISHARMONIC SUFFIXES 323

	q'olb'ee-	'accept a fiance'
/u__	xjuk'b'ee-	'guide, teach to work'
	xmutz'b'ee-	'wink'

10. -nV

     -naa
     /i__   tz'iynaa-   'line up'
            txiknaa-   'hurt again'
     /a__   majnaa-   'lend'

     -nee
     /a__   q'axnee-   'warm one's self by the fire'

11. -mV

     -maa
     /i__   siqmaa-   'blow the nose'

     -muu
     /a__   taqmuu-   'cut at intervals; fold tortillas'
            yaqmuu-   'cut logs in pieces'

12. -wV

     -wee
     /a__   tzaq'wee-   'answer'

     -wii
     /u__   sukwii-   'glean after harvest'

APPENDIX II
EXCEPTIONS TO MORPHOPHONEMIC RULES

1. -VV 'Stem Formative' (4.1 #3)

    The rules are:

    a. → a / $\begin{Bmatrix} VV \\ V7 \end{Bmatrix}$ C__   b'iitza- 'sing'

                           ma7la- 'measure'

    b. → uu /CuC__   b'ujuu- 'degrain'

                        muquu- 'bury'

    b'. at times and often in free variation, a u in the root → a /__uu (stem formative), for example: sakuu- ~ sukuu- 'tie up badly'

    c. → ii /V C__   iyajii- 'toughen up plants and

             [-stress]   seeds' (from iiyaj 'seed')

                           xb'alamii- 'dress' (from

                                xb'aalan 'clothes')

    d. → vowel length with transitive roots which terminate in a vowel or vowel plus glottal stop.

                        b'ii- 'hear'

                        tx'aa7- 'bark, bite'

    e. a y glide is inserted between nontransitive stems which terminate in a vowel and the stem formative.

                        b'eeya- 'make a road' (from

                           b'ee 'road')

                        meb'ayii- 'adopt' (from meeb'a

                           'orphan')

    f. VV → V /__(y)ii   meb'ayii- 'adopt' (from meeb'a)

    g. → oo /_ _ _ (i.e. after a CVC root in which the vowel is any but u)

Exceptions to the rules:

a. → aa (Many of these are derived from nouns)

EXCEPTIONS TO MORPHOPHONEMIC RULES 325

    ab'xaa-   'hear badly'   najaa-   'occupy a house'
    alamaa-   'domesticate'   q'amaa- 'say'
    apaa-   'withstand'   samaa-   'send', <u>but</u>:
    aq'naa-   'work'   samoo-   'return'
    awaa-   'plant'   tze7aa- 'accept'
    elq'aa-   'rob'   saqchaa- 'play'
    munaa-   'plant seedlings' sewaa- 'carry something discoid'
    munulaa- 'serve the community'

b. → ee
    neb'ee- 'savor'

c. → ii /CVC__
    axii- 'degrain corn by kopii- 'untangle'
      hand'
    b'ilii- 'spin'   sch'ii- 'read'
    chib'ii- 'spin'   tzqii- 'know (<u>conocer</u>)'

d. → a /CVC__
    b'aq'a- 'grind sugar- b'icha- 'call chicks'
      cane'
    b'ub'a- 'heap up'   b'uqa- 'smoke'
    chila- 'play a rattle'   ch'aja- 'splash in the water'
    ch'ana- 'make noise in jatz'a- 'eat dry food'
      water or mud'
    jutza- 'dance with slow jula- 'insert something in a
      short steps, without   hole'
      noise'
    kach'a- 'chew gum'   karsa- 'card'
    (s)kata- 'stroke the   k'ila- 'fill pots'
      beard'
    k'loja- 'group people   lanka- 'walk slowly in gravel
      or animals'   without shoes'
    lika- 'urinate (children)' plaja- 'make bundles'

q'eb'a- 'cross over'   saq'a- 'fight (children)'
sjuma- 'eat grains or   smuk'a- 'eat grains or toasted
   toasted food'   food'
t'eja- 'cut with dull   (xh)t'oja- 'jump like a frog'
   blade'
tzak'a- 'eat toasted   tzuk'a- 'eat toasted food'
   food'
tz'ub'a- 'kiss'   wab'a- 'place on feet; accom-
                                 pany walking'
(x)wit'a- 'jump'   xb'iq'a- 'wash hands'
xb'laq'a- 'wallow (ani-   xpotz'a- 'braid'
   mal) when stung'
xwaq'a- 'crack nixtamal'   xyoq'a- 'amass'
xhipa- 'make skeins'   xhoq'a- 'fill water jars'
xhtiky'a- 'damage,   xhuq'a- 'poke the ground for
   tease'   nothing'
yek'a- 'show'   yob'a- 'hang from nail, stick,
                                 or rope'

2. -al 'Abstract Noun' (4.2 #47)
   The rules are:
   a. → iil / V   C__
                [-stress]
   b. VV(7) → V/__ii
   c. ∅ → y / V__ {al}
                    {iil}

Exceptions to the rules: (only the stem is given)
   a. → il
   jeetz' 'lane'   jb'aal 'rain'
   t'eb' 'thick'   q'ay 'rot'
   yaab' 'sick'
   b. → -eel
   sib' 'smoky'

c.   → aal

chi7 'sweet' (varies between <u>tchi7aal</u> and <u>tchi7yal</u>)

meq'maj	'hot'	nimaq	'big' (<u>tmaqaal</u>)
q'achq'aj	'tasteless'	q'iinan	'rich'
q'u7chma	'rotten wood' (<u>tq'u7chamaal</u>)	seeka	'sellable' (<u>tsekaal</u>)
nim	'a lot'	txub'txaj	'content; savory'

d.   al ~ aal (Colors)

<u>al</u>		<u>aal</u>	
kyaq	'red'	kyaq	'hot'
xhq'an	'yellow'	q'an	'ripe'
saq	'clean'	saq	'white'
cha7x	'raw, blue' (<u>tcha7xal</u>)		
cha7x	'humid' (<u>tchaaxal</u>)		

e.   Others:

tajlaal	'sum'	ajwaalal	'20 days of service in the cofradia'
tajwiil	'owner'	tib'laal	'color, form'
tq'ijlaal	'birthday'	t-xlekamaal	'shadow'
tch'iinel	'helper'	tlaneel	'cover'
tqaniil	'notice'	tq'ab'aal	'care for a crop'
tsameel	'ingredient'	ttzee7yil	'ingredient'
ttz'ab'il	'ingredient'	tyajlaal	'scarcity'
chib'jaal	'muscle'		

APPENDIX III
TEXT

The following story was recorded and transcribed by Juan Ordóñez, translated into Spanish by Juan Ortiz, and analyzed and translated into English by me. It is of the trickster genre, but can't refrain from adding a bit of origin myth at the end.

                t-i7j   Luuch
        3s-RN/thematic Pedro

             About Pedro

1. juun xjaal ojtxa Luuch t-b'ii b'ix nim o-∅-b'eet
   ONE PERSON BEFORE Pedro 3s-NAME AND A LOT past-3sA-WALK

   Once upon a time there was someone named Pedro, and he

t-witz   tx'otx'   2. at-∅-tzan   juun
3s-RN/on LAND   LOC PRED-3sA-well ONE

walked a lot in the country.   Well, one day he met a

q'iij n-ch-ok   nooj[1] txqan aryeeral   t-witz   t-miij
DAY prog-3pA-dir FULL GROUP MULE-DRIVER 3s-RN/on 3s-MIDDLE

group of mule-drivers in the road, and there he was boiling

b'ee, b'ix luu   n-∅-loqa-n   t-xaar per nti7 sii7
ROAD AND THERE prog-3sA-BOIL-ap 3s-JUG BUT NEG FIREWOOD

his jug of water but there wasn't any firewood or fire (to

b'ix-mo q'aaq' t-i7j   t-jon-aal-x[2]   xaar
AND-OR FIRE 3s-RN/thematic 3s-ONE-abs n-encl JUG

do) it, the jug was boiling fiercely by itself.

```
n-Ø-loqa-n          weena.  3.  tza7n  Ø-teen  t-ee-7³
prog-3sA-BOIL-ap  A LOT          HOW    2sA-BE  LOC PRED-3sA-2s
                                "How are you, Pedro?
Luuch,  walaan-ta          t-xaar⁴  chi-chi-tzan  xjaal
Pedro   EXCELLENT-2s emph  2s-JUG   3pA-SAY-well  PERSON
your jug is pretty good," the people said to him.
Ø-Ø-ok              ky-q'ama-7n   t-ee       4.  walaan-ta
past dep-3sA-dir    3pE-SAY-ds    3s-RN/dat      EXCELLENT-3s emph
                                                "It's excellent,"
Ø-chi-tzan,    qa  Ø-x-el         ky-laq'o-7n-a
3sA-SAY-well   IF  3sA-dir-pot    2pE-BUY-ds-2p
he said, "if you want to buy it, buy it!"
Ø-ky-laq'oo-n-x-a        5.  n-Ø-tzaj-tzan         ky-laq'o-7n
3sA-2pE-BUY-imp-dir-2p       prog-3sA-dir-well     3pE-BUY-ds
                            So then the mule-drivers
aryeeral    ja7la,  b'ix  n-chi    kub'  tzoqpaj  t-uj    b'ee,
MULE-DRIVER NOW     AND   prog-3pA dir   ESCAPE   3s-RN/in ROAD
bought it, and they moved along the road, and when they were
ma   chi  miija-n            b'ee t-e⁵    chiki-q'iij  n-Ø-kub'
rec  3pA  REACH MIDPOINT-ap  ROAD 3s-RN   MID-DAY      prog-3sA-dir
at the middle of the road at midday, they put their jugs
ky-q'o-7n    ky-xaar  t-jon-aal-x      t-witz     tx'otx',
3pE-GIVE-ds  3p-JUG   3s-ONE-abs n-encl 3s-RN/on  GROUND
down by themselves on the ground, so that their food would
t-u7n                   t-tzq'aaj ky-chi7,  b'ix  nti7  Ø-tzaj
3s-RN/in order to       3sE-COOK  3p-FOOD   AND   NEG   3sA-dir
cook, and it didn't boil, it was for nothing.
```

330   APPENDIX III

```
loqa-n, noq gaana     6. n-∅-tzaaj-tzan      ky-q'ooj
BOIL-ap ONLY IN VAIN     prog-3sA-COME-well 3p-ANGER
                         The people became angry$^6$,

xjaal, jat-tzan   walaan    t-xaar Luuch, per ii-na
PERSON WHERE-well EXCELLENT 3s-JUG Pedro  BUT THAT-affirm

"Where is Pedro's good jug? But he should have waited

∅-teen neej tz'e7y-ka-na-ta-jo         t-witz$^7$, mejoor
3sA-BE WAIT BURN-but-affirm-3s emph-dem 3s-RN/on BETTER

(for us) to understand, it's better that we watch it again

ii    t-kub' kweent-∅   t-i7j     juun-tl   el   t-u7n-j
THAT 3sE-dir WATCH-pas? 3s-RN/pat ONE-other TIME 3s-RN-because

because he did us wrong, maybe he is a robber, because he

naach n-t-b'iincha-n    q-i7j,    b'ala eleq'-ta-jo,
BAD   prog-3sE-MAKE-ap 1p-RN/pat MAYBE ROBBER-3s emph-dem

sure beat us this time," they said.

maj o-o7-xa-x             qo-kub' moo7ya-n-∅$^8$ jun el
WELL past-emph-encl-encl 1pA-dir WIN-ds-pas?   ONE TIME

t-u7n    chi-chi-tzan 7. aax-tzan      nn-∅-ook
3s-RN/agt 3pA-SAY-well   THE SAME-well prog-3sA-ENTER
                         They met Pedro again, the

nooj juun-tl    el   Luuch ky-witz,  n-chi    tzaj-tzan
FULL ONE-other TIME Pedro 3p-RN/on prog-3pA dir-well

people came and joined the group, (and said) "It is certain

yoqpaj        xjaal, ii-na     t-b'ant ch'in    mooda
JOIN A GROUP PERSON THAT-affirm 3sE-MAKE A LITTLE WAY

that he should make a plan about it," and they drove
```

```
t-i7j            b'ix lajo-7n              txqan nim-aal cheej
3s-RN/thematic   AND  DRIVE MULES-part     GROUP DEM    MULE

the mules.⁹

ky-u7n      8.  b'ix tzan-la     n-ku7-x           t-xtaanka-n¹⁰
3p-RN/agt       AND  well-doubt  prog-dir-dir      3sE-BAG (vb)-ap

                And Pedro put himself into a sack at dusk.

t-iib'       Luuch  t-uj        saaka aj    t-qoqaax
3s-RN/refl   Pedro  3s-RN/in    SACK  WHEN  3sE-NIGHT FALLS

9.  ii-na           t-xi7      xoo-b'aj         t-uj         a7,
    THAT-affirm     3sE-dir    THROW-proc pas   3s-RN/in     WATER

    "Throw him in the river¹¹, so that he learns his lesson

t-u7n               t-tz'e7y    t-witz⁷   t-u7n-j         puuro
3s-RN/in order to   3sE-BURN    3s-RN     3s-RN-because   PURE

because he's nothing but a liar," said the people.

sla7j,  chi-chi-tzan xjaal    10.  a-tzan     t-e⁵      Luuch
LIAR    3pA-SAY-well PERSON        DEM-well   3s-RN     Pedro

                                   So Pedro tied the opening

nn-∅-ok          t-k'alo-7n t-zi               saaka   t-u7n
prog-3sA-dir     3sE-TIE-ds 3s-RN/at opening   SACK    3s-RN/inst

of the sack with a cord and the opening remained at his head.

jun ky'ijaaj b'ix ma    ∅-kyaj-a           t-txii7     t-uj       t-wi7
ONE STRING   AND  rec   3sA-REMAIN-?       3s-MOUTH    3s-RN/in   3s-HEAD

11.  n-chi       tzaj-tzan yoqpaj           aryeeral         n-∅-xi7
     prog-3pA    dir-well  JOIN A GROUP     MULE-DRIVER      prog-3sA-dir

     Well, then the mule-drivers went and threw him in the
```

ky-xoo-7kj   t-uj   a7,   b'ix mii-l-pa-la   chi
3pE-THROW-proc 3s-RN/in WATER AND NEG-?-even-doubt 3pA

river, and they didn't even think about (the fact that)

naa7-n   t-i7j   aj qa ky-ee   ky-saqb'aaq[12]
THINK-ap 3s-RN/thematic REL pl 3p-RN/pat 3p-ROPE

it was their own ropes that they went and threw.

Ø-Ø-xi7   ky-xoo-7kj   12. b'ix
past dep-3sA-dir   3pE-THROW-proc   AND

                                                  And Pedro even

oo-taq-pa-la   Ø-jaa-tz   Luuch t-uj   saaka
past-perf-even-doubt 3sA-GO UP-dir   Pedro   3s-RN/in   SACK

got out of the sack, and immediately he fled in the night.

b'ix b'i7x   Ø-iky'   oq   t-uj   qoniiky'an-tl
AND IMMEDIATELY 3sA-dir FLEE 3s-RN/in   NIGHT-other

13. ma-tzan   Ø-jaa7w-al[13]   q'iij, qoo-qa,
     rec-well 3sA-GO UP-spec term SUN   LET'S GO-pl

     When the sun rose, "Let's go," said the people,

chi-chi-tzan xjaal, ma-a7   Ø-jaa7w-al-ta   q'iij
3pA-SAY-well PERSON rec-emph 3sA-GO UP-spec term-3s emph   SUN

"the sun has risen now."

14. jaa-tzan   t-e7   q-ryaat, chi-chi-tzan, b'ix
     WHERE-well LOC PRED-3pA 1p-ROPE 3pA-SAY-well AND

     "Where are our ropes?" they said, and this was because

aa-l-pa-la-jo   oo-taq   Ø-ku7-x
DEM-?-even-doubt-dem past-perf 3sA-dir-dir

Pedro had put them in the sack which the people had gone

```
t-tetz'o-7n            Luuch t-uj-aj        saaka Ø-Ø-xi7
3sE-INSERT FORCEFULLY  Pedro 3s-RN/in-dem   SACK  past dep-3sA-dir
```
and thrown away.

```
ky-xoo-7kj         xjaal   15. noq-tzan   Ø-i-jaw
3pE-THROW-proc     PERSON      ONLY-well  past dep-3pA-dir
```
                    Well, they were surprised and

```
mees-j¹⁴       b'ix  Ø-i-jaw              ooq' t-i7j
SURPRISE-pas   AND   past dep-3pA-dir     CRY  3s-RN/thematic
```
cried about their ropes.

```
ky-saqb'aaq  16. a-tzan    t-e¹⁵ Luuch nn-Ø-iky'      tzoqpaj
3p-ROPE          DEM-well  3s-RN Pedro prog-3sA-dir   ESCAPE
```
                And Pedro left again, and found a patron.

```
juun-tl    el,   n-Ø-kaana-n          t-uk'a        jun patroon
ONE-other  TIME  prog-3sA-MEET-ap     3s-RN/com     ONE PATRON

17. n-Ø-xi7-tzan              t-qaa7na-n,  qapa   at-Ø
    prog-3sA-dir-well         3sE-ASK-ds   MAYBE  LOC PRED-3sA
```
    And then he asked, "Maybe there's some work with

```
ch'in      w-aaq'an-a t-uuk'al-a,   Ø-chi-tzan
A LITTLE   1s-WORK-1s 2s-RN/com-2s  3sA-SAY-well
```
you?" he said.

```
18. at-Ø-ta                  aq'uuntl,  Ø-chi-tzan      patroon
    LOC PRED-3sA-3s emph     WORK       3sA-SAY-well    PATRON
```
    "There's work," said the patron, "but you'll be a

```
per pastor kuch k-ok-al        teen-a, ax-la           b'a7n
BUT HERD   PIG  2sA-dir-pot    BE-2s   THE SAME-doubt  GOOD
```
pig herd." "That's fine," he said, and answered.

Ø-chi-tzan   Ø-xi7   t-tzaq'we-7n   19. n-Ø-xi7-tzan
3sA-SAY-well 3sA-dir 3sE-ANSWER-ds   prog-3sA-GO-well
                                                     So then he went

pastoor-al ja7la, n-ch-iky'   t-ii-7kj   kuch,
HERD-inf   NOW   prog-3pA-dir   3sE-BRING/TAKE-proc   PIG

to herd, he took the pigs, he went and sold them, who

n-ch-e7x   t-k'aa7ya-kj, jaa7-la   tuumal   20. jun-tzan
prog-3pA-dir   3sE-SELL-proc WHERE-doubt ...WHERE   ONE-well

knows where.   He had

Ø-Ø-b'ant,   n-ch-el   t-ii-7n[16]   t-jee7[17]
past dep-3sA-MAKE prog-3pA-dir 3sE-BRING/TAKE-ds   3s-TAIL

an idea; he cut off the pig's tails and there was a swamp

kuch, b'ix at-Ø   txqan t'al   xooq'l   n-chi
PIG   AND LOC PRED-3sA   A LOT LIQUID MUD PUDDLE   prog-3pA

and he put the tails in it.

ku7-x   t-tx'apo-7n   t-uj   21. ma-tzan
dir-dir   3sE-INSERT FORCEFULLY-ds 3s-RN/in   rec-well
                                                           So Pedro

t-xi7   Luuch q'am-al   t-e   t-uk'   patroon, patroon,
3sA-GO   Pedro TELL-inf 3s-RN/pat 3s-RN/com   PATRON   PATRON

went to tell the patron, "Sir," he said, "the pigs are

Ø-chi-tzan   li   ma-a7   ch-e7x   b'aj-kya   kuch t-uj
3sA-SAY-well   INJ rec-emph 3pA-dir   FINISH-3p emph PIG 3s-RN/in

stuck in the swamp, what are we going to do?" he said.

t'al   xooq'l,   tii   k-ook-al   q-u7n[18],   Ø-chi-tzan
LIQUID MUD PUDDLE   WHAT   3sA-ENTER-pot 1p-RN/agt   3sA-SAY-well

22. qapa-x-ta,   Ø-chí-tzan   patroon, n-Ø-xí7-tzan
    MAYBE-encl-3s emph 3sA-SAY-well PATRON   prog-3sA-GO-well

"Maybe so," said the patron, and he went to see it, and

lo-1   t-ee,   ma Ø-poon   li
SEE-inf 3s-RN/pat rec 3sA-ARRIVE THERE INJ

when he arrived there, the pig's tails were stuck in it.

tx'apo-7n-qa-kya   nim-aal t-jee7 kuch   23. qap
INSERT-part-pl-3p emph DEM   3s-TAIL PIG   MAYBE

                                              "Maybe it's

chiix   chi-jaa-tz, Ø-chi-tzan   patroon, n-Ø-ja-tz
POSSIBLE 3pA-GO UP-dir 3sA-SAY-well PATRON   prog-3sA-dir-dir

possible to get them out,"[19] said the boss, he pulled them

t-b'aqo-7n,   mii7n mii7n Ø-chi-tzan   Luuch Ø-Ø-xi7
3sE-PULL UP-ds   NO   NO   3sA-SAY-well Pedro past dep-3sA-dir

up, "No, no," said Pedro, "they will only break," and

t-q'ama-7n, noq-an-x   chi ja-tz   b'oq-1[20]
3sA-SAY-ds   ONLY-?-encl   3pA dir-dir   PULL UP-pas

that's exactly what happened.

kukx-ka-tzan   Ø-Ø-ook   t-i7j-jo
LIKE THIS-but-well   past dep-3sA-ENTER   3s-RN/thematic-dem

24. nn-Ø-iky'   tzoqpaj juun-tl   el   Luuch,
    prog-3sA-dir ESCAPE ONE-other TIME Pedro

Pedro got away again, he met another patron, and when

n-Ø-kaana-n   t-uk'a   juun-tl   patroon, ma
prog-3sA-MEET-ap 3s-RN/com   ONE-other   PATRON   rec

he arrived there he asked, "Maybe you want to buy some

Ø-poon   n-Ø-xi7   t-qaa7na-n, qapa   t-aj-a
3sA-ARRIVE THERE prog-3sA-dir 3sE-ASK-ds MAYBE 2sE-WANT-2s

cows," he said.

Ø-looq'a-n-a   t-i7j   txqan waakxh, Ø-chi-tzan
2sA-BUY-ap-2s 3s-RN/pat GROUP COW   3sA-SAY-well

25. b'ala jaa7-ka, Ø-chi-tzan   patroon,   jte7-tzan
    MAYBE YES-but 3sA-SAY-well PATRON   HOW MUCH-well

"Maybe so," said the boss, "how much?" "Who knows?"

t-wi7 t-u7n, per maaxa-la   Ø-chi-tzan   Luuch
3s-RN 3s-RN BUT UP TO-doubt 3sA-SAY-well Pedro

said Pedro.

26. q-la-7tz-chaq,   Ø-chi-tzan   patroon   27. ma
    1pE-SEE-proc imp-dist 3sA-SAY-well PATRON   rec

"Let's go and see them," said the boss.   When

chi kaana-n neqaa7-yiin, luu-qa-kya   waakxh at-e7
3pA MEET-ap CLOSE-atten THERE-pl-3p emph COW   LOC PRED-3pA

they got close by, there were the cows and they weren't

b'ix nyaa7 waakxh-qa-jal,   sinoke
AND NEG   COW-pl-cl/nonhuman BUT RATHER

cows, but instead bottle gourds; Pedro had cut open their

xhii7-na-qa-jal,   oo-taq   Ø-b'aj t-qeeta-n
BOTTLE GOURD-emph-pl-cl/nonhuman past-perf 3sA-dir 3sE-CUT-ds

mouths.

Luuch t-tzii7   28. yob'a-n-tzan-qa-jal
                    HANG-part-well-pl-cl/nonhuman

They were hanging in the branches of the

```
txa7n         t-q'ab' tzee7, b'ix tzin-tzan      n-chi
3s-RN/at edge 3s-HAND TREE    AND  SURELY-well  prog-3pA
```

tree, and they were mooing a lot, so the patron counted the

```
muuya-n-jal          weena toons n-∅-7ajl-eet-tzan       pwaq
MOO-ap-cl/nonhuman A LOT THEN   prog-3sA-COUNT-pas-well MONEY
```

money into Pedro's hand, so Pedro took off yet again, who

```
t-uj       t-q'ab' Luuch t-u7n       patroon, yaj-xa-tzan
3s-RN/in   3s-HAND Pedro 3s-RN/agt   PATRON   AND-encl-well
```

knows where he went.

```
nn-∅-iky'      tzoqpaj-tl    juun-tl    el   Luuch jaa7-la
prog-3sA-dir ESCAPE-again ONE-other TIME Pedro WHERE-doubt

tuumal    ∅-pon-a    b'aj    29.  yaj-xa-tl         n-∅-xi7
...WHERE 3sA-dir-?  FINISH         AND-encl-again prog-3sA-GO
```

And then the boss went

```
patroon lo-l    ky-ee    t-waakxh jatuma oo-taq     chi kyaj
PATRON SEE-inf 3p-RN/pat 3s-COW   WHERE  past-perf 3pA dir
```

to see his cows where he had bought them and they weren't

```
t-laq'o-7n b'ix tz'iinan-qa-jal,   o-∅-7eel-ka-x²¹
3sE-BUY-ds AND  NEG-pl-cl/nonhuman past-3sA-GO OUT-but-encl
```

there, he was looking for them.

```
t-u7n        30.  jaa7-tzan    t-e7      n-waakaxh-a,
3s-RN/agt         WHERE-well  LOC PRED-3pA 1s-COW-1s
```

"Where are my cows?" he said, and there

```
∅-chi-tzan,  me7aal-qa-kya-jal,       noq  nim-aal
3sA-SAY-well NEG-pl-3p emph-cl/nonhuman ONLY DEM
```

wasn't anything, only the bottle gourds were mooing in the

xhii7-na   n-chi   muuya-n txa7n   t-q'ab'
BOTTLE GOURD-emph prog-3pA MOO-ap 3s-RN/at edge 3s-HAND

tree branches; all of a sudden he looked up.

tzee7, n-∅-jaaw-tzan   ∅-meeltz'a-j   t-witz[22]
TREE   prog-3sA-GO UP-well 3sA-TURN OVER-pas 3s-RN/on

31. luu-qa-jal   oo-taq   ch-ok   yob'a-n,
    THERE-pl-cl/nonhuman   past-perf   3pA-dir   HANG-ap

There they were hanging, and like that it remained.

kukx-tzan   ∅-kyaj   t-i7j-jo
LIKE THAT-well 3sA-REMAIN   3s-RN/thematic-dem

32. nn-∅-iky'-tzan   tzoqpaj Luuch jaa7-la   tuumal
    prog-3sA-dir-well   ESCAPE   Pedro WHERE-doubt ...WHERE

Pedro fled again, who knows where he went, all because

∅-pon-a   b'aj, t-u7n-j   nim   t-xiim-b'il   b'a7n
3sA-dir-? FINISH 3s-RN-because   A LOT   3s-THINK-inst   GOOD

of a lot of ideas once upon a time.

ojtxa   33. me-tza-l   o-∅-b'ant   b'ix-qa nti7
BEFORE   NEG-well-doubt   past-3sA-MAKE   AND-IF NEG

        Who knows if this happened or not.

34. nn-∅-ok-tza-l   nooj[23] dyoos t-witz,
    prog-3sA-dir-well-doubt   FULL   GOD   3s-RN/on

Pedro met God, and he said to Pedro, "You will stay

n-∅-xi7   q'ama-7n-∅   t-e   Luuch, b'an t-ee7[24]
prog-3sA-dir SAY-ds-pas? 3s-RN/dat Pedro GOOD LOC PRED-?

to hold the whole world, because you're excellent, you're

```
aat-∅-a          kyj-el²⁵       tzyuu-1  t-witz   tx'otx',
LOC PRED-2sA-2s  REMAIN-pot     GRAB-inf 3s-RN/on EARTH
```

a good person and good at talking, you'll hold the whole

```
t-u7n-j          walaan-ta,     b'a7n  xjaal-ta     b'ix
3s-RN-because    EXCELLENT-2s emph GOOD PERSON-2s emph AND
```

world like that," he told Pedro.

```
b'a7n-ta      ∅-yoola-n,     kyja7-tzan        aat-∅-a
GOOD-2s emph  3sA-TALK-ap    LIKE THAT-well LOC PRED-2sA-2s

k-tzyuu-1     kyaqiil-ka²⁶   t-witz    tx'otx',   ∅-chi-tzan
2sA-GRAB-pot  WHOLE-2p emph  3s-RN/on  EARTH      3sA-SAY-well

∅-∅-xi7      t-q'ama-7n     t-e       Luuch
past dep-3sA-dir 3sE-SAY-ds 3s-RN/dat Pedro
```

35. jaka-la   ∅-tzy-eet-wa   w-u7n²⁷   ∅-chi-tzan
    YES-doubt 3sA-GRAB-pas-1s emph 1s-RN/agt   3sA-SAY-well

   "Yes, I can hold it," said Pedro.

36. kyja7-tzan   ∅-kyaj   Luuch tzyuu-1 t-witz
    LIKE THAT-well   3sA-REMAIN Ledro GRAB-inf 3s-RN/on

   Thus Pedro stayed to hold the world, but he's a rock

```
tx'otx',   per aa-tzan-jo      aj  xaq ja7la  37. kyja7-tzan
EARTH      BUT DEM-well-dem    DEM ROCK NOW       LIKE THAT-well
```

now.   This is what

```
n-∅-xi7         q-b'i-7n,            tzyu-7n    tx'otx' t-u7n
prog-3sA-dir    1p-HEAR/KNOW-ds      GRAB-part  EARTH   3s-RN/agt
```

we hear, that the earth is full of rocks, maybe thus it

```
xaq, b'ala ax       o-∅-b'ant       iky-jo,     t-u7n-j
ROCK MAYBE THE SAME past-3sA-MAKE   LIKE THIS-dem 3s-RN-because
```

passed, because only from generation to generation they

340   APPENDIX III

noq nkolokol   t-kyaj   jun q-b'i-b'1   ky-u7n
ONLY STEP BY STEP 3sE-REMAIN ONE 1p-HEAR-inst 3p-RN/agt

left a message for us[28], and we are cultivating it a little

ojtxa, b'ix kajo-7n-x-tzan   ch'iin   q-u7n
BEFORE AND CULTIVATE-part-encl-well A LITTLE 1p-RN/agt

now, and it can't be lost, that's all.

ja7la yaa milaay-x-tzan ∅-naaj, o7kx ∅-teen-jo
NOW NOW NEG-encl-well 3sA-LOSE ONLY 3sA-BE-dem

NOTES

1. Idiom: 'meet'.
2. This abstract noun formed on the root juun 'one' means 'by itself, alone'.
3. I don't know what exactly is going on here; the form should be t-a7-ya. Or, if tee7 is analyzed as a relational noun (-ee), what is the 7? 7 can be a person enclitic, but only first person.
4. The -ta on walaan is a postposed person marker for emphasis. Normally this indicates third person if there is an explicit third person noun, and second person if there isn't. There is no person enclitic on xaar, possibly because second person has been marked already on walaan?
5. This is an instance of te used for something other than possession, patient, or dative marker.
6. Lit: 'The people's anger was coming.'
7. Idiom: 'understand, learn'.
8. The agent marker is missing from this verb, but the agent is indicated by tu7n. This seems to be more like a passive than an "indefinite agent."
9. Lit: 'driven a group of mules by them'.
10. The suffix -n on t-xtaankan is the antipassive, rather

than the directional suffix, because this is a reflexive
construction. No absolutive is indicated (e.g.,
n-∅-ku7-x) because there is never a change in form
corresponding to a change in person.
11. Lit: 'That he be thrown in the water.'
12. Saqb'aaq 'rope' is from saq 'white' and b'aaq 'bone'.
13. Jaaw 'go up' + -7...al refers to the specific termination
point of a sunrise.
14. Meesj is a frozen passive.
15. Another instance of te for neither possession, patient,
nor dative. It probably marks some discourse function.
16. Idiom: 'cut or remove'.
17. Tjee7 kuch (singular) does not correspond with ncheel tii7n
(plural patient). Mam speakers are sloppy about third
person agreement.
18. Lit: 'What will enter (happen) by us?' This is an
example of an intransitive verb with an oblique agent,
where the meaning is transitive.
19. Lit: 'they come up'.
20. Since this passive implies lack of agent control, it
changes the meaning from 'being pulled up' to 'being
broken'.
21. Idiom: 'look everywhere'.
22. Idiom: 'look up suddenly'.
23. Idiom: 'meet'.
24. See note 3.
25. This should have second person marking (kkyjela); perhaps
it is deleted because of the preceding pronoun.
26. I think this is the emphatic enclitic for second person,
but it should be -kya and it doesn't agree in number (it
is plural, while Pedro is of course singular). -ka
rather than -kya is an older form, and the lack of

number agreement could be sloppiness. <u>Ktzyuul</u> should have a person enclitic to make it second and not third person.

27. There is no person enclitic; it is on the preceding word instead. The scope of the emphatic person enclitics can include several words, which would be marked separately for person if there were no emphatic.

28. Lit: 'our message stays by them'.

BIBLIOGRAPHY

Aissen, Judith. 1979. El pasivo en tzotzil. Paper and hand-out presented at the Mayan Workshop IV. Mexico: Palenque.

Ayres, Glenn. 1977. Es el antipasivo siempre una voz? Paper presented at the Mayan Workshop II. Mexico: San Cristobal de las Casas.

Bricker, Victoria R. 1978. Antipassive Constructions in Yucatec Maya. Papers in Mayan Linguistics, ed. by Nora C. England, 3-24. Columbia, MO: University of Missouri.

------. 1981. The Source of the Ergative Split in Yucatec Maya. Journal of Mayan Linguistics 2,2: 83-127.

Brintnall, Douglas E. 1979. Race Relations in the South-eastern Highlands of Mesoamerica. American Ethnologist 6.638-52.

Campbell, Lyle with Pierre Ventur, Russell Stewart, and Brant Gardner. 1978. Bibliography of Mayan Languages and Linguistics. (Institute for Meso-American Studies, 3.) Albany: State University of New York.

Canger, Una. 1969. Analysis in Outline of Mam, a Mayan Language. Ph.D. dissertation, University of California, Berkeley.

Craig, Colette G. 1977. The Structure of Jacaltec. Austin: University of Texas Press.

------. 1979. The Antipassive and Jacaltec. Papers in Mayan Linguistics, ed. by Laura Martin, 139-164. Columbia, MO: Lucas Brothers.

Dixon, R.M.W. 1979. Ergativity. Lg 55.59-138.

Durbin, Marshall and Fernando Ojeda. 1978. Basic Word Order in Yucatec Maya. Papers in Mayan Linguistics, ed. by Nora C. England, 69-77. Columbia, MO: University of Missouri.

England, Nora C. 1975. *Mam Grammar in Outline*. Ph.D dissertation, University of Florida.

------. 1976a. The Development of the Mam Person System. *IJAL* 42.259-61.

------. 1976b. Mam Directionals and Verb Semantics. *Mayan Linguistics I*, edited by Marlys McClaran, 201-11. Los Angeles: University of California American Indian Studies Center.

------. 1976c. Mam Text. *IJAL Native American Text Series* 1.88-97.

------. 1976d. Verb Categories in Mam. *Florida Journal of Anthropology* 1.1-8.

------, (ed.). 1978a. *Papers in Mayan Linguistics*. (University of Missouri Publications in Anthropology, 6; Studies in Mayan Linguistics, 2).

------. 1978b. Space as a Mam Grammatical Theme. *Papers in Mayan Linguistics*, ed. by Nora C. England, 225-38. Columbia, MO: University of Missouri.

------. 1980. Eating in Mam. *Journal of Mayan Linguistics* 1,2.26-32.

------. In press. Ergativity in Mamean (Mayan) Languages. *IJAL* 49.

Greenberg, Joseph H. 1966. Some Universals of Grammar with Particular Reference to the Order of Meaningful Elements. *Universals of Language*, 2nd. ed., ed. by Joseph H. Greenberg, 73-113. Cambridge, MA: MIT Press.

Kaufman, Terrence. 1969. Teco-A New Mayan Language. *IJAL* 35.154-74.

------. 1974. *Idiomas de mesoamérica*. (Seminario de Integración Social, 33). Guatemala: Editorial José de Pineda Ibarra.

------. 1976a. New Mayan Languages in Guatemala: Sacapultec, Sipacapa, and Others. Mayan Linguistics I, ed. by Marlys McClaran, 67-89. Los Angeles: University of California American Indian Studies Center.

------. 1976b. El proyecto de alfabetos y ortografías para escribir las lenguas mayances. Guatemala: Proyecto Lingüístico Francisco Marroquín and Ministerio de Educación.

Larsen, Thomas W. 1979. A Preliminary Look at Aguacatec Narrative Discourse. MS.

Larsen, Thomas W. and William M. Norman. 1980. Correlates of Ergativity in Mayan Grammar. Ergativity: Toward a Theory of Grammatical Relations, ed. by Frans Plank, 347-70. London: Academic Press.

Lengyel, Thomas E. 1978. Ergativity, Aspect, and Related Perplexities of Ixil-Maya. Papers in Mayan Linguistics, ed. by Nora C. England, 78-91. Columbia, MO: University of Missouri.

Maldonado Andrés, Juan and Juan Ordóñez Domingo. 1976. Practicas y experiencias obtenidas en programas de alfabetización efectuados en una comunidad indígena del área mam. Mayan Linguistics I, ed. by Marlys McClaran, 11-18. Los Angeles: University of California American Indian Studies Center.

Maldonado, Juan, Juan Ordóñez, and Juan Ortiz. In press. Diccionario Mam de San Ildefonso Ixtahuacán. Guatemala.

Martin, Laura. 1978. Mayan Influence in Guatemalan Spanish: A Research Outline and Test Case. Papers in Mayan Linguistics, ed. by Nora C. England, 106-26. Columbia, MO: University of Missouri.

McQuown, Norman A. (ed.). 1967. Handbook of Middle American Indians, vol. 5, Linguistics. Austin: University of Texas Press.

Norman, William M. and Lyle Campbell. 1978. Toward a Proto-Mayan Syntax: A Comparative Perspective on Grammar. Papers in Mayan Linguistics, ed. by Nora C. England, 136-156. Columbia, MO: University of Missouri.

Oakes, Maud. 1951. The Two Crosses of Todos Santos. (Bollingen Series, 27). New York: Pantheon Books.

Peck, Dorothy Miller. 1951. The Formation of Utterances in the Mam Language. M.A. Thesis, Hartford Seminary Foundation.

Pinkerton, Sandra. 1978. Word Order and the Antipassive in K'ekchi. Papers in Mayan Linguistics, ed. by Nora C. England, 157-68. Columbia, MO: University of Missouri.

------. 1980. Ejectives and Implosives in the Quichean Languages. MS.

Reynoso, Diego de. 1644. Arte y vocabulario en lengua mame. Reprinted, n.d., France.

Robertson, John S. 1980. The Structure of Pronoun Incorporation in the Mayan Verbal Complex. New York: Garland.

Robertson, John S., John P. Hawkins, and Andrés Maldonado. n.d. Mam Basic Course, vol. 1 and 2. U.S. Peace Corps.

Rubin, Joan. 1968. National Bilingualism in Paraguay. The Hague: Mouton.

Silverstein, Michael. 1976. Hierarchy of Features and Ergativity. Grammatical Categories in Australian Languages, ed. by R. Dixon, 112-171. Canberra: Australian Institute of Aboriginal Studies.

Smailus, Ortwin. 1979. Pronouns and Ergativity in Colonial Yucatec. Paper presented at the Mayan Workshop IV. Mexico: Palenque.

Smith-Stark, Thom. 1976a. The Antipassive in Jilotepequeño Pocomam. MS.

------. 1976b. Some Hypotheses on Syntactic and Morphological Aspects of Proto-Mayan (*PM). Mayan Linguistics I, ed. by Marlys McClaran, 44-66. Los Angeles: University of California American Indian Studies Center.

------. 1978. The Mayan Antipassive: Some Facts and Fictions. Papers in Mayan Linguistics, ed. by Nora C. England, 169-87. Columbia, MO: University of Missouri.

Sywulka, Edward Frederick. 1948. The Morphology of the Mam Language of Guatemala, C.A. M.A. Thesis, University of Oklahoma.

------. 1966. Mam Grammar. Languages of Guatemala, ed. by Marvin Mayers, 178-85. (Janua Linguarum, series practica, 23). The Hague: Mouton.

Valladares, Leon A. 1957. El hombre y el maíz: etnografía y etnopsicología de Colotenango. Guatemala: Universidad de San Carlos.

Vogt, Evon Z. (ed.). 1969a. Handbook of Middle American Indians, vol.7, Ethnology, part I. Austin: University of Texas Press.

------. 1969b. Zinacantan: A Maya Community in the Highlands of Chiapas. Cambridge: Belknap Press.

Wagley, Charles. 1949. Social and Religious Life of a Guatemalan Village. American Anthropological Association Memoir, 71.

------. 1969. The Maya of Northwestern Guatemala. Handbook of Middle American Indians, vol. 7, Ethnology, part I, ed. by Evon Z. Vogt, 46-68. Austin: University of Texas Press.

INDEX

Absolutives, 41, 45, 55, 58-64, 66, 68, 69, 75, 77, 78, 96, 110, 112, 123, 164-167, 169, 174-176, 177-180, 187, 193, 197, 198, 199, 200, 204, 211, 213-214, 218-219, 220-222, 228, 235, 236, 238, 243, 257, 258-264, 269, 274, 301, 317, 341

Adverbials, 131-132, 232-233, 234-236, 259, 262, 264, 269-271, 274, 310-312

Adverbs, 139, 163, 189-193, 239-240, 255, 274; Manner, 90-91, 190-191, 239, 270, 287; Temporal, 89-90, 191-193, 239-240, 249, 262, 284-287

Affect: Roots, 93, 95, 102, 104, 105, 106, 107, 120, 130, 131, 135, 136, 138; Stems, 111, 130-131, 133, 137, 138; Verbs, 65, 111, 130, 233-236, 269-270, 274; Words, 81, 84-85, 121, 233-236, 257, 269-270, 274

Affixes, 38, 40, 49-51, 52-54, 54-64, 68-71, 78, 80, 81, 83, 97, 98-138; Applicative, 102-103, 137; Causative, 47-49, 103-107, 115, 134, 135, 136, 137, 200; Intransitive, 15, 49, 52, 59, 64, 96, 101, 107-116, 134, 135-136; Nominal, 117-124, 134, 135, 136, 137, 138; Passive and Antipassive, 101, 110-115, 134; Possessive, 68-72; Processive, 101, 107-109, 114, 134, 135; Transitive, 15, 47, 50, 134-135; Versive, 111, 136, 137

Affrication, 21, 36, 38, 39

Agent, 55, 60-64, 110, 112, 113, 114, 139, 155-156, 164-165, 177, 179, 181-182, 186, 187, 188-189, 194, 198-209, 211-222, 225-227, 244-245, 250, 252, 259-264, 277-279, 280-281, 290, 294-295, 299, 300-301

Aguacatec, 6, 7, 155, 262-263, 317

Aspect, 40, 55, 58, 60, 161-

<u>164</u>, 173, 174-176, 191-193, 228, 231, 240-249, 255, 264, 265-266, <u>275-297</u>, 303, 306-308; Dependent, 58-59, 85, 150-151, <u>161-164</u>, 215, 226, 228, 230, 231-232, 242, 243, 244, 249, 250, 253, 266-267, 272-273, <u>275-297</u>, 302
Aspiration, 25, 36, 38, 39
Assimilation, 26-29, 36, 39
Bilingualism, 12-15
Case, <u>71-74</u>, 139, 153-155, <u>164-165</u>, 182
Causatives, 47, <u>103-107</u>, 115, 134-137, 153, 182, 188, 200, 251
Classifiers, <u>158-160</u>
Clitics, 38, 39-40, 45-46, 52, <u>56-64</u>, 66, 76-77, 86, <u>96</u>, 143, 145, 165, 169, 174-176, 187, 196, 228, 238, 248, 254-255, <u>304-316</u>
Complements, <u>298-302</u>
Consonant Clustering, 37, 38, 39, 43, 93, 97
Dative, 72, 73-74, 155, <u>183-184</u>, 195, 222-224, 230, 253, 281
Definite/Indefinite, 83-84, 147, <u>151-153</u>, 291
Demonstratives, 76, 91, 139,

140, 145, <u>149</u>, 151-152, 197, 229, 230, 232, 238, <u>241</u>, 255, 290, 291, 297
Directionals, 40, 41, 59, 60, 65, 96, 108, 114, 125, 138, 161, 165, <u>167-172</u>, 173-176, 187, 188, <u>197</u>, 206, 207, 208, 255, 260, 262-264, 298, 299, 300, 318, 341
Dissimilation, 26, 36
Eastern Mayan Languages, 6, 7, 8
Ejectives, 25, 26, 37, 39
Emphasis, <u>157-158</u>, <u>165-167</u>, 194, 232-233, 235-236, 285-286
Ergatives, 22, 23, 40-41, 55-58, 60-61, 78, 96, 125, 141-142, 153, <u>164-167</u>, 174-175, 177, 187-188, 193, 198-199, 208, 209, 211, 228, 233, 235-236, 243, <u>258-264</u>, 274, 275, 306, 316-318
Ergativity, 56, <u>164-167</u>, 177-182, <u>198-199</u>, 209-211, <u>258-264</u>, 301-302; History of Ergative System, 261-264
Existentials, 75-78, 156-157, 177, <u>238-242</u>, 245-246
Flaps, 24, 29
Fricatives, 24, 26, 27, 36
Focus, <u>143-144</u>, 150, 157,

INDEX 351

164-165, 177, 181, 193, 208, 216-218, 221, 225, 226, <u>227-138</u>, 244, 259, 262, 264, 269-270, 272, 274, 275, 276, 277, 278-280, 284-285, 288, 295, 296, 297

Glottal Stop, 22, 32, <u>34-36</u>, 37, 41, 45, <u>51-54</u>, 78, 81, 100, 132-133, 135-136, 309, 324

Glottalization, 24, 25, 26, 32, 34, 37, 38, 41, 42, <u>51-54</u>

Implosives, 26, 37, 39

Infinitive, 108, <u>123-124</u>, 135, 136, 138, 189, 224, <u>298-302</u>, 318

Inflection, 16, 55, 60, 64, <u>78</u>, 85, 86, 123, 141, 161-167, 174-176, 189, 214, 240, 245

Instrument, 72, 73, 118, <u>184-185</u>, 186, 195, 231, 252, 279, 281

Interrogatives, 71, <u>87</u>, 148, 192, 196, 214, <u>248-254</u>, 256, 276, 280, <u>313-314</u>

Intonation, 32, 35, 196, 313

Intransitivity: Roots, 15, 55, 64-65, <u>93-94</u>, 103, 104,

106, 121, 123, 135, 178; Stems, 15, 83, 101, 103, 109, <u>110-123</u>, 134-136, 174, 178, 181, 324; Verbs, 15, 49, 52, 55-60, <u>64-65</u>, 80, 83, 118, 123, 126, 131, 151, 161, 164-167, 169, 172, 173, 174-176, 177, 178, 179, 180, 182, 188, 198, 199, 200, 204, 209, 211, 222, 233, 235, 259-264, 270, 272-274, 298, 303, 316, 341

Ixil, 6, 7, 8, 209, 211, 231, 262

Jacaltec, 5, 7, 8, 211, 261, 317, 318

Kekchí, 193, 209

Laryngealization, 32, 37

Literacy, 11-12, 42

Locatives, 71-73, 75-78, 88, 89, 119, 134, 136, 139, 153, 156, 159, 177, 182, 185, 189, 190, 195, 238-241, <u>245-246</u>, 273, 311

Measure Words, 46, 81, <u>86</u>, <u>131</u>

Metathesis, 46, <u>50</u>, 150, 291, 296

Mode, 59-60, 78, 101, 162-163, <u>172-174</u>, 174-176, 197, 257-248; Imperative, 101, 175-176; Potential, 65, 88, 101, 191, 192, 256, 259, 265,

276, 287, 289, 318
Nasals, 24, 28-29, 38-39, 43, <u>54</u>
Negation, 88, 218, 221, 228, 242, <u>244-248</u>, 272, 276, 281
Neutralization, 29, 32, 33, 37, <u>44-45</u>, 50, 51, 96
Numbers, 83-84, 121-122, 127-128, 131, 132, 140, 144-148, 197, 228, 256, 291
Occlusives, 24-32, 36, 37, 38, 39
Onomatopoeia, 85
Orthography, 24, 30, 33, <u>40-41</u>, 316-317
Particles, 71, <u>86-93</u>, <u>95-96</u>, 120, 121, 139, 148, 150, 189, 242, 244, 248, 254-255, 256, 259, 265-266, 275, 286-287, 304, 305, 306, 311, 312
Patient, 55, <u>60-64</u>, 110, 112, 114, 139, 155-156, 164, 177, 179, 181-182, 188-189, 194, 198-209, 211-222, <u>222-224</u>, 227-230, 244-245, 250-251, 259-264, 278-275, 280-281, 294-295, 299, 300-301
Person Marking, <u>55-59</u>, <u>60-61</u>, 66, 77, 78, 123, 125, 141-144, 153, <u>155-157</u>, 158,
161, <u>164-167</u>, 238, 241, 299, 302, 306; Dependent, 85, 151, 243, <u>258-274</u>, 288-290, 291, 297-298, 302, 304
Possession, 35, <u>66-71</u>, 120, 121, 122, 123, 125, 139, 140, 141-144, 146, 147, 151, 153, 154, 155, 164, 186, 195, 251
Pronominalization, 75, 149, <u>155-158</u>, 179, 182, 186, 194, 197, 200, 208, 228, 238, 241, 242, 257, 259, 274, 318
Quichean Languages, 6, 7, 8
Reduplication, 85, 86, 99, 233
Reflexivization, 186-187, 341
Relational Nouns, <u>71-75</u>, 139, 141, 142, <u>153-155</u>, 156, 157, 158, 159, 182-189, 190, 195, 211, 222-224, 231, 241, 242, 251-253, 267, 277, 279, 280, 281, 284, 290, 299, 300, 340
Relative Clauses, <u>149-151</u>, <u>272-274</u>, <u>282-284</u>, <u>290-298</u>
Resonants, 24, 29, 53
Roots, 33, 39, 40, 43, 45, 47, 49, <u>55-97</u>, 98, 100, 101, 102-138
Sentence: Non-verbal, 177, <u>238-244</u>; Verbal, <u>177-238</u>
Split Ergativity, <u>258-264</u>

INDEX 353

Statives, 75-77, 78, 88, 125, 145, 149, 151, 156, 157, 158, 159, 227, 232, 237, 241-243, <u>244</u>, 245, 257, 270, 303
Stems, 33, 49, 50, <u>98-138</u>, <u>174</u>
Stress, 32-33, 36, <u>37-38</u>, 39, 40, 41, 43, 44, 45, 46, <u>49-50</u>, 67
Subject, 55, 64, 139, 155-156, <u>164</u>, 177, 179, 188, 198-200, 211, 238, 243, 259-264, 299, 301
Teco, 6, 7, 8
Transitivity: Roots, 15, 47, 55, 60-64, 81, <u>93</u>, 100, 101, 102, 103, 105, 107, 112, 121, 123, 127, 130, 131, 133, 134-135, 161, 178-181, 200, 233; Stems, 15, 47, 50, 101, <u>102-110</u>, 112, 115, 118, 122, 125, 127, 130, 131, 133, 134-138, 174, 178-179, 200-207, 209; Verbs, 15, 47, 55-64, 78, 80-81, 82, 96, 113, 118, 119, 123, 125, 126, 127, 129, 161, 164-167, 170-173, 174, <u>175</u>, 177, 180, 181, 188, 193, 198, 199, 207, 208, 209, 211, 215, 216, 227, 232, 243, 250, 251, 257, 259-264, 274, 276, 278, 298, 300, 301, 317, 318
Universals, 37, 195-198, <u>256</u>
Voice: Antipassive, 61, 64, 101, 110, 111, 134, 165, 178-179, 187-189, 198-199, <u>209-222</u>, 226, 229, 242, 243, 244, 250, 251, 257, 277, 280-281, 290, 293, 294, 295, 298, 340; Passive, 46, 101, 112, 113, 114, 115, 134, 170, 178-179, 180, 188-189, <u>198-209</u>, 226, 227, 230, 277, 280, 340, 341
Voicing, 25, 26, 36, 37, 39, 41
Vowels: Disharmony, 46, <u>47-49</u>, 103-104, 105, 107, <u>319-323</u>; Dropping, 29, 33, 37, <u>43-44</u>, 45, 93, 143; Harmony, <u>46-47</u>; Synthesis, 45-46
Western Mayan Languages, 6, 7, 8, 209
Yucatec, 5, 193, 209, 261

www.ingramcontent.com/pod-product-compliance
Lightning Source LLC
Chambersburg PA
CBHW020635230426
43665CB00008B/185